INDEPENDENT REVIEW INC.

bringing governance and competitiveness together

Independent Review Inc. (IRI) is dedicated to the idea that any company can benefit from sound governance while fulfilling its compliance and disclosure obligations and still making money. It also believes that every company is different and demands a different solution. A customized soution will usually require the specialist knowledge, expertise and depth of experience that IRI can provide.

IRI specializes in reducing the exposure of public company directors to simple errors and omissions, small mistakes that should be avoided. For example, boards must now have a written charter plus a code of ethics, they must have policies on board operations, on disclosure and they need a whistle-blower policy. Every standing committee must have a charter. Director orientation is highly recommended, as is regular board assessment. There are a lot of issues to cover while simultaneously attending to corporate strategy, management oversight and creating wealth for shareholders. IRI can assist you in developing all of them, from a totally independent viewpoint.

IRI serves the governance needs of private companies, not-for-profit organizations, government agency boards and commissions. It works from a firm conviction that good governance is largely distinct and separate from the issue of compliance as this term is applied to reporting issuers. The IRI team includes senior executives, former regulators and experts in law and accounting, a well-rounded inventory to deploy on behalf of clients.

IRI provides a "Sounding Board" service for boards of directors seeking a sober, second opinion on any governance issue. It provides advice to small- and medium-size companies that are, or are planning to go, public; and it provides corporate secretarial support to all companies.

In addition to this spectrum of governance offerings, IRI has developed a particular expertise in the issues facing the mutual fund industry, where it has assisted numerous investment fund families to set-up and run Independent Review Committees under NI 81-107.

To avail yourself of our specialist sound governance services please call Don Hathaway or W William Woods on 416.849.1928

www.independentreviewinc.com

Chairs and Tables:

Corporate Governance for Directors of Small- to Mid-sized Companies

Donald B. Hathaway

Sponsored by

INDEPENDENT REVIEW INC.

Published by

ISI *publications*

Chairs and Tables:
Corporate Governance for Directors of Small- to Mid-sized Companies

ISBN: 978-0-9782645-5-0
Copyright © 2008 Donald B. Hathaway
All rights reserved.

About the Publisher

This book is published by ISI Publications Limited. All enquiries should be directed to ISI Publications at info@isipublications.com or call:

UK	Hong Kong	Toronto
Tel: 44 1892 548881	Tel: 852 2877 3417	Tel: 416 849 1926

All ISI titles can be reviewed and purchased online at:

BOOKSonBIZ.com

THE ON-LINE BUSINESS BOOKSTORE

Printed in Canada

Acknowledgements

Writing a book was a daunting prospect, to say nothing about the amount of work entailed, but I had a lot of help and encouragement.

The biggest motivation came from Mary-Ann, my wife and partner in life, who kept putting it on the agenda at our morning coffee meetings until I gave in and got started, when she became the leader of the cheering section. This certainly would not have happened without her.

The Institute of Corporate Directors played a role, too. It is an inspiring organization, and the ICD Director Education Program convinced me that corporate governance and compliance are often separate issues, a theme in this book. Preparing for the DEP revealed the lack of a book dedicated to small businesses, and it is not a coincidence that I decided to write *Chairs and Tables* shortly after completing that program.

I was eventually able to talk to over 40 people, and their names are in Appendix One. I have given them a collective name, "the Wise", for they are, and generous of both their time and wisdom. Thank you, all of you, for your contributions and for the distinctive opportunity to spend time discussing the core of this book.

I offer a note of thanks to the many directors with whom I have had the pleasure of sharing a board and the many attendant experiences. Some were good, some were not, but all were opportunities to learn. Over the last 25 years, I have been on the board of about two dozen small companies, so I have a lot of tee shirts, but we learned some important lessons together.

Thank you to the many others who helped, especially Sarah for her enthusiasm and endless encouragement, Carol for editing and wisdom, Ellie for layout and good humour, Jeremy for sales and William for showing the way.

I am grateful to ISI Publications for its open and flexible style and its willingness to provide the appendices on its website, making them immediately available to those who need them.

Finally, the book recognizes the many amazing contributions of small companies, those wonderfully individualistic generators of more jobs, more innovative ideas and more taxes than all the rest of the organizational family put together.

Contents

Chairs and Tables

Chapter Six: Advanced Carpentry — Building a Better Board.......83

Chapter Seven: Conundrums Faced.....................................115

Chapter Eight: Special Relationships.................................137

Contents

Foreword

Gone are the days when boards were populated by those with little to do and less to say. Back then, boards had minimal effect on those rare occasions when they attempted change. It was an era when Irving Olds, a former chair of Bethlehem Steel could pronounce that, "Directors are like parsley on fish — decorative but useless". In stark contrast, today's boards are legal entities that have accepted a trust. Richard Leblanc and James Gillies insist that the board of directors is of paramount importance to the best interests of the corporation. Their book, *Inside the Boardroom*, informs us that under the law the board carries a legal responsibility for the business and its performance. I agree — so if you crave intellectually demanding issues, all having intersections with many stakeholders, you should give serious consideration to joining a board of directors.

It could be a company, a charity or a not-for-profit for they all have a lot in common, plus the obvious differences. Any of them will have a special appeal for those who wish to consume their spare time, perhaps all of their time, and are not dismayed by a bit of risk. Actually, it might be a lot of risk if your choice is to sit at the boardroom table of a publicly-traded company, and should you choose to sit in the chair, this book will add a dollop of empathy for your choice.

While considering whether the world needed yet another text on corporate governance, I scanned the shelves of my favourite bookstore, and it was clear that most authors had concerned themselves with larger companies and their more publicized issues. There were a few directed at the boards of charities or not-for-profit organizations, but notably absent was any attempt to deal with the issues more particular to the boards of small businesses. I found several great books written by people more qualified than I am, addressing corporate governance from many vantages, but missing from the field is the recognition that small companies face the same governance issues as their larger colleagues although they must do so with constrained resources. I will try to shed some light on those problems.

What do I mean by a "small" company? The number of definitions is about equal to the number of authorities, so for the purposes served here, let us agree that any company with annual revenues under $100 million is small. By this definition, there are many, many small companies in North America; in fact, more than 95% of all incorporated companies fall below that threshold. These small public companies face all the demands of the big guys, but without their resources. Consider that the out-of-pocket costs for a company with annual revenues of $50 million are about $1.5 million, simply to exist as a public entity. That subtracts about 3% from the bottom line and does not count the time, effort, stress and strain, all drawn from a small group of people. So, while the unique problems of large corporations deserve deference and the greatest respect, this book recognizes that complexity can come in small packages and the regulators are blind to size.

Public listings aside, the book is meant equally for the directors of the several hundreds of thousands of small companies that are not now, nor may ever be, listed on a stock exchange. Some are held very closely and privately, perhaps by the members of a family or a tightly-knit group of business partners. For these companies, governance has traditionally been provided by the shareholders' agreement, because they need not answer to anyone other than the owners, as long as they operate within the laws of the land. All are in business for economic gain, no matter how those are realized by the owners, and the effective pursuit of those returns is most often described by the time-worn term "good management".

Readers will discover that the view expressed in this book is that good management and good governance have so much in common that a greater recognition of their overlapping processes and methods would be salutary. No argument, they are applied under different circumstances, for different reasons, and with different constraints. Perhaps the most significant difference between the two is the emphasis on, and methods of, disclosure (notice that I did not say compliance, which comes later). I suggest that owners, management and directors would all be well served if disclosure was a central responsibility in all organizations, of all sizes, public and private alike. After all, the owners of a private company, who have put its care and feeding in the hands of professional managers and who have appointed directors to watch over those managers, want "disclosure" just as much as they would if they were shareholders in a public company.

In my opinion, the objective of corporate governance is to ensure that investor and shareholder decisions are informed, owners are alerted to risks, and it is easy to obtain important insights into the stewardship of the company and its operations. Good corporate governance ensures that the organization operates in a manner transparent to its stakeholders. Period. Full stop. It matters not whether we are talking about those elected to the board of the local ratepayer's association, the owners of a NASDAQ stock traded over the counter, or the directors of a Toronto Stock Exchange (TSX) listing. It is now broadly recognized that corporate governance is an essential safeguard for the stakeholders of any organization.

The burden of compliance, as this term is understood for a publicly-listed company or fund, is a separate issue; and it may have little to do with corporate governance, although we have fallen into the habit of confusing the two terms. A few chapters further along you will discover examples when compliance was enforced, but at the expense of the shareholder. That is not good governance.

Foreword

Please observe that I have no position on public versus private. I consider the decision to go public, or for private equity to become the owners of a public company, as one of the most important decisions to be made, a highly strategic one with profound implications and, therefore, exactly the preserve of the board. Choosing that direction is one of the fundamentals of corporate governance and, therefore, it is inappropriate to have a preference for public or public in the absence of the known requirements of the company and its shareholders.

Part of the thinking and planning for this book included re-visiting some of my old "friends", all well-worn volumes living in my personal library, one of them being *Inside the Boardroom* by Richard Leblanc and James Gillies. It is an excellent book and I recommend it highly. When I returned to it and re-read Chapter Nine, I was struck by the authors' characterization of the chair of a board, calling on the Latin phrase "*primus inter pares*", meaning first among equals. Since I knew this to mean that the person was not only the most senior among those of the same rank, but also carried overtones of special authority. I almost abandoned the project on the spot!

Having recovered my composure and taken the decision to plunge onward, I decided to seek out a few thought leaders and recognized experts in corporate governance and ask them to help me. It is a wonderful endorsement for the devotion and dedication of this group that very few refused. Their collective wisdom is found in Chapter Twelve, *A Word from the Wise*. I have not attributed individual quotations from the interviews. Instead, and because some of their remarks were especially pertinent, I have included statements from those interviews as words from "the Wise" without further identification. If you find the odd pithy remark by one of them and the speaker is identified, it is because that particular utterance was in a public forum and, thus, it is fair game to be repeated.

I hope to make this book useful to as many readers as possible, some of whom may be considering accepting their first directorship of either a public or a private company. While much of it would be useful to a small business in either Canada or the US, it is simply not feasible within a reasonable number of pages to cover the continent, so this version is for those with Canadian operations.

I have attempted to balance substantive information, even a touch of the thinking behind governance, with the teachings of experience. While this is not a how-to-do-it manual, I have included materials that should be useful to those responsible for managing or supporting the operation of a board of directors. On this point, I would consider it a great compliment if readers decide to use something from the book. Yes, it is under copyright, so you may not use the book or any part of it for direct commercial benefit, but if ideas, tables, appendices or whatever are useful to you in your role as a director, please be my guest. You can obtain Word versions of the appendices by going to www.isipublications.com.

Chapter One:

The Context of Corporate Governance

Capturing the absolute essence of a situation in a few words is a rare talent — and Kurt Eichenwald has it. He also captured our imagination and engendered mutterings of "Why didn't I think of that?" when he titled his wonderful book on the Enron scandal *Conspiracy of Fools*. It was so blindingly perfect — once Eichenwald spelled it out. Yes, there were a few crooks, but the real villains were the many, many people who were, to put it as kindly as possible, fast asleep at the switch. They were fools, and there is absolutely no reason for any director to follow in their footsteps.

The "First Sage of Business", Peter Drucker, once famously said: "In every single business failure of a large company in the last few decades, the board was the last to realize that things were going wrong." It is guaranteed that Eichenwald would agree, and that idea will reappear from time to time in this book, usually when the issue of the Duty of Care (DOC) is raised, for that duty will be portrayed as both essential to the job of the corporate director and equally as a bulwark against attack from various quarters. But I will stop there, for the DOC is simply one aspect of being a director, albeit a critical one. This book is really about the roles and responsibilities of directors, chairs and entire boards of small companies. It will display a special affection for the chair of any "small cap" company. Let us start by placing corporate governance in its legal, ethical, and regulatory context and, of course, within its sphere of operations, the board itself.

In the interest of those coming to a board for the first time, I will start with an abbreviated primer. Some readers may wish to skip the next few pages.

The Legal Context

The media, depending on their political bent, would persuade us that companies are governed solely by "the suits" or by "big business", or by forces so devious that they remain conveniently unidentified and unexplained. Aside from such popular fiction, real-world corporations are "governed" formally by a board of directors empowered by the shareholders to manage

Chairs and Tables

the business and by the government though legislation and regulation. This starts the moment that a new company is incorporated and gets its charter — a formal contract between the owners and the government — allowing those owners the right to operate their business with limited liability, as long as they obey certain rules.

As an aside, one might say, "Aye, there's the rub!" for those "certain rules" do not have certainty. For those with time on their hands, wander through the Canada Business Corporations Act (CBCA), or any of its provincial counterparts, and discover that they have precious little to say about governance. Given the prominence of governance and all related issues circa 2008, one might expect more. Disappointment looms, for these musty tomes have changed remarkably little in the last one hundred plus years. That is not to say, however, that the rules and regulations, the operating manual if you like, has remained static. One of the most serious governance issues is determining how to pick a pathway through the statutory minefield created by scandal and over-reaction. But that issue can wait, for it is certainly not going away.

What is corporate governance anyway? Well, David Leighton and Donald Thain in their excellent book, *Making Boards Work*, suggest that it is the "political science" of the business world. As such, it provides both theory and practice for electing or appointing directors, who thus become responsible for the corporation as a whole, particularly for planning and strategy, setting policies and taking the decisions to implement them.

Further, "those who rule" derive their legitimacy and power from the fact that they have been elected by the owners of the business to represent their interests. The shareholders usually choose delegation to their agents (also called directors) as the means of removing themselves from tasks and responsibilities that may be beyond their skills or something that they simply prefer to avoid. The CBCA states that:

> "Subject to any unanimous shareholder agreement, the directors shall manage, or supervise the management of, the business and affairs of a corporation."

So, starting with the charter, which the government issues to the owners, who in turn elect the directors, there are three layers of governance, and as we cross its threshold to see how the company operates on a day-to-day basis, we find management plus all other employees, adding two further layers. We now have the five constituent parts defined by Leighton and Thain — I trust they agree with my version of how they relate, one to another, within corporate governance as we now understand it.

Reality is not as neat and tidy as the chart, for there are many areas of overlap and interdependency. For example, a senior executive is likely to be a shareholder and may also be a director, especially in a private company. Further, this somewhat complex structure lives and operates within a yeasty environment of politics on multiple levels; social forces emanating from the

The Corporate Governance Structure

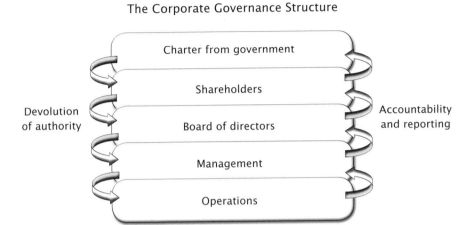

Devolution
of authority

Charter from government

Shareholders

Board of directors

Management

Operations

Accountability
and reporting

community, special interest groups and the media; the national and local economies; and technological change. That global environment is but the outer matryoshka (one might speculate as to the identity of the irreducible core, usually a baby in the traditional Russian dolls), with the next doll the legal framework defined by government and implemented by the legislative, administrative and judicial systems, then the company and so on. The five hierarchical layers provide accountability for modern, western-world corporations. In the exact middle of that hierarchy and responsible across all of it is the board of directors.

Governance 101

The whole governance process builds from two established facts, both enshrined in law in our system, that is, shareholders have property rights and the board is their agent. Directors must agree to be elected and they sign a consent that says they agree. Once they are elected, they are bound to act as agents of the owners — they are the "go betweens", the interpreters of what the owners want and how it should be achieved. Directors accept two major duties to the corporation and it is fundamental that new directors understand that these duties are to the company first and, after that, to shareholders and all others.

The first duty is as a fiduciary and it is useful to clarify exactly what this means. The Shorter Oxford Dictionary says that "fiduciary" is a noun, meaning "something that secures trust" or "a person who holds a position of trust with respect to someone else". That is clear. A fiduciary duty is a legal relationship between two or more parties and is the highest standard of care imposed by either equity or common law. Directors may not put personal interests before their duty to the company, and they must not profit from their position as a fiduciary, unless the beneficiary (the company) consents.

Chairs and Tables

The courts have developed a basic test for determining whether fiduciary obligations arise from a relationship: first, the fiduciary has the ability to exercise some discretion or power; second, the fiduciary can unilaterally exercise that power so as to affect the interests of the beneficiary; and third, the beneficiary is in a position of vulnerability at the hands of the fiduciary. Since fiduciary originates with the Latin word fides, meaning faith, this duty is often called the Duty of Trust (DOT).

Next is the DOC as it will be called hereafter. This seems more difficult to clarify, and a dictionary is not much help, but DOC is actually a relatively simple and objective concept. It is usually understood to be the expectation that directors will act in the manner of a reasonably prudent person in comparable circumstances, exercising their judgment and doing the best they possibly can. Difficulties arise from our interpretation of "reasonably prudent" and "comparable circumstances". I include both phrases deliberately due to their prominence in governance writing, debates and law.

Directors are expected to meet the standards of a "reasonable person", an important concept of the "negligence tort". The law of torts has developed over centuries, and since it is based on precedents and the judge's interpretation of them, it could be described as a judge-made law. This allows a court to adapt to the circumstance and, thus, what might be considered reasonable in a particular situation. Chapter Three is all about DOC and why it is both hard work and the director's friend.

Directors derive their legitimacy from the fact that they have been elected by the owners, who have granted them the power to act on their behalf. With authority comes accountability, and directors are not only legally empowered but responsible for increasing the value of the company entrusted to them. As noted previously, the company operates within a legal, economic, political and social context, and the board of directors is given the authority and responsibility to control and guide it within the constraints imposed by that environment. Over time, the performance of the board is measured by the increase in shareholder value, that is, the worth of the company.

The board puts the company in the hands of the best available CEO and a supporting cast of top officers, placing them in charge and delegating to them the authority to manage the company, with all that implies. The role of the CEO is to run the company every day, and he or she is held accountable by the board to ensure that the company performs according to plans which the board has approved. The board has the mechanisms to enforce that accountability, usually through one or more standing committees, which are responsible for ensuring that the appropriate systems are in place. Such systems normally include monitoring, reward and censure, and are usually designed and developed by management and brought to the board for approval. Alternatively, one of the board's standing committees may take a leading role in the design work, perhaps with the assistance of an external subject matter expert. Either way, this is another example of the manner in which directors and executives alike frequently find themselves not only addressing the same issues, but perhaps sharing in their resolution, particularly in small companies.

In its trustee and guidance roles, the board monitors and evaluates company results, and it takes action through its capacity to compensate, support, discipline and, if necessary, to remove management, if its performance does not meet the expected corporate goals. An important aspect of this oversight is to ensure that all of this is accomplished with high ethical standards.

The board is responsible for fulfilling fiduciary and legal requirements, meaning adherence to the laws and regulatory requirements, payment of taxes and statutory deductions, and the preparation and maintenance of minutes, documents, contracts and records. This means ensuring that the company acts at all times in accordance with relevant laws and regulations, while adhering to high ethical and moral standards, which can become a perplexing task if the company ventures into the international sphere, where what is considered locally as "moral" may be at odds with home base. In addition, the board is responsible for acting as necessary in unusual circumstances. In emergencies or crisis situations such as raids, severe financial troubles, insolvency, death or removal of the CEO or chair and so on, the board or a special committee may have to take direct control of the company to make major decisions and take action on behalf of the owners.

Lastly, it is important to note the board's responsibility for the management of corporate governance. Only the board is qualified to manage its own function. To upgrade the work and performance of the board continuously means: defining the job; implementing the job definition; monitoring, assessing and evaluating the work and process of the board as an operating unit and of its members individually; and doing everything needed to ensure the competent performance of all its duties.

Given that the legal duty of the board is to act as agent for the shareholders in overseeing the affairs of the corporation, how do its responsibilities translate into a practical "job description" for a director? As the legally empowered intermediary between shareholders and management, the board must relate to both of these groups within the political structure of the firm. On behalf of the shareholders, the job of the board is fiduciary, acting as stewards for those owners in safeguarding and maximizing the value of the company's assets. Prospective investors and other stakeholders expect that DOC will be in place. For management, directors offer high-level advice and guidance on the strategic management of the corporation. Directors govern by taking responsibility for the overall strategic direction of the company, mitigating risks, resolving big issues and overseeing the necessary decisions and initiatives flowing from the strategy and the annual plan.

As you might expect, communication is an important task of the board. Indeed, the demand for "transparent disclosure" has placed so much emphasis on communications — read "disclosure" — that it can easily impinge on the more fundamental responsibilities of strategy, risk management and oversight of the senior team. It is not enough simply to have an effective communication process *per se*; the real responsibility is its content. In this instance, the medium is not the message (but wait and directors will get a turn!). The information flowing from a company is meant to allow all interested parties to monitor the company's performance and then evaluate the results against what was expected or promised. It must also compare and contrast how other companies did, how the economy performed and so on, providing a context for the company and its accomplishments. The board is held accountable for the completeness and accuracy of that information and the timeliness of its availability. From there, it is easy to understand why boards are now responsible for selected and specific management processes, perhaps the most critical being "Internal Control over Financial Reporting" (ICFR), but more of that later, other than to note that ICFR is again an example of where the boundary between board and management is hazy, or where managing and governing use the same tools in different ways and for different purposes.

Where are We Going?

Small companies are at least as dependent as their larger cousins on a robust capital market system; in fact, they want that market to be in nothing but rude good health. Such a healthy disposition follows from confidence, which rests on trust, which implies transparency and, as a character with a wonderful bald dome once said, "Etcetera, etcetera, etcetera". Another factor is that Canadian companies are North Americans, in fact, they depend on the continental market for their growth and prosperity whether they are importers, exporters or some combination of the two. It is a small wonder that the Sarbanes-Oxley Act (SOX) had a profound effect on the regulatory landscape on both sides of the Canada-US border, but even before SOX, Canada was set on the path to improved governance when Peter Dey delivered "Where Were the Directors?" in 1994 (see Appendix Seven, *Sources and References*). Since 1995, and thus well before SOX, the Toronto Stock Exchange (TSX) required all TSX-listed companies to disclose the extent of their compliance with the 14 corporate governance guidelines which it published at that time. These became the basis for the so-called "harmonized guidelines" which aligned compliance in Canada with Section 404 of SOX.

As power shifted away from the stock exchanges and into the hands of the regulators, eg, the Canadian Securities Administrators (CSA), more layers of compliance were added. In January 2004, the CSA published a draft Multilateral Instrument on Disclosure of Corporate Governance Practices and a Multilateral Policy on Effective Corporate Governance. In November 2004, it published a revised National Instrument (NI 58-101) on practices and National Policy (NP 58-201) on effectiveness. These address board composition, the board mandate, committee charters, position descriptions (for the CEO, the board chair and the chairs of standing committees), orientation and continuing education for directors, codes of business conduct and ethics, and board assessments. These were drafts in 2004, but they rolled into place for filings beginning in 2005 and are now an accepted fact of life for all reporting issuers. Amendments arrive in a steady stream and wisdom dictates currency with the evolving disclosure requirements.

We are caught in an "evolving door", to mix a metaphor, and our regulatory destination is somewhere in the mists of the future. Speaking to the Empire Club on "Revolution in Financial Services" in February 1986, then Chairman of the Ontario Securities Commission (OSC), Stanley M. Beck, Q.C. stated:

> "In typically Canadian fashion, we have commissioned a seemingly endless series of reports to diagnose and to prescribe. The result is a babble of conflicting advice, with both provincial and federal governments yet to take any significant action. But financial markets do not wait upon dithering governments, and the structure of the Canadian financial market continues to change in response to international forces from which we are not immune."

As if this were not enough, there are two overall approaches, perhaps philosophies, affecting the manner in which the roadmap is drawn. As a generality, the approach south of the 49th parallel is based on rules, while the Canadian tack relies on a set of principles. (I hasten to add that the Americans have principles and the Canadians obey the rules!) These tendencies were established in the early history of each country. For example, Noah Webster lobbied the US Congress to make it a legal requirement to use "simplified spelling", as it was then described, which would have made the US the only country in history where deviant spelling would be a punishable offence. Perhaps this was simply part of the understandable desire for a distinctive American approach, given the Revolutionary War and the fervent desire to banish English ways and thinking. On the other hand, Canadian law and thus regulation has been, from colonial days, based on English law and its traditional reflection of underlying and commonly held principles. These have not been codified to the same extent as in the US, so the Canadian practice is to return to first principles rather than apply pre-conceived regulations. For directors, an apparent divide is in "generally accepted accounting principles" (GAAP). In spite of the word "generally", US GAAP are hag-ridden by minutia, whereas the Canadian variety, although certainly a detailed set of instructions, frequently require a lot of interpretation based on an understanding of those underlying principles. This can lead to difficulties when two seemingly eminent authorities disagree and proffer differing interpretations. The company and its directors are in the middle, forced to choose between the two experts, and there are penalties if they get it wrong.

Speaking of interpreting, perhaps this is the time to differentiate three words that recur not just within these pages, but in every aspect of business life. They are governance, disclosure and compliance.

> **Governance** is an amalgam of legal authority and collaborative processes to allocate an organization's resources and direct its affairs to the attainment of those purposes for which the organization exists. The origins of the word suggest the notion of "steering", ie, a group, a company or perhaps an entire country. National governments of

many types are the embodiment of how an entire country manifests itself in the world, regardless of our opinion of the manner in which that is accomplished. For corporate governance, there is the crucial distinction between providing direction versus the traditional "top-down" approach of a government driving an entire society, ie, corporate governance is the political science of business. As an attempt at a general statement about it, the rational purpose of governance is to assure that an organization produces a worthwhile pattern of good results while avoiding an undesirable pattern of bad ones. Note that this is reasonably consistent with most definitions of management.

Disclosure is most frequently used to mean providing information. When a reporter writes a newspaper story, the contents are said to have been disclosed. That is one form of voluntary disclosure. When a person involved in a legal action is questioned under oath, they are said to have been deposed, and they have disclosed their information because they did not have a choice, much like the continuous disclosure required of publicly-listed companies. We associate disclosure with public issuers and seldom apply it to a private company, because we have come to place the word consistently in the context of compliance as the regulators mean it to be used. The point made here is that disclosure also includes revealing the same information, in the same manner, to the owners of a private company. Management and, one hopes, the directors, have the proximity to possess the facts and figures vital to those shareholders. In this case, professional management and the board of directors act towards the company's owners as if they are the "regulator".

Compliance generally means conforming to a specification, standard or law, and presumably, it is clearly defined (would that this was so!). As used in the business context, compliance means the provision of defined information to satisfy the regulations or standards imposed by external bodies such as the CSA and its members, or a stock exchange. Compliance could also mean conforming to standards such as GAAP or ISO 9000 (the family of standards for quality management systems maintained by ISO, the International Organization for Standardization, and administered by accreditation and certification bodies) or meeting a security requirement when doing work for a government.

Governance, disclosure and compliance share certain concerns, but my worry is that they are too often seen as having an inordinately large degree of overlap, to the point that they are sometimes used interchangeably to the detriment of clarity and, thus, good governance. All three also have commonalities with certain management processes, and this adds to the confusion. As the three are transposed into synonyms, "transparency" suffers, which is, of course, another frequently used word and something of a grail for all and sundry.

Only a couple of pages back, I managed to use all three words in one sentence, "the Toronto Stock Exchange — required all TSX-listed companies to disclose the extent of their compliance with the 14 corporate governance guidelines which it published at that time". I am still content with that, but I sincerely hope that the manner in which we conduct business becomes increasingly easy to understand and, thus, more transparent while we sort the strands in the bowl of spaghetti called regulations. We might profitably consider whether some of the "box ticking" variants in the governance regime actually make a contribution to the company and its shareholders.

This diagram is representational rather than accurate, but it does illustrate a way to think about the relationships.

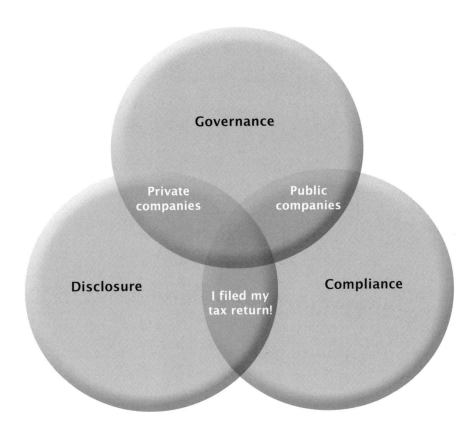

In concluding this very general description, I want to reflect a thought presented first in the Foreword to this book, I trust that one of its tenets is clear: high standards of governance are essential safeguards for the stakeholders of any and all organizations. It is, therefore, the job of the board and its members to deliver that safeguard, a task that could be seen as two duties and five responsibilities. The next chapter will go beyond that glibness and provide a serious description.

Chapter Two:

The Profile of a Corporate Director

A stroll in the aisles of any bookstore with a few shelves devoted to the business world presents an incredible proliferation of management, leadership, governance and other business-related books that have poured forth in recent years. You will have your own view as to the usefulness of many of these. A few proffer advice as to what would constitute the "compleat director", but this book will not attempt the same feat because I do not believe it can be done. Every organization is different, with its unique vision and plans to achieve a uniquely defined goal. This implies that the specs for a director to provide guidance along a chosen path must necessarily vary to match the road. Thankfully, the pool of talent from which directors can be drawn is equal to the many varieties needed, but a director's profile must be drawn with the organization and its plans in mind. One size fits all simply will not do.

Chapter Twelve of this book is entitled *A Word from the Wise*, which draws on the experiences and insights of those who were willing to share their knowledge as the background for that chapter. They are the thought leaders and experts whom I refer to as "the Wise". They agreed universally on a few essential ingredients related to either personal characteristics or experience, or both, but beyond that their suggestions were situational and hence, widely different. The old tendency to favour a former CEO did surface, but it got very few votes, and those were accompanied by the caveat that boards need a more diverse set of backgrounds across their directorships. The interviewees were divided in their opinion as to whether industry knowledge and experience are absolute necessities or simply nice to have, and they were not completely united on the fundamental qualities of a director. Some characteristics were universally admired. Integrity, wisdom, maturity and judgment topped the list. To paraphrase a sentiment expressed variously by those interviewed, "A great education and a lot of experience may never be used unless the director can make a wise choice and then have the capacity to get others to agree with the decision".

Chairs and Tables

One person cannot accumulate the experience or knowledge of the Wise, but one perk of writing a book is that the author can always have the last word. Here is my "last word" on the profile of a director, so far as this is feasible, starting with a couple of assumptions about all directors on all boards.

The Author's View

I wrote this book primarily for the directors of small companies, and it is just as impossible to draft a single, one-size-fits-all profile for those directors as for any others. That said, the essentials — not the "nice to have" qualities, but the *prerequisites for everyone* on the board — are nowhere more important than for those on the boards of smaller organizations, where resources might not be as plentiful or as deep, while simultaneously the company's size or its earlier stage of development could mean more risk. There are basic preconditions for all directors and the situation dictates the choice of specific competencies. The profile that follows is in three parts, each a step in thinking about a given person for a board. The first layer consists of prerequisites, followed by a core of personal traits or characteristics, and my belief is that at least two or three should be present in each director, with all of them available across an entire board. Finally, there is the third layer, specific to the situation and the reason that there are at least as many director profiles as there are boards.

Prerequisite Competencies

The word competency is used as a collective for all traits, characteristics, skills, experiences or other aspects that might distinguish an individual during a board's selection process.

Wisdom and integrity are fundamental. Yes, there are many contenders for the job, and it is likely impossible to choose one over another except in particular situations, but if a choice must to be made there is no substitute for being wise and honest. Please allow a clarification. I understand wisdom to be the ability to use the sum of one's combined experience and knowledge to govern all actions and decisions. This is a lot like saying that wisdom is developed by learning from many experiences, including mistakes, implying that a certain passage of time is needed. I believe that it is practically impossible to acquire wisdom without prolonged learning by experience. As it accumulates, personal wisdom comes to include individual ethical guidelines, social mores, personality, perspective on life, social attitudes, and so forth. I am admitting to the use of "wisdom" as a very broad term, embracing multiple elements that, while their individual merits may be argued separately, in real life are bound to bear on any serious decision as an apparently inseparable set of motivators. So, as it is used here, wisdom is a term that others may dissect so as to choose among its components. I prefer their combination.

Integrity means actions based on consistent internal principles. When someone acts on the basis of a set of principles or a set of core values, and their actions always reflect those fundamentals, we ascribe the virtue of integrity. While those values or principles may change over time, or we might disagree with some of them, as long as that person's actions are consistent with them, we believe that individual to have integrity. The concept of integrity is directly linked to responsibility and accountability, since implementation spawned by principles is being carried forward in an acceptable manner to achieve a specific outcome. We sometimes say, "She has the courage of her convictions"; she has the courage to act. As an aside, one of the Wise, when discussing director certification, said, "You cannot teach courage". It is one of life's comforts to know with virtual certainty the manner in which someone will respond because we know that person's values and therefore how they will act.

The next essential is that all directors must be financially literate. This is not an "added feature" like call waiting, it is a mandatory skill fundamental to the director's job. While the ability to spot a flaw or inconsistency in the financial statements would be a prized competency anywhere, it is positively golden in the director of a small company, and those with the talent are sought by one and all. If you have difficulty understanding financial statements, either become educated or avoid boards, at least those where fiduciary responsibility has its customary meaning. Going further, if you cannot spot a fatal flaw yourself, you must be able to understand it when someone else draws it to your attention. This is a business, after all, it exists to make a profit and directors have accepted the responsibility for that result. If the company is publicly listed the directors carry added risk; therefore, become comfortable with basic corporate finance or stay away. For all boards, private or public, each director is responsible for his or her personal DOC; ergo they must be financially literate.

If you wish to brush up on some neglected skills, it would be worthwhile looking at some of the tutorials available through Investopedia.com. Find your way to "Advanced Financial Statement Analysis" written by David Harper — it is available in a printer-friendly version of 66 pages.

I suggest that the truly competent director should be able to go beyond the consolidated financial statements to understand the numbers that tell the tale of how the organization operates, and especially how it spends or earns money. We have all accepted the fact that financial statements are the primary means of communicating financial information to the external stakeholders. Fair enough, but they are historical documents telling the story of the previous quarter or year. By the time they have been approved and published, they become the barn door for a horse that has galloped into the next county. If "the financials" are the customary insight into the company, you should ask for more. Directors should receive and be able to understand at least an overview drawn from the managerial accounting system, an extract from the plans, forecasts and internal reports used by the

CEE Suite (This term is used through this book to mean the CEO and his or her direct reports, ie, the CFO, the CTO, the CMO and those with an executive vice president title.) to run the business. Without understanding how the CEE Suite makes decisions, it is unlikely that you will be able to understand risks as they appear on the horizon, when something can still be done to avoid them. This information is the basis for penetrating — and helpful — inquiries by the directors, but they must possess the knowledge and insight to frame those questions.

As an aside, I have wondered for years about people who seem proud of their innumeracy, proclaiming that, "I don't know anything about numbers!" But I digress.

A director must have the time and the inclination to devote to the task. It should be unnecessary to state this, but research reveals many who have an unmanageable burden and do not recognise it. Those who say, with careless disregard, "I sit on about 10 boards", are kidding themselves and doing a disservice to others. Their reach exceeds their grasp, for unless the boards referred to are trivial, it is simply impossible to sit on 10 boards and perform well. Elsewhere in this book (see Chapter Five) there is a summation of the time spent on corporate governance (read: doing the job of a director) that advises the new director to find 250 to 350 hours per year if he or she is a director who also chairs a standing committee of a publicly-traded company. You will certainly consume all those hours and likely many more as a director of a small company, for you will find yourself involved in multiple ways as you veer across the white line between governance and management. It is for this reason that you should question prospective directors closely about their discretionary time prior to asking for their commitment to the board. Make no mistake, being a director is not an honorary role and having time that can be allocated exclusively to the board is a basic criteria. Equally obvious is the commitment to the organization in question, given the availability of time.

The director must have a genuine interest in the company and its sector. This assumption may seem evident as well, but it is such an essential quality in directors of small companies that it bears repeating. Why does it deserve more emphasis for those on such boards? There are three good reasons. First, you will be expected to bring a lot to the party and a strong personal interest will make it more likely that you can do that, because you are active in the industry, read trade publications, maintain contacts, go to trade shows and so forth. The prerequisite is an abiding interest that motivates your involvement, which is likely the result of direct experience in the sector. Second, since we are thinking about small companies, you may be asked to advise rather than oversee certain operational aspects, at least in the company's earlier stages. Your interest must be the source of your reward, for the board fee will provide only for the oversight tasks. The third and final reason is that your interest in the sector should lead to a deeper understanding of its inherent risks. This is not "familiarity breeds contempt"; it is a higher tolerance through a more thorough knowledge, allowing you to accept those risks that are peculiar to the industry and are simply a consequence of being in it. It will allow you to concentrate on issues that you can affect and put aside the immoveable risks that are a natural part of the industry.

Core Competencies

After the prerequisites, there is a constellation of essentials that are more or less equally important, called "core competencies" as a collective term. Colin B. Carter and Jay W. Lorsch choose six essentials — including intellectual capacity, interpersonal skills, instinct, interest, integrity and a commitment to contribute — in *Back to the Drawing Board* (Harvard Business School Press, 2004).

It is easy to agree with all six, but there are other attractive characteristics and, without attempting an exhaustive list, it would be hard to argue against any of good instincts, a commitment to contribute, confidence, balance, intellectual capacity, high performance standards and the like. The problem with lengthy lists of attributes is that it becomes almost impossible to choose, and choose we must when selecting a director. You will have your own list of favourites; here are mine:

1. **Consensus builders are invaluable.** Their gift is close to being essential, but perhaps it is not needed in every director. Consensus builders lead or smooth the process that not only seeks the agreement of most participants, but attempts to resolve or mitigate the objections of the minority to achieve the most agreeable decision. It is difficult to discern this competency in advance, but if you can get insights from other situations, and the prospective director has the happy knack of helping a group to reach common ground, do whatever you must to recruit her or him to your board. By the way, consensus builder moves from "nice to have" in a director to essential in the board chair.

2. **Creativity** will support the board's role in corporate strategy, either as a contributor while strategy is developed or as one who "gets it" when management presents the strategic plan for board approval. The director who consistently generates new ideas or concepts, or who can discern new associations between the ideas or concepts that we have at hand, is a treasure on a board.

    "Creativity, as has been said, consists largely of rearranging what we know in order to find out what we do not know... Hence, to think creatively, we must be able to look afresh at what we normally take for granted." (source unknown)

3. **Breadth of knowledge** ranks high on my list because I believe that those who have a comprehensive view of the world are likely to have the faculty to place issues in their context more readily than those with a narrower base of knowledge and understanding. Perhaps because my original education was as an engineer — ie, straitjacket narrow — I quickly came to appreciate a more eclectic preparation. It seemed to lead to an understanding of issues, whereas this newly graduated engineer was ill-prepared. We need not find the fabled "renaissance" scope of knowledge in every director, but more is better.

4. **High personal standards** help to set the tone at the top. Directors ought to be exemplars, a possibility only when they are chosen because they set strong standards of performance and then meet them. The directors are more visible than they realize, especially in smaller organizations, and their performance, good, bad or indifferent, is only too plain for all to see. Further, a board is like any small team, each member must play a part and play it well, or the responsibility will fall to another director and that will shortly erode the team concept.

5. **Interpersonal skills** are like the spoonful of sugar in the old song, they ease the way for thorny issues. Respect, good manners and a positive outlook combine into someone that we enjoy working with, where we would prefer to avoid the difficult individuals in our midst. Resolving the tough issues before a board demands a lot; it should not include resorting to a lengthy string of deleted expletives.

6. **An appreciation of governance** completes my list of core competencies, and its appearance as the last entry is intended to emphasize rather than detract. Small companies are often led by an owner-operator who has little interest beyond satisfying the legal minimum. Governance is seen as an obstacle, something of a nuisance, to be taken in small doses if it cannot be avoided. That mentality is a burden to the board and a risk to the company; it is certainly something to be avoided.

While the chart on the following page sums up my thinking on the profile of a corporate director, the prerequisites and core competencies would suit not-for-profit boards too. One might add others to the six core competencies in the table, and they might be chosen with the situation in mind or, as in this example, those which would be universally appropriate. For example, those who possess a generosity of spirit are valuable people, for they may make their business contacts available or act as a mentor or help with financing, actions not likely to be required by the board charter, but immensely valuable contributions nonetheless.

The Profile of a Corporate Director

The Profile of a Corporate Director

Prerequisites	Core Competencies	Situational Competencies
• Integrity	• Consensus building	• Industry knowledge
• Wisdom	• Creativity	• Functional skills
• Financial literacy	• Breadth of knowledge	• Executive experience
• Time	• High standards	• Specialist experience
• Interest	• Interpersonal skills	
	• Appreciates governance	

After these, one can turn to the competencies leading to the choice of a particular person as a director in a specific situation. The chart suggests four categories of experience, knowledge and skill, and of course there could be many more. The right hand-side of the chart should be driven by the company's business and strategic plans, with their implications arrayed against the current directors in a matrix, so that needs become obvious. The requirement could be quite specific, for example, a board seeking a new audit chair might specify an accounting designation for that director, or demand a given number of years of experience in a reporting issuer in the same industry.

Selecting a director is a topic addressed in more detail in Chapter Six, *Advanced Carpentry: Building a Better Board.*

Chapter Three:

The Duty of Care as Job One

I am seriously tempted (tempted, but not fully convinced), to advise one and all to forget directors' and officers' (D&O) insurance and, in its stead, place their faith in the DOC. Think about it. Review the many examples on either side of the Canada-US border where assorted executives and directors have found themselves facing legal actions arising from those very roles. In an uncomfortably large proportion of those instances, either the insurance policy had a flaw which left the plaintiff without coverage or, though the basics were covered, the attendant costs were not repaid until after the completion of the suit, a potentially disastrous situation for those caught in the toils of the action. This is to say nothing of the hours of frustration, stress and anxiety accompanying the whole discordant mess. Add to this the problem of affordability for the small company, the challenge of buying enough insurance to make it truly useful instead of a chimera that cannot withstand a true test. Take a realistic view of what D&O insurance can and cannot do, and consider that there has yet to a case where the director was found guilty if he or she could show with reasonable conclusiveness that they had been attentive to their DOC. You must have both, but "DOC" is the director's bulwark.

First, do you recall that off-the-cuff remark about two duties and a few tasks? DOC is one of those duties, and the tasks or responsibilities are how to accomplish it. To reiterate: every director of every board is personally and individually responsible to the corporation for a fiduciary duty and a DOC. An indispensable book on corporate governance by Carol Hansell, *What Directors Need to Know* (Thomson Carswell, 2003. Reprinted by permission of Thomson Carswell, a division of Thomson Canada Limited.) has this to say.

> *"Every director has two basic duties to the corporation — a fiduciary duty and a duty of care. These are very powerful concepts in law. A court will deal harshly with a director who has acted in a manner contrary to one or both of these duties, but will be very reluctant to question the decisions made by a board in a manner consistent with these duties."*

Chairs and Tables

In this chapter, I want to address the DOC and we should start with the simple question: what does the "DOC" mean? What does it take to make it happen? How would we know it when we see it? What steps would you take to satisfy yourself that the DOC has been done? How would you respond to a new director's questions on the DOC? Well, part of the answer lies in taking care of the five tasks, because in accomplishing them, a director goes much of the way to fulfilling the DOC. The following pages are an overview of those tasks, and they will get a more thorough treatment through the remainder of this book.

The Big Five

Let us admit at the outset that there may be more than five responsibilities, or perhaps there are fewer, or at least their demands on a director's time and attention may not be equal. But clearly, some are more important than others and so can be seen as the core of a director's responsibilities, those present for all directors of all organizations. Why five? As noted earlier, I visited a few old friends as part of the preparation for this book, that is, I reviewed my small collection of texts and articles on corporate governance, plus there were, of course, the insights of the Wise. Based on this modest bit of research, I can report to you that agreement on the key responsibilities of the board is hardly universal.

Opinions on what a director does are well portrayed by the old parable about the blind men describing an elephant. By this I mean that if your apprehension about the elephantine responsibilities of a director is shaped by your view that directors are the agents of the shareholders, then you will probably see their first responsibility as acting on the owners' behalf to monitor the behaviour and performance of the CEE Suite. Otherwise, the owners would supervise directly, rather than choosing to elect directors and remove themselves from the fray. If your stance is that of a lawyer you would probably emphasize fulfilling the legal framework that is the consequential side effect of incorporation. Those who are management gurus think that directors are there to give strategic oversight and promote the company to the world at large. Still others think of directors as a pipeline to capital and business alliances. And so it goes, from strategy to CEO succession to coaching and sounding board, many roles and responsibilities, all combined and recombined as the company grows and develops.

In my view, the "Big Five" are strategy, resources, risk and corporate performance, all operating through a disclosure and communications process with the rest of the world. They comprise the essential core of a director's responsibilities to the organization. I expect to draw criticism from some quarters by placing corporate performance among a director's responsibilities in such a direct way, but it is difficult to see an alternative given the stewardship responsibility of the director. I do not intend to imply that directors are to cross over into management, to have annual targets for sales or revenue, or anything of the sort. But shareholders invest for gains, and I suggest that many would prefer to see stewardship expressed so that it has a more direct linkage to at least the long-term results for the company than has been visible until now. In small companies, coincident roles create overlapping goals, since owner, director and executive are terms that may fit one person, especially during a start up or just after a merger or acquisition.

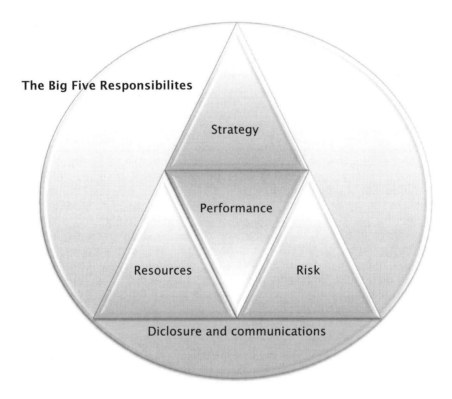

The Big Five Responsibilites

Strategy

Performance

Resources

Risk

Diclosure and communications

Presenting the Big Five as a "job description" would reveal that there is a lot to be done to fulfill each of the five responsibilities (in fact, Appendix Two provides sample job descriptions). For example, the "resources" responsibility includes populating the CEE Suite and helping fill the organization's coffers, but it could also mean helping to secure a key patent or the operating characteristics of a power plant the company expects to build. Managing risk obviously includes financial and marketplace hazards, but it also covers operating on the straight and narrow. Finally, there is the collective responsibility for communications and disclosure, congenital twins who sometimes disagree.

The point is not whether a director's job can be carved into different shapes that fit into a neat graphic. The purpose of this chapter is to emphasize those things that *must be done* if a director's DOC is to be accomplished satisfactorily. We will start with corporate performance, which is accomplishing those things for which the organization exists.

Corporate Performance

Businesses — small or large, public or private — have a central purpose: they exist to multiply the value of the investment made when they were created. Along the way they accomplish many other things, such as creating jobs, paying taxes and doing good things in their communities, all part and parcel of what a company should do. None of this need obscure the true rationale for incorporation: to pool capital, to limit or spread risks and to create a return on shareholder investment. For that matter, creating shareholder value and doing good works go hand in hand when aligned by a thoughtful strategy and pushed by the tone at the top. This statement of the blindingly obvious is true for large and small alike, but their mix of responsibilities may be somewhat different. Allow me to explain.

The scope and scale of smaller organizations allow directors to "connect the dots" more readily than might otherwise be the case, so the performance of an individual and his or her contribution to a corporate goal are usually under a microscope. For example, the directors of a large enterprise are likely to see sales as an aggregate number, perhaps presented by region or product line. Those on the board of a small company may know the targets and progress of every sales person. The disparity with the larger company goes further. While the key word for directors of large companies is oversight, in smaller ones there is a mix of responsibilities, and directors often contribute in a more direct manner. While this does not mean that directors have a sales quota, it is not uncommon for directors to place their Rolodex in service. On one board where I serve, it is expected that directors will introduce the VP of sales to a new prospect once every quarter — a goal for the directors if you will — and the chair of the board keeps a scorecard. The company is growing quickly and, while the ongoing general support of the board is expected, directors will no longer carry this specific and individual responsibility when revenue reaches the $50 million mark. In the meantime, more than three years have passed, and five directors have facilitated more than half of the gross of excellent sales leads. Most became a sale with a lower cost of acquisition and a shorter cycle.

The directors' independence has not been impaired. The reward for their quarterly sales role is the certain knowledge that they made a difference when it was needed, that the revenue growth admired by the street was on their watch, and they were on the team. No commissions, no bonuses, but everyone won, especially the shareholders.

The directors of other small companies can relate similar experiences. They recount examples of securing financing, recruiting key employees, coaching and mentoring, and many other direct, personal contributions that cannot be placed under the umbrella of oversight. These are hands-on contributions and the expectation of them, of viewing them as a part of a director's responsibilities, is a significant difference from what is expected of a director of a large company.

Having noted this difference, it is important to also add that none of this reduces the oversight aspect of the director's responsibilities. Board supervision still focuses on management's accountability for performance. It ensures that purpose and strategy are defined, and expects everything to flow from there, that plans are organized and implemented, objectives are met and the company competes successfully. This is another way of saying that the requirements that merit the continuing support of shareholders and investors are satisfied.

That same oversight requires the board to have a direct role in the delicate business known as goal setting and review or performance management or some similar tag. More will be said on performance later, but two words of caution at this stage. First, the CEE Suite is often heard to say "leave me alone and fire me if the results are bad", which may work, except that the feedback is usually too slow in the results-sensitive world of the small company. The board cannot — or certainly should not — wait until year-end. When the evidence finally becomes clear, it may be too late and there could be serious damage that will be difficult and costly to rectify. Second, just imagine the absolute impossibility of this task if the CEO and the chair of the board is one and the same person. While about 75% of the boards of larger Canadian companies have split the chair and CEO roles, duality remains a temptation in smaller companies. Avoid it. Although a family-owned, privately held company may have the same actors in the roles of owners, operators and directors, there are now many who seek out independent points of view and, occasionally, an outsider as chair.

Directors have a special sensitivity to all things financial and tend to ask more questions about financial matters than all others together. Directors constantly ask variations of the "How do I know?" question, as in "How do I know if we will make the quarter? What does the year look like? Have you heard anything about the Synopsis Contract?

If there is a single theme when directors talk about their boards, it is information, or more accurately, the lack of it. Those from large companies tell of doorstops in the guise of "board books" arriving so as to require digesting a page per minute to prepare for the next meeting, hardly an informative approach. The reverse is a seeming inability to pull out the most pertinent data, an affliction of large and small enterprises alike, usually aggravated by systems (electronic and human) that are incapable of communicating, leaving summaries to be brought together through "blood, sweat and tears".

On a positive note, all accounting systems now run on a software program of some sort, as do most inventories, work flow systems and the interface with current and prospective customers. This should allow a summary for the board to be fully self-extracting, once it is in place, and at this point one should mention the "corporate dashboard". For those unlikely few who have yet to encounter the beast, a "corporate dashboard" is a summary of the key performance indicators (sometimes shortened to KPI). The dashboard ought to provide directors with an overview of finance, sales, operations, human resources, research and development and so forth. It should give a tactical view of the company's performance at a point in time, a comparison of actual results with what everyone thought possible before the start of the year. In their most useful versions, dashboards are always current and can be accessed via the company website.

My purpose is not to extol the virtues of corporate dashboards, but to address what they should tell you. By the way, if you check a few websites you will discover that there are myriad varieties available, apparently off-the-shelf and ready to use, but *caveat emptor*. You probably do not want a replica of the dashboard of your car so you can "drive your business", but I assure you it can be found, right next to one that bears a striking resemblance to the instrument panel in an aircraft. Certainly there may be some value in graphics or wonderful designs with multiple fonts, but the real value is the information, and it can be found in the answers to three simple questions:

1. What goal was stated in the business plan?
2. What has been accomplished to date?
3. How do you explain the difference between the two?

Closely related to the business goals and also on the director's desk, are the targets for the inhabitants of the CEE Suite, so keep them in mind when the dashboard is being designed. Your board will find it useful to devote some time to discuss and perhaps argue about which goals are critical, but that time is well spent, since it is also a part of business planning. Document the metrics for the dashboard, think about them for a few days, discuss them with the management team, talk about them some more, and only then turn them over to the company as a request for action. At the same time, think about how you and the other directors want to view the data. Do you prefer charts and graphs, spread sheets, other graphics, what? This is invaluable advice to those in the company who must decide how to store the goals in the dashboard database and then pull data from functional files to allow the actual-to-projected comparisons.

Last, but not least, include every possible insight into the underlying drivers of performance, many of which are not financial. For example, it is widely accepted that the cost of replacing a key employee is at least one-half the amount of that person's annual compensation — so — what do you know about employee commitment to the company? If your chief competitor offers a 10% increase will the employee jump at once? Or, what do you know about customer satisfaction? Every new customer costs something and that first sale consumes added time and effort — so what is the risk due to unhappy customers? Another example is the supply chain, the lifeline that allows your company to use just-in-time inventory. How dependable is that linkage, really, and how do you know? There are many non-financial drivers and business is still learning what they are and how to gauge their effects, but the nightly newscast will tell us that many stakeholders are very interested in business ethics, environmental stewardship and corporate social responsibility. Performance is crucial, but it is driven and measured in many ways that have little to do with dollars, at least not immediately.

Strategic Oversight

Strategy is perhaps the most important overall responsibility of any board. It sits at the top of the Big Five pyramid, rather like the light at the entrance to the harbour, for it guides all those venturing forth and all vessels return to it. As an aside, others may present the tasks in a different order, so please note that this particular sequence does not necessarily imply more or less importance. However, as the Red Queen said to Alice in *Through the Looking Glass*, "If you don't know where you are going, any road will take you there", so let us start with that. Ensuring that there is a clear vision of where the company is going and how it will get there without travelling the road to disaster is the linchpin of the Big Five. The board is responsible for a strategic action program that will take the company from where it is today to where it should be, as measured by profitability, growth and competitive strength. All the board's duties coalesce in corporate strategy.

The day-to-day work of strategic management is delegated to the CEE Suite. As you might expect, their practices will differ depending on the strengths and personal work styles of the CEE team members — eg, one CEO will lead the strategy development while another will facilitate it, and a third may stay above the fray and be an arbiter. Your task, the practicalities of your DOC when it come to strategy, means nothing less than understanding, monitoring, evaluating, controlling and guiding strategic management across the company. Nor is it fulfilled when the annual plan is approved. The strategy must become a practical, operational element, the source of the metrics at the base of your responsibility for the company's performance.

In a nutshell, the board's responsibility is to ensure that the company has a coherent, effective and competitive strategy and is successfully implementing it. The director's task is to understand clearly what the shareholders want and what would be minimally acceptable. That is why they are directors. Anything less either lacks understanding or turns a blind eye to fiduciary obligations, current standards of care and reasonable business competence.

I will return to corporate strategy, the directors' roles in it, and the board's responsibilities for it, in Chapter Eleven, *Strategy in Small Packages*.

Resources

As the directors and the senior team work on strategy, they consider how the company is going to get leverage from its resources, those physical, financial, intellectual and technological assets that they intend to use to create and sustain a competitive advantage in the marketplace. The first, and in my view the most important of those resources, is the CEE Suite itself. There is old expression in Boston, something like "How are you going to get the washing done?" This small group of people gets the wash out. As directors, we keep our hands out of the wash tub, but we have a deep and abiding interest in everyone around it, that is the president and CEO and everyone who reports to that position.

The job starts with populating the CEE Suite, modest though it might be.

Finding and then working with the CEE Suite is a crucial task for any board, with tricky dimensions for smaller companies. While conventional wisdom limits this oversight to the CEO, my personal opinion is that it should include the rest of the officer cohort as well. Many of the Wise agreed that the act of determining the profiles of the executive team and then matching them with the best candidates is itself crucial to corporate strategy. Once the best possible team is in place, the board must use the tools at its disposal to ensure that the team does its job. In down-to-earth, working terms this means influencing or perhaps even operating within the processes and tasks that hire, appoint, monitor, evaluate, counsel, coach, mentor, discipline, support, pay and, if necessary, fire and replace the members of the CEE Suite. The management resources and compensation (MRC) committee should capture this in its charter and functional leaders should be well aware of the linkages on topics like goal setting, performance management, structure and the like.

Since the rest of the top managers all report to the CEO, the board usually acts on his or her advice in dealing with them, but many boards now exert a strong influence on the manner in which that is done. The CEO is the primary focus and interface when carrying out this part of DOC. Developing strategic leadership in the CEO — or acquiring one who has it — is an inextricable part of inculcating strategic management into the CEE Suite and the company. Choosing the CEE Suite and securing strategic management are mutually reinforcing tasks, either positively or negatively.

"Part and parcel of this is getting the structure right. Organization design is about how work gets done."[1] Remember the adage, "form follows function"? Given that boards have overall accountability for the company, it should follow that the board ought to include structure as a concern. The field of organizational behaviour has conducted research since at least the early 1960s, and the results are clear. When an organization is "purpose built", financial results, employee satisfaction and customer approval all benefit and the structure is a natural part of strategy implementation. The board should be involved in major organizational changes, perhaps approving them if these changes could expose the company in some manner, eg, a strategic alliance carrying reputational risk. A new company offers the opportunity and the problem of organization design to match strategy, perhaps without the tendency to think about specific individuals instead of the needs of the company.

1   Ron Capelle, "The Accountability of the Board of Directors for Organization Design". Reprinted with permission from the February, 2007 edition of the ICD *Director* newsletter, published by the Institute of Corporate Directors (www.icd.ca).

Then there is management succession, a key factor in risk reduction, but almost impossible for the small company struggling to afford enough talent to function every day, much less gain redundancy. The board can play an important role if it includes a director with the experience who could step in while recruiting a permanent replacement — and who is able to keep "hands off" at all other times. Directors should expect criticism if they have not grown a successor to the CEO, but they should also know that they are likely to be berated if they spend money on that bit of risk reduction. *Ainsi soit-il.*

Returning to the role of the CEO, recognizing that the board must be actively engaged in supervising the process of strategic management implies taking the lead in appointing a CEO. Of course, this act does not take place in a vacuum, meaning that the CEO is chosen to lead management in evolving a strategy and then lead its execution. The qualities sought in a prospective CEO are, to a large extent, determined by the company's strategy and future direction. Assuming that strategy calls for vigorous overseas expansion, for example, suggests that the chosen CEO should have international experience, adapt easily, perhaps have another language, etc. If the company strategy calls for growth through consolidation in its sector, it would be salutary for the CEO to have an unusually strong grasp of finance, deal making, mergers, integration of acquisitions and so on.

By the same token, the strategic direction of the company provides a framework for evaluating the performance of the CEO. Without a clear strategy, it becomes almost impossible to monitor and evaluate performance on a continuous basis. The board cannot be passive in this. It cannot leave the development of strategy to the CEO; the board's job is not only to see that a strategy is in place, but also that the strategy is one that has been developed by board and management together, and is wholeheartedly subscribed to by both parties. Monitoring the CEO performance is the means by which the board carries out its duty of due diligence in ensuring the implementation of that strategy, and its amendment as necessary.

Financial resources are the second leg of the corporate resources stool, balancing people and technology, and they command an extraordinary amount of the board's time and attention. Small wonder that directors pay attention, given the prominence of financial measures in corporate performance, to say nothing of how shareholders and the media pounce with a special fervour on anything to do with money. It was the board's scrutiny — or lack thereof — of Enron's financial manoeuvres that suggested the title of Kurt Eichenwald's book, *Conspiracy of Fools*. Those egregious events were recalled in an October 29, 2007 *Forbes* article, "F is for Fudging", and it includes other prime examples such as Petrohawk's accounting for oil and gas reserves and Proctor & Gamble's $57 billion acquisition of Gillette. Closer to home, let me ask your opinion of a decision to buy three companies within a few months, total acquisition costs US$7.9 billion, to gain negligible revenue, large operating losses and a huge chunk of goodwill to sit on the balance sheet? I suggest that tough questions would have been in order when Nortel did exactly that and grabbed Qterra, Xros and CoreTek in a matter of months in 2000. To quote Peter Dey again, *"Where were the directors?"*

It would take a world-class understatement to posit that corporate finance is simple. It is not. Its complexity is growing, regulation is tightening and the push for board oversight is ever stronger. This is the primary reason for the earlier position that financial literacy is a minimum standard and is a basic requirement to be a director. Small companies are not immune, quite the reverse, for it is unusual for the founder of a small business to be financially sophisticated and the directors will find that they must close the ring of competencies protecting the company. As growth leads to more professional management in the CEE Suite, the availability of operating competency builds, but with scope comes complexity, so the requirements of the board at best remain level and they probably increase. As the moment of the initial public offering (IPO) approaches, the company and its board come face-to-face with the regulatory systems and compliance looms large. The demands on the directors increase by a couple of orders, and financial concerns tend to become the major preoccupation of the board. In fact, shifting onto non-financial responsibilities and giving them the attention they need often takes something of a leap of faith at this stage — so that the over-burden on finance may become a risk because of its selfishness.

Private companies have the same concerns about financial resources, the issues are simply arrayed differently. The directors' contribution, apart from personal investment, should include advice, contacts and insight. The first instance relies on the accumulated wisdom of those with more experience, surely a strong criteria for selection onto the board of a small or early-stage company. Such directors have gone this way before, and they can proffer invaluable advice on financial issues during those critical first years when the CFO may be getting his or her first experience in a corporate setting. Further, the director's seniority in the business world should translate into contacts with a large slice of the financial community. Creativity is expected from the founders, but the best idea, described in a perfect business plan, is the sound of a tree falling in the forest unless it is heard by someone who matters (read: an investor), and at least some of the directors should be able to make that happen.

Intellectual properties are products of the mind. Some would say the concept includes "the way we do things" or "know how", a major resource hiding under an umbrella term. Many companies are founded to exploit a technology and others use their knowledge to differentiate themselves from others in the market. Directors joining the boards of such companies should spend some serious effort to ensure they truly understand exactly what the company has — and what it does not have.

It is important to start with an understanding that the law regards intellectual property (IP) as referring to various legal entitlements which attach to inventions, writing, brand names, recorded media and many others. Such entitlement is a guarantee of access to the benefits from the IP because of rights which can be claimed or by legal agreement. Those rights may be exclusive in relation to the subject matter of the IP. IP laws confer certain exclusive rights relating to the particular form or manner in which ideas or information are expressed or manifested, but not to the ideas or concepts themselves. A director might expect to find that the company has these rights.

A copyright gives the holder the exclusive right to control reproduction or adaptation of creative and artistic works (eg, books, movies, music, paintings, photographs and software) for a certain period of time. Historically, this was between 10 and 30 years, depending on jurisdiction, but recent years have shown that a copyright may not provide the protection it once did, and then only after an expensive and time-consuming defence.

A patent is granted for a new and useful invention in exchange for disclosure of the invention. It gives the patent holder a right to prevent others from using the invention without a license from the inventor for a certain period of time (typically 20 years from the date of a patent application). The procedure and requirements for granting the patent and the degree of exclusivity gained vary widely according to national laws and international agreements. The exclusive right granted in most countries gives the patent holder the right to prevent or exclude others from making, using, selling, offering to sell or importing the invention.

Patents, like all forms of IP, are fraught with risk and can be a major governance issue. There have been many instances of "parallel invention", the inadvertent creation of a technique or a device that, while perhaps not an exact duplicate, is sufficiently close to someone's IP that a lawsuit is the result. Consider the Research in Motion (RIM) versus Eatoni Ergonomics affair. The BlackBerry 7100, launched in 2004, introduced SureType, the RIM technology that allows users to press a single key and have the device determine whether they want, for example, a Q or a W to appear on the screen. Eatoni claimed that this was exactly what it discussed when it applied for patent 6,885,317 in December 1999, long before RIM released the 7100. It pointed out that its system had been used since early 2002 by equipment makers using the Digital Enhanced Cordless Telephony standard (DECT). RIM attempted to have the Eatoni patent declared invalid, but Eatoni counter-sued, alleging patent infringement and asking the court to ban the sale of the allegedly infringing products. The US District Court of

Northern Texas instructed the two companies to try mediation first, and the negotiations proved successful.

The two companies signed an agreement in which Eatoni, which specializes in designing hardware and software for keyboards, granted RIM a license to use its technology and RIM, in return, made an equity investment in Eatoni. "The parties met in accordance with the court's mediation process and common goals were identified, which led to the settlement," RIM and Eatoni said in a statement. The claims have been mutually dismissed and other details are confidential.

A trademark is a distinctive image used to distinguish products or services and some are world famous, eg, the font used by Coca Cola or the Nike "swoosh" logo.

An industrial design right protects the form of appearance, style or design of an industrial object (eg, the "stubby" beer bottle or the plaid in a kilt).

A trade secret is sometimes equated with "confidential information" and so is non-public information concerning the commercial practices or proprietary knowledge of a business. Disclosing such information to the public may be illegal, eg, the launch date of a new product.

Patents, trademarks, designs and "know how" are sometimes collectively known as industrial property, especially when they are created or used for industrial or commercial purposes, but protecting them is both difficult and expensive. Securing a patent is a tortuous process that takes time and effort — and money. IP laws and enforcement vary widely from jurisdiction to jurisdiction, and patents may be needed in each, adding to costs. There are inter-governmental efforts to harmonize intellectual property laws through international treaties such as the World Trade Organization's (WTO) Agreement on Trade-Related Aspects of Intellectual Property Rights (TRIPS), agreed in 1994, while other treaties may facilitate registration in more than one jurisdiction at a time. Disagreements over medical and software patents and the severity of copyright enforcement have, so far, prevented consensus on a cohesive international system.

Directors have some tough decisions. Should scarce dollars be spent on a patent before commercial prospects have been established? How much added risk is incurred by the revelations of the patent filing? How quickly will the business spread beyond its home market, dictating the need for protection in other jurisdictions? Is the best protection the first mover advantage? Will the way in which the company applies the technology and maps it to key business processes be more protection than the law?

Protecting and enhancing the company's assets are responsibilities that attract risk. The emphasis is more often on protect than it is on enhance, but in either case the board will be involved whenever the issue at hand is "material", which is another judgment call. The issues likely to be seen as major, and thus material, form around management, ownership, investments, acquisitions, divestments, raids or insolvency. When the issue is so serious as to move it well beyond the materiality threshold, it assumes such significance and is such a threat to the company that the board assumes the decision-making role. For example, in the event of a hostile takeover bid, the shareholders might want direct and immediate control through the action of a special committee of the board.

A board has done its job of protecting and enhancing the company's assets when it has paid close attention to all *material* decisions, actions, policies and functions. Board approval is mandatory for any material "act or omission" (the Ontario Business Corporation Act, Section 147, calls this "the oppression remedy") that affects the interest of any "security holder" of the corporation. In practical terms, it means that specific board approval is required for all capital expenditures and all acquisitions, divestments or other acts or omissions that affect the purpose and strategy of the business. In this context, "material" is usually defined as a proportion of total assets, ordinarily 1% or 2%, or as affecting investors' decisions to buy or sell a security of the corporation.

In summary, the director's responsibility for resources requires insights that vary with the resource and, within that, with the different application or uses of that resource in the business. General management experience is probably the best preparation, and in its absence, curiosity and a very steep learning curve if DOC is to be delivered.

Managing Risk

The popular board game with the eponymous name claims that, "risk is a game of world domination, where the object is to conquer the world. To win, you must attack and defend — attacking to acquire territory, and defending to keep it from your opponents". Businesses, especially small ones, often feel that everyone else in the game is attacking while they are frantically defending.

> *"Driven by the fear of major business failures and under increasing compliance-related pressures, companies are focusing on their exposures, and risk management has become part of the essential fabric of the corporate governance structure."*[2]

Large enterprises have the resources to devote full-time attention to the identification and mitigation of risks; small companies rarely do. Their "Enterprise Risk Management" (ERM) system is quite likely something that someone in accounting does after lunch on Thursday. ERM systems are expensive and usually beyond the means of the average small company.

---

2   Thomas McGrath, Global Managing Partner, Client Services and Accounts, Ernst & Young, 2005

This is not to say that the CEE Suite and the directors are unaware of risk, quite the contrary. The problem is more likely that they have identified specific risks, but these come with known probabilities, making it possible to dream that the company lives under that part of the distribution curve where calamities never intrude. The busier and more intensely engaged the CEE Suite, the more likely they will conclude that "it probably won't happen". Well, it might not, but if this is the prevailing view at your company both you and it are going to face a nasty situation and it should not be a surprise. It is not a question of *if* it will happen; it is a question of *when*. While it is absolutely true that your small company may not have an ERM system nor that risk *per se* is a specific accountability for an individual, it has not gone away nor has it been reduced. As a director, mitigating that risk, whatever it may be, is part of your responsibility.

First, understand the rules of the game. New arrivals on the board should ask questions, and everyone in the room had better understand their own legal obligations and those of the company. Revisit or make the acquaintance of the CBCA and its relevant provincial counterpart, eg, the Alberta Business Corporations Act (ABCA). Beyond those foundations, seek out the legislation that regulates your company and its industrial sector. You can expect regulations for environmental issues, employment standards (certainly the Canada Labour Code), trade and tariff restrictions, hazardous materials, building codes and other generally applicable regulations to affect some part of your business. Directors need at least a general knowledge of the legal context, with enough depth to know when to ask for more details and for an expert opinion. A working knowledge of the rules of the game is akin to financial literacy, in that it is not a "nice to have", it is an essential.

The management of risk is an inevitable accompaniment to strategic oversight, for whenever a board talks about its plans the conversation has to include the opportunities and their accompanying risks. Considering strategy without looking at risk simply cannot be done for, in the words of a once popular song, "you can't have one without the other". The Joint Committee on Corporate Governance (established in 2000 by the Canadian Institute of Chartered Accountants or CICA) put it like this:

> *"Board's involvement in strategic planning and the monitoring of risks must recognize directors are not there to manage the business, but are responsible for overseeing management and holding it to account. Where lines are clear, and roles are respected, effective boards will contribute to the development of strategic directions and approve a strategic plan. They will oversee the processes that management has in place to identify business opportunities and risks. They will consider the extent and types of risk that is acceptable for the company to bear. They will monitor management's systems and processes for managing the broad range of business risk. And most important, on an ongoing basis, they will review with management how the strategic environment is changing, what key business risks and opportunities are appearing, how they are being managed and what, if any, modifications in strategic direction should be adopted."*

The Duty of Care as Job One

The final sentence in the quotation should be taken as an action item for every director. While the oversight of risk can be a tough nut to crack, there is really little choice. Executives and directors alike are accountable personally when something goes awry, and when that happens they will wish to demonstrate that they have been diligent. If your company wants to attract an institutional investor it may exact an explicit description of your company's risk-reward profile as a condition of investment, which a high net worth individual might emulate as well. After all, their fiduciary duties demand it. As a board reviews strategy and adjusts it in the face of change, the risk profile shifts with the altered strategy and the board has the challenges of monitoring and disclosing.

As a director on the board of a small company, you face something of a dilemma. Let us suppose that the CEE Suite has asked its auditors for an estimate on an ERM system and learned that the assessment to establish a baseline could cost as much as $35,000 to $50,000 and that developing processes on behalf of the company, with systems tweaking and implementation, could add an equal amount, and probably more, to the bill. As they consider their decision they realize that the ERM system would be a significant percentage of the earnings forecast for the year, and they may well choose to delay until the future. Fair enough, and under the circumstances this may be the correct decision, but the dilemma has not gone away.

Executives and directors alike are now accountable personally if something goes awry, ie, when the other side of that probability statement becomes the reality. When that happens, they must be able to demonstrate that they considered all aspects before making business and strategic decisions, that they did everything in their power to be aware of and manage the risks associated with those decisions (see Chapter Ten, *The Director and the Law*). The challenge for the smaller company is to be able to support the contention that DOC was fulfilled.

The best advice to directors is, "heal thyself". When the board asks the right questions it lays the stepping stones on the pathway to a resolution of the dilemma of how to reach well-considered decisions without an expensive ERM system. To get started, find a copy of the CICA publication, *20 Questions Directors Should Ask about Risk* written by Hugh Lindsay, it is a great aide. The responsible director doctrine is gaining ever more weight, a trend that is likely to continue, and probing management's decisions is now virtually taken for granted. While directors may want a lot of distance from company affairs when things go wrong, they should understand — clearly and fully — that this dodge is less and less likely to be viewed favourably by any court hearing a liability case. The directors are expected to do everything within reason to implement the policies and systems that either avoid or solve the situation. No train wrecks, please, we are all passengers.

Well-honed questions go beyond defensiveness and become an important tool, a board contribution to management process. As a caution, to be truly useful on all accounts a director's inquiries must be based on a very solid knowledge of the company and its operations, and driven by experienced insight. It would take many pages to come close to a comprehensive list of questions, if that is even possible, but here are a few to help along the way.

1. What would happen if the Ministry of Labour asks us to demonstrate that we are in compliance with workplace safety standards? What is the trend of our Worker's Compensation Board premiums? (ie, in Ontario, this would be the Workplace Safety and Insurance Board).

2. How many of our eggs are in one basket — what percentage of our revenue comes from our biggest customer? What is the percentage from the five largest customers?

3. How does our employee turnover compare with the industry average? Which of our technical groups are being targeted by recruiters?

4. Our backlog of work is diminishing — what is in the sales pipeline and when will those prospects become contracts? When will we be able to issue invoices and recognize revenue?

5. If we spend $XX million in buying the widget division of Acme, what is the internal rate of return and when will we break even on the investment?

6. Why does the new bid for the National Contract have a gross margin so much lower than the usual figure?

7. Who is the major local competitor for the office planned for Saskatoon? What is their share of the market? How long will it take for the new office to reach break even? How is the cost of housing affecting out ability to hire or transfer employees?

8. The truck route into our new plant crosses an arm of a conservation area. How long will the environmental assessment take? Are we reasonably certain that permission to build will be granted? What is the contingency plan?

9. Is the contract to supply that value added reseller (VAR) in Germany in dollars or euros? Are we hedging foreign exchange?

10. What is our sensitivity to increased energy prices?

The list could go on, but its limitations have been admitted so we will stop at this point.

There will be instances when the company is "blind sided" by an act that is almost impossible to predict, ERM or not, as in a risk to reputation. For example, who would have expected that the wife of a well-known race car designer would walk into a photocopy shop with the intention of copying a rival's intellectual property? In June 2007, that is exactly what happened when Trudy Coughlan, the wife of the McLaren team's chief designer was caught in the act. The fine of US$100 million is the largest in sports to date. Did Team McLaren know of the attempt? Would it have countenanced an act of espionage? Certainly not, but the memory of the incident will linger with the industry and its fans regardless of the future presence or absence of the Coughlans.

The variations and origins of risk are almost endless, as potentially any issue could become serious if either dealing with it or disregarding it might create materiality. For example, I was on the board of a company that used an Alberta Stock Exchange shell to become public through a reverse takeover (RTO). Due diligence on the "shell" was thorough, while the company prepared for the RTO. Several years after the fact, a letter arrived from the Department of the Environment for the State of Nevada, asking for a decision on the money we had on deposit with it, some $25,000. On reviewing the due diligence process we realized that the investment bank employee who had reviewed this topic had discovered the need for the deposit, but not the fact that the money had already been placed in trust with the State of Nevada. In the context of the deal the amount did not seem material, at least to the person doing the work, and he simply did not question the Department of the Environment's need for a deposit. Our CFO wondered how to account for the newly discovered cash, but the risk was, of course, the environmental issue. He found that the deposit had been required because a road was being developed in an environmentally sensitive area. Now, 11 years later, rainwater was leaching arsenic from the exposed rock and carrying it into a nearby stream. The only thing that saved us from what could have been a serious liability, even after that many years, is the scarcity of rain in that part of Nevada.

This was a simple situation which became dangerous only with the passage of time and our unwitting ignorance of its existence. Since neither the board nor management learned of the Department of the Environment's interest, an inexperienced junior looked at the money, but ignored the truly material issue. When the RTO was in process it would have been difficult to imagine why the board would have intervened in greater depth and thus discovered more than those who were conducting the due diligence on its behalf. Later, we all understood that our review and approval at the time had missed the risk, and we could have faced a class-action lawsuit on environmental grounds. It was well outside company premises, not a customer or a supplier, not covered by company policies — so — a grey area that was skimmed. A lesson was learned and, fortunately, the tuition was nominal.

Fraud is a risk that has metastasized into a monster with an attitude. Left alone it can consume the company — remember the Nick Leeson scandal and its aftermath at Barings Bank? Leeson was a whiz kid who rose quickly at Barings in London and was sent to manage a new futures market in Singapore. London was soon delighted with the huge profits that he was raking in on behalf of the bank. Since Leeson claimed that he was executing purchase orders on behalf of a client, not the bank, Barings believed that it had no

Chairs and Tables

exposure. But there was a dark secret. Leeson had set up an error account to cover a freshman team member's mistake. After the damage had been repaired, Leeson kept the account to cover his own losses, which escalated as he threw good money after bad in a vain attempt to trade his way out of the mess. In the final three months, he bought more than 20,000 futures contracts worth about $180,000 each as he tried to move a market that refused to budge. When the wheels fell off, Barings had lost $1.3 billion and three quarters of it was from Leeson's trades.

Barings had to inform the Bank of England that the 233-year-old investment Bank, which proudly counted Queen Elizabeth as a client, was bankrupt. The $1.3 billion in liabilities was more than the entire capital and reserves of the bank. In a classic twist of fate and irony, Nick Leeson is now a popular speaker on — you guessed it — risk management!

Closer to home, there was the Greymac Affair. It began when Cadillac Fairview sold about 11,000 apartment buildings scattered around Toronto to Lenny Rosenberg, who "flipped" them to his friend Bill Player for a $42.5 million profit. Player immediately resold the buildings to Saudi investors, or so the story goes, for $500 million. The story remains unclear, even after a dramatic court case and Terrence Belford's book, *Trust: The Greymac Affair* (James Lorrimer & Company, 1983), but one fact is clear: a lot of depositor's money was in play to pay for unseemly profits.

Recently, there was Ian Thow, a smooth-talking mutual fund salesman in Victoria. He lived the good life for quite a while. He had a $4.6 million mansion, he drove a fleet of luxury vehicles and private jets whisked him to exotic destinations whenever he wished. He spread his wealth around too, appearing at gala fundraisers and writing big cheques to popular charities. Then, in the small hours of September 8, 2005, Ian Thow crossed the border into the US, an easy passage since he is an American citizen. The salesman was gone, and so was $32 million.

Fraud costs Canadian companies between $25 billion and $30 billion every year, at least according to our best guess (Association of Certified Fraud Examiners: *Report to the Nation on Occupational Fraud and Abuse*, 2004) after grossing up the known cases to account for those that go undetected. The majority of it is "an inside job" perpetrated by employees of the victim or by those in a position of trust. While it is true that a smart and dedicated fraudster is impossible to stop because the crime cannot be detected in advance, in many cases it is perpetrated over months or years, and the signs are there for the directors to see. It is tough to defend against a simple grab-and-run episode, but the instances just recounted all took place over extended periods, during which the guy running the scam was only too pleased to be praised for what appeared to be unbelievable results. Well, they were too good to be true, and that characteristic might have been the needed warning to stop the theft with less damage, while simultaneously having a better chance of seeing someone held accountable. Fraud is often motivated by greed, and if the company avoids the same sin it has the key to early detection.

Communications and Disclosure

For those who have just joined us, welcome to the director's dilemma. As a new director you must now learn how to be transparent and discreet on demand, a bimodal division of roles made tricky by the simple fact that while you are delivering the message you are also part of the medium. Disclosure is a serious task, with an example described in an article in the *Globe and Mail* by Jacquie McNish on October 12, 2007.

The newspaper describes a case (*Kerr v. Danier Leather Inc*) in which a class action was brought against the Danier Leather company and some of its senior executives alleging that their disclosure had failed to provide proper warning to investors. Danier had launched an IPO in 1998 to raise $65 million. In its prospectus, the company predicted a profit in its fourth quarter but unseasonably hot weather kept customers away from leather apparel and sales slumped, sending the share price spiralling downward. Certain investors took exception and sued, starting nine years of court battles. In 2004, the Superior Court of Ontario ruled that Danier had misled shareholders, but that decision was overturned by the Ontario Court of Appeal in 2006 because, over time, the profit forecast came true. Encouraged by the first decision, the appellants took the case to the Supreme Court of Canada, which found for the company.

The *Globe and Mail* said that, "the Supreme Court of Canada has waded into the murky waters of public company disclosure rules". Murky, indeed, but perhaps this decision, which is certain to be quoted as a precedent, will make the "bright line" a little brighter still. In its decision, the Supreme Court of Canada stated:

"The Securities Act is remedial legislation and is to be given a broad interpretation. It protects investors from the risks of an unregulated market, and by its assurance of fair dealing and by the promotion of the integrity and efficiency of capital markets it enhances the pool of capital available to entrepreneurs. The Act supplants the "buyer beware" mind set of the common law with compelled disclosure of relevant information. At the same time, in compelling disclosure, the Act recognizes the burden it places on issuers and sets the limits on what is required to be disclosed."

By "setting the limits" one assumes that the Supreme Court found that the bad weather and subsequent sales decline were unforeseen events that could not reasonably have been anticipated when the company wrote the prospectus. Because the sales slump was temporary and Danier ultimately was able to deliver a profitable quarter, the court ruled that the company had no legal obligation to report the temporary setback. The paragraph just quoted continues:

"When a prospectus is accurate at the time of filing, s.57 (1) of the Act limits the obligation of post filing disclosure to notice of a "material change", which the Act defines in s.1 as "a change in the business,

operations or capital of the issuer that would reasonably be expected to have a significant effect on the market price or value of any of the securities of the issuer". An issuer has no similar express obligation to amend a prospectus or to publicize and file a report for the modification of material facts occurring after a receipt for a prospectus is obtained that do not amount to a "material change" within the meaning of the Act. A "material fact" is defined in the Act more broadly than a "material change" and includes "a fact that significantly affects, or would reasonably be expected to have a significant effect on, the market price or value of securities". A change in intra quarterly results is not itself a change in the issuer's business, operations or capital and, for that matter, does not necessarily signal that a material change has occurred. Sales often fluctuate (as here) in response to factors that are external to the issuer. The trial judge rightly found that Danier experienced no material change. Consequently, no further disclosure was required and there was no breach.

There are two crucial items in this: the difference between a "material fact" and a "material change", and the disclosure rules around them. The Supreme Court found that while a material fact may have become known, there was no material change that required disclosure.

Then there is the matter of the predicted profits. Companies routinely make forecasts, combining data with experienced insight in a business judgment, whereas disclosure is a matter of legal obligation. The Supreme Court said:

"The Business Judgment Rule is a concept well developed in the context of business decisions but should not be used to qualify or undermine the duty of disclosure. The disclosure requirements under the Act are not to be subordinated to the exercise of business judgment."

Generally, a corporation is a legal entity distinct from its shareholders (*Salomon v. Salomon & Co., Ltd.*, [1897] A.C. 22 (H.L.) (the Business Judgment Rule)) and when a court disregards this principle it is said to be "lifting the corporate veil". While this principle has not been followed consistently, *Kerr v. Danier* takes it further by pronouncing that forecasting is a matter of business judgment, but disclosure is a matter of legal obligation and, further, the exercise of business judgment takes precedence over the duty of disclosure as required under Section 130(1) of the Ontario Securities Act.

Given the attention paid to *Kerr v. Danier*, directors would be well advised to read the details of the decision and monitor how it is applied. The fact that it started well before Enron and its cousins and then concluded well after SOX, Bill 198 and ICFR means that it reflects, to some extent, the evolution of thinking about disclosure through this evocative period. The 2004 decision, the 2006 appeal and the Supreme Court's final resolution of the matter should be part of your work on DOC. This is an important case and it will become part of the background of many future actions relating to communications and disclosure.

The Duty of Care as Job One

As the agent of the shareholders in overseeing management, the board is responsible for maintaining two-way communications between the shareholders and management whether the company is private or public. In a company with a controlling shareholder, representing and protecting the minority shareholders is especially important. The board must ensure that external reporting is optimal — timely and fully adequate — and that the shareholders' views and wishes are communicated to management. Under all business corporation acts, the main accountability event is the annual shareholders' meeting and the main accountability document is the published annual report. It discloses the required comparative financial statements, management's discussion and analysis (MD&A) of financial conditions and results of operations; the auditor's report; and any other information demanded by the company's articles, by-laws, shareholder agreements in private companies and, of course, all regulatory bodies.

Please remember that you and your colleagues on the board are responsible for the culture of integrity that must guide everything your company does and in a public company you must disclose how this is accomplished. You are expected to play an active role in ensuring that disclosure occurs as required, and that the internal systems to support that disclosure are in place and effective. If your company is not a reporting issuer, observe the parallel and ensure that the same quality of disclosure reaches the owners of the company. Everyone will be well served by your actions.

Board Mandates

Where we once relied on the incorporation statute to define the responsibility of a board, the current approach is to be more specific by means of a written and formally approved mandate. In many instances, the mandated statement is published widely in documents and on websites. The basic responsibility of the directors is to exercise their reasonable business judgment on behalf of the corporation, but in discharging this obligation, directors rely on, among others, the company's officers, legal counsel, auditors and other outside advisors. This reliance has developed edginess as directors face increasing personal risks due to errors or omissions committed by others, especially the corporate officers. The board mandate has become more than a list of responsibilities, in some ways it now defines the minimum, while the further extent of the envelope is still being pushed outward by "scope creep".

Here is a typical list of the general responsibilities for the board.

- evaluation and compensation of the CEO;
- evaluation of the senior management team;
- review of succession planning for the CEO and senior officers;
- consideration of long-range strategic issues and risks to the company;
- review of the company's execution of long-range business plans;
- approval of major business decisions;
- review and oversight of public disclosure;

- review of the effectiveness of internal controls and information systems;
- development of effective corporate governance principles and guidelines;
- establish committees of the board and define their roles and responsibilities;
- establish expectations and responsibilities for directors;
- evaluate the performance of the board, its committees and members;
- review compensation of the board; and
- approve policies of corporate conduct that promote and maintain the integrity of the company.

There are "only" 14 items on that list, but if you attempt to sort them among the five responsibilities of a director, you will discover that several fit into at least two slots. Their interdependence is typical of the complexity of directorship.

There is an example of a board charter in Appendix Three.

DOC as Good Management

All this may present DOC as an almost impossible task, but while it certainly takes time and effort, it is actually rather simple or at least it can be described simply as knowing and understanding everything about the company so as to bring that wisdom to the exercise of the director's fiduciary responsibility. A few years ago, the then Chief Justice James Farley admonished one audience as follows:

> "Directors **must** know the business, they cannot act without knowing the company **intimately** — so get off your butts and stop merely reading the board package and get to know **everything** about the company. Your duty is to the corporation, know it well."

The words emphasized in that quote are my interpretation of Farley's tone and body language as he spoke. He meant every word. DOC is about knowing what is going on in and around the company, and the Chief Justice was delivering a clear message: You cannot be wilfully blind and keep yourself in the dark. Several of the Wise expanded on that theme and offered concrete examples of what knowing the company intimately means for them. One well-known authority on good governance practices advises directors to meet customers and suppliers as well as the senior team and investors. He agrees with the five major responsibilities of a director, seeing each as a roster of things a director needs to do to accomplish DOC. Listening to him during our interview, I thought, "This guy is Jim Farley's admonition in action".

I had the privilege and good fortune to have two wonderful mentors when I first started to learn about corporate governance. Ernie Spence had been a friend and colleague on the Faculty of Administrative Studies at York University (now the Schulich School of Business), and I turned to him for advice on strategy and governance when I first became a partner in, and a director of, a start-up. He taught the importance of keeping strategy in front of the board and knowing the operating metrics as the means to understand risk. Mary Alice Stewart was the chair of the board of directors of CJRT-FM Inc. when it first emerged from its start as a student-run radio station with a scorching 100 watts of broadcast power. I was one of the earlier directors on that board, and it was my first serious directorship. Mary Alice was its first chair, and she taught me the importance of managing the process of the meeting and why an agenda was simultaneously fixed and flexible.

Both Ernie and Mary Alice were unswerving in their belief that good governance and good management spring from the same source and are directed towards the same ends, a persuasion that has remained convincing. After all, governing and managing an organization both derive their legitimacy from the same act of incorporation, both are part of the hierarchy of responsibility that flows from that act and both have identical corporate goals. Executives report to the board and through it to the owners, whereas the directors' accountability is direct, but it is to those same shareholders. Given the close scrutiny of modern disclosure and the shared accountability for the certification process of public companies, good management and good governance have been brought even closer together. The DOC instills and improves good management practices as well as being the cornerstone of good governance.

There are substantial reasons for this belief. They start with the vantage from which a director views the organization and discharges the responsibilities of independent oversight aided by privileged inspection. Directors are able to stand apart from operational issues and the day-to-day pressures besetting the CEO and the rest of the executive team, but they still have as much information available as they wish and if they have questions they will be answered. They are able to examine internal processes; indeed the directors can accept or reject how some of those processes have been designed and how they function. Having participated in many meetings as ICFR processes were developed in public companies, I have seen first hand that directors in such circumstances have a direct and powerful influence on this particular set of fundamental management processes. In these working sessions, the directors' focus was identical with management, although they often had differing views. For example, a CEO might want a different level of signing authority than the chair of the audit committee wishes to grant, but in the end, they are both addressing one operational detail of a normal management function. The combined effect is that management and board leaders alike brought their combined talents to bear on developing and later testing the ICFR procedures. They reach into every nook and cranny of the company either to examine or extract data used for financial controls and, in the process, touch many non-financial policies and procedures.

And, as noted previously, what is now termed the certification process for a public company is a lot like the control policies of a private one, especially if it is in the hands of professional management rather than owner-operators, where the latter will have wished to put controls in place to act in their stead. Directors are able to apply to such a task a breadth of experience and knowledge unavailable within most management teams and certainly not those of smaller organizations. They have the wisdom and counsel of their board colleagues, a "brain trust" brought together to serve common purposes, and their requests for information or insights often lead to improvements in a management process. As an example, providing a "dashboard" of information for board use means that it is available to management, and the thinking and development of the support processes for the dashboard will sharpen management's view of operations. The dashboard may simply be one aspect of DOC, but its side effect is better management.

The final point supporting the efficacy of DOC on management practices is the emphasis that corporate governance places on risk assessment, an aspect of business life often given, at best, subdued time and attention by the owners of smaller companies, who seem inclined to "go for it" in situations where entrepreneurialism has evolved into foolhardiness. Further, and especially in smaller organizations, it seems that risks are downplayed if they arise from issues such as health and safety, the environment, quality control, local by-laws and others not related in a very direct way to technology, a customer or sales. Certainly, it is rare to find managers in such companies who even know about transactional level activities and their controls, or lack thereof. They are simply "below the radar". The applied experience of a board as it examines risk will almost certainly provide reasons for improvement to management processes.

DOC as a Shield

This chapter opened with an aside, to the effect that DOC is as valuable to a director as insurance, a less than fully serious comment, but one imparting a solid truth and a lot of advice. The Business Judgment Rule is a shield often used as a defence when a director's decision becomes the subject of litigation. In cases of a legal proceeding against directors the Business Judgment Rule is an effective defence when it can be shown that their decisions were taken while acting in an informed manner and in good faith and that the resulting decision was reasonable within the context of the situation. The directors are not held to make either a "perfect" decision or even the "best" decision, but simply a reasonable decision based on knowledge, good faith and the situation at the time.

Chapter Four:

Start with a Compass

A currently popular phrase, "tone at the top", has become a short-hand reference to the belief that the ethics and values of leaders are likely to spread and be emulated throughout the organization. In this sense, they are a compass, for they provide direction as surely as a lodestone can find north. This is not a simple "monkey see, monkey do" act of imitation, although that may be a partial explanation. The wrong tone includes more subtle acts, such as giving tacit approval or implying permission by conveniently or deliberately omitting specific instructions. This chapter is positioned immediately after the basic overview because ethical behaviour is the essential ingredient, the catalyst, for any hope of what is acceptable as good corporate governance. While this statement is, or should be, universal it is even more pertinent to smaller companies where leaders are easily heard and observed, and where *laissez faire* is more likely to flourish.

The concept of ethics has ancient roots, reflecting an early concept of "moral philosophy". Today it is the branch of philosophy studying the values and customs of a person or group, including ideas such as right and wrong, good and evil, responsibility and so forth. We discover quickly that practices accepted readily in one setting may be viewed quite differently in another. Business is left to determine, and then apply, ethical concepts and principles within a commercial context, and that is rarely easy. Executives and directors struggle to comprehend the various moral or ethical problems that can arise, understand any special duties or obligations that apply and find the right course if they are to avoid lawsuits, bad publicity and the loss of worth earned over the years.

Ethical dilemmas often have origins in simple decisions. Let us take the example of a small manufacturer that chose Winnipeg's St. Charles area for its low cost real estate and proximity to Winnipeg International Airport, lying just to the east. Restaurants and coffee shops were few and far between, so the company included an on-site cafeteria in its plans. Company officials, reasoning that they were not in the restaurant business and wanting to avoid time lost to travel during the noon lunch hour, decided to operate the cafeteria at break even. This plan paid dividends immediately, as employees appreciated the convenience and low cost of lunch in the company cafeteria, and a pleasant and convivial atmosphere grew. Morning and afternoon coffee was served, and then breakfasts were added to accommodate the company's flexible working hours. The company hired a former restaurant operator to run the cafeteria, and his experience ensured a great menu of delicious foods, with terrific coffee, bagels and Danishes for the morning and afternoon breaks. The operator's experience also meant that prices stayed the same or were reduced during the company's first five years in St. Charles. With the cafeteria effectively a non-event in the operating budget, the company saw it as a trump card in attracting and retaining its workforce.

It was at this point that a small restaurant opened in the area and shortly thereafter complained that the company's cafeteria was unfair competition, alleging that company subsidies locked up a sizeable population of people who might otherwise be its customers. At a meeting meant to diffuse the situation, the restaurant owner hammered on three points:

- Do your customers know that they are subsidizing employee meals and therefore pay higher prices for your products as a result?

- Is it right that your subsidy prevents my success and so eliminates services to area businesses that do not have a cafeteria?

- Do you treat the subsidy as a taxable benefit and report it as such?

The company was represented by its president and CEO, its CFO and the chair of the board. The dispute was eventually settled, more or less amicably, but the chair carried the questions away from the first meeting for discussion with the other directors. The resolution is a topic for another time, but in the interim, what would you have recommended? Is there an ethical response to each question?

"Ethics is — knowing the difference between what you have a right to do, and what is the right thing to do."[1]

There are those who believe that if an act is legal, it is ethical. Justice Stewart obviously does not agree with that — and neither do many others, including me. Ethical behaviour goes well beyond merely complying with the law. Ethics is like good manners, it requires voluntary compliance. You may have a legal right to burn our nation's flag, but that does not make it the right thing to do. Racial discrimination was legal at one time, but it was always wrong and so is gross or insulting behaviour. In business, pre-emptive hostile takeovers are legal, but most would agree that they are the wrong thing to do.

---

1   Potter Stewart, US Supreme Court Justice

Start with a Compass

It is frequently easy to be evasive and simply avoid an issue, especially if circumstances are obscure. A company could say that maintaining high ethical standards is untenable when competing in a global marketplace where the definition of "ethical" varies widely from country to country. There are three very strong reasons to reject this view. First, it contradicts many of the values held in high regard by many companies, such as integrity, equality, accountability and so forth. Second, such thinking will lead to actions that are against the law. Third, it is bad business to attempt to guarantee a sought-after, short-term outcome rather than follow a demanding ethical compass and be better served over the longer term.

Ethical behaviour is not simple. Not only does one have to know the right thing to do, one must also have the intestinal fortitude to do it. Ethical people believe in honouring their word, respecting the law, acting honestly, respecting other people's property, displaying loyalty and working hard — but even these virtues are not sufficient unto themselves. Consider these four examples.

- **Optimism** is certainly not unethical in the usual sense, but unbridled enthusiasm to the point of misrepresentation is a crime in business. Too much of a good thing, one might say, is likely to mislead the listener. When you stand before a group of prospective investors and become fervent in your optimism over the prospects for those who become shareholders you tread a thin line, and it is not only easy, but probable, that you will step to one side.

- **Information** is valuable, but using it is ethical only as long as you are entitled to possess it. Many of us stoke our ego by imparting "the inside scoop", without considering if we are allowed to know what we know, and if allowed, is it then appropriate to share that information with others? In this vein, public companies have "red out" periods, for those are times when at least a dozen people know the results at the end of a quarter well in advance of the release of that information to the general public.

- **Profit** is valued when it is earned and it is genuine. The scandals that plagued us a few short years ago had many roots, but the common motivation was money, especially if the amount of revenue or profit that a company seemed to possess would have a significant and salutary effect on someone's bonus package. We live and thrive in a capitalistic economy. But the fruits had better truly be from our labours and not by any other means.

- **Loyalty** is prized and appreciated, as long as it is not misplaced. Blind obedience leads to "I was only following orders", while collusion — and the absence of questions — are synonymous with it.

Four virtues, each prized in and of itself, and we usually admire them. But as the examples show, that admiration depends on a context that does not adulterate the value of the characteristic. Otherwise, what should be a virtue is not.

Making It Work

The tone at the top is not a nine-to-five issue. It cannot be, for the defined role of an executive or director is not confined to "working hours", and this complicates the situation. There is a strong tendency to think of time as discontinuous, meaning that we believe that we can view our lives as discreet bundles of the stuff labelled business, family, community, personal and so forth. Many would claim that they live that way, while worrying over whether their lives are "balanced". This would seem to imply that the bundles are about the same duration, or at least have the same weight. Perhaps some accomplish this feat, but others understand that the boundaries are hazy at best and they must contend with instances made difficult because the lines between work and play are blurred.

Not only do we view time as packages on a conveyor belt, but we also attach selected behaviours or customs to them. We are more or less formal, we use different words and phrases, and certainly we have a wide range of behaviours. An easy example is how we dress for work or play, or for that matter for differing occupations or one of our many varieties of play. We adjust easily when we cross an obvious boundary, such as my squash club's rule that we must change to street clothing before entering the lounge. Issues arise when the boundary is too hazy to be seen, when we may think it has gone but it is still there.

Legitimacy Matrix

Company Policies in Real Time		The relationship of the conduct to the company	
		Related	Unrelated
Locale of the conduct	Inside the company	**Strong influence**	**Moderate influence**
	Outside the company	**Moderate influence**	**Little influence**

This becomes pertinent to governance when the behaviour of an employee or director creates risk for the organization. The diagram below is an over simplification, but it will serve to make the point. It portrays the degree of influence of a company's policies and rules when they are applied to behaviour in all the situations that may be encountered. These behaviours are either physically within company premises or outside of them, and they are seen either as closely related to the company and its world, or they seem unrelated.

This simple construct recognizes that the influence of company policies is likely to diminish when the employee is off-site. Similarly, a policy is more likely to be ignored if the employee judges it to be unrelated to the company and its business, even when on company premises. In other words, corporate policy is less likely to influence the behaviour of an individual if he or she is not "at work" — eg, if their activity is part of sports or volunteer work. In this way corporate policy is rather like a parent attempting to influence a child's behaviour when the youngster is out of sight and beyond the range of the human voice.

The model helps by sorting behaviours into four groups, and the colour shading suggests what they mean. For example, an employee at work is very likely to pay attention to company policies that are specific to the business; the policies have a strong influence and behaviours fitting into the white cell are less likely to be an issue. Similarly, those in the grey cells need some cautionary attention while those in the black cell are problematic. Companies cannot address all possible issues, no matter what we might wish, but neither should we emulate an ostrich, so setting priorities is in order. The grid can be used like early-warning radar or the rumble strip at the edge of a highway, alerting us to policy topics likely to be problematic, when the problems will arise, and what level of risk they are likely to incur. Applying the legitimacy matrix will also provide a "stress test" for any given policy, because using it as a framework for thinking will "paint" a blip of risk while it is still at a distance and evasive action can succeed. The directors of small companies might consider setting aside all those issues which are likely to be "in the clear", meaning they are in the white cell where someone else is caring for them, ration their time on the grey areas and spend their scarce time and resources on the Black Zone.

Black Zone Issues

It is beyond the ambit of this book to attempt a comprehensive documentation of the entire set of possible Black Zone risks. Instead of the all-time checklist of errors and omissions, the following section opts for heightened awareness of the three large sets of issues most likely to cross ethical lines and place their progenitors at risk. These culprits are conflicts of interest, in all their variety, the set of practices clustered around entertainment, gifts and payments, and the wonderful way that humans have of behaving like humans.

Obstreperous and thorny by nature, these issues thrive in the less-defined climate of the Black Zone. They can come into play at any time, usually without warning and often from an unexpected quarter. Worse, entirely new and parallel Black Zones materialize where none existed when the stakeholders change and new values and opinions redefine the boundaries. Many small companies start life as family concerns or they are owned by two or three good friends. Their culture is relaxed and informal. There are no rules about entertaining customers or using the corporate golf membership for family and friends, or granting favourable payment terms to a supplier who just happens to have gone to high school with the owner. *Laissez faire* is an attractive style and may even be a "best practice" in some circumstances. Black Zone issues frequently materialise as a small company travels the path from private to public, or even from family-owned and -operated to professional management. *Laissez faire* cannot extend to large companies and it should be discontinued either when a family-owned enterprise brings in professional management or when a small company becomes a public issuer. In these circumstances, at least one of the major categories of Black Zone issues will loom large on the horizon.

Conflicts of Interest

You should not be surprised that conflicts of interest comprise the first, the most common and the largest set of Black Zone risks. After all, it is hardly newsworthy that conflicts of interest are such variegated species, thriving in every habitat imaginable. They are the definition of ubiquity. That is because their apparent innocence is often the result of a well-honed rationalization, or because the risk has been deliberately downgraded in advance. We are blind to many conflicts of interest because we wish to be. We explain them away in advance, taking an active part in sewing the cloak that disguises them. Later, we find ourselves saying, "I never realized that a situation like this could ever develop". If you feel prone to this tendency, I suggest a very small but pithy book by Harry G. Frankfurt, *On Bullshit* (Princeton University Press, 2005).

Instead of opting for ostrich behaviour it is infinitely better to consider the whole set of possible conflicts in a proactive way and provide clear guidelines for one and all. You cannot cover every eventuality, but you can be specific on the majors and set a framework to judge the minors. Here is how one company opens this topic in its code of ethics, which all employees are required to read and then sign as having read and understood.

> *"All employees have a duty to avoid financial, business, or other relationships which might be opposed to the interests of the company or might cause a conflict with the performance of their duties. Employees should conduct themselves in a manner that avoids even the appearance of conflict between their personal interests and those of the corporation."*

Most large public companies have written and published their "code of conduct" or "values statement" in an attempt to clarify what is expected from employees. Some have made their views known for years, while others have gone this route as a matter of self defence, hoping to avoid liability for some gaffe when it occurs; and it will occur. Difficulties rear their heads when some action is not thought through, when it appears to be within bounds, but is not. Here is an example, as always, carefully disguised.

This is a story about a construction company in the northeastern part of the United States. It had built a great reputation for its ability to design and deliver storm sewer infrastructures to smaller municipalities, always on time and on budget. As it grew, the company decided that its strong reputation could be the basis for creating a brand that would propel it into other geographies and even into related market sectors, such as water treatment systems. It hired an advertising firm that had been successful in creating brand images for other companies and work got underway.

The ad firm wanted to gain an appreciation of its client's image in its home market and its work plan included a series of interviews with current or prospective customers of the company. As a small agency, it generally sub-contracted a lot of the less creative work and such was the case with these interviews, which were handed off to a small market research company. The advertising agency and the market research firm both believed that results would be improved if those being interviewed were offered an honorarium, either personally or paid to a charity of their choice. They discussed their plan with the company's vice president of marketing and everyone agreed that the direct feedback was important. Three weeks later, the company was accused of offering a bribe to a potential customer.

When the news hit the boardroom there was astonishment followed by "How could this have happened?" From that time until the eventual happy ending was about three months. The point of the anecdote is not whether an ethical barrier had been breached, for not only was the accusation withdrawn, but the customer admitted that there had been an overreaction by the potential recipient of the misunderstood honorarium. The value of this cautionary tale is how it exemplifies the Robbie Burns maxim about the best laid plans. An apparently innocent decision, part of a normal business process, risked the company's reputation and consumed months of extra time and effort to reconcile the parties and return to square one.

Could this debacle have been avoided? Of course, but only if the company had recognized the Black Zone before it drove into it. The company actually crossed at least three rumble strips as it entered the dangerous territory. All of this began when company executives decided to embark upon the branding exercise, an investigation of its image in the market to be followed by an action plan dictated by the research. This was hardly unusual as a generality, but it was unique in the history of this company, ergo, experience and existing policies did not cover it, a sure sign of a Black Zone ahead.

There was a second, but apparently inaudible, rumble when the marketing consultant was allowed to choose and engage a sub-contractor without the scrutiny of a company official. The customer interviews were arranged and conducted by someone hired by a contractor to work as a sub-contractor. This is the very definition of a Black Zone; a sub-contractor twice removed from company supervision, blissfully unaware of company rules and practices, engaging customers in an opinion-laden discussion for which they were to be paid.

That "honorarium" was questionable, or it should have been, the moment that it was considered. The customer interviews were scheduled during normal hours of work and were to take place on customer premises, so clearly the employee to be interviewed was being offered money in addition to his or her usual salary. Payments to a customer employee, no matter the circumstances, should be viewed as dark cell candidates, simply because they can be misconstrued so easily.

In other words, the warning rumbles were there and the whole unfortunate mess could and should have been avoided. Could this situation have been forecast? Unlikely, since prescience is generally in short supply. But rather than attempting to cover all contingencies by specifics, suppose this policy had been in place:

> *It is the policy of this company to know and understand the policies of customers and prospective customers, and these will be applied as a minimum standard, with company policy as the operational standard when it is the more restrictive.*

That policy would have helped the marketing department recognize the possibility that the interview fee could be misunderstood, but that leaves two other warnings that were unheard or ignored through inexperience. Perhaps an executive or boardroom discussion of the matrix would have heightened their awareness of the impending risk. North American companies operate in a hyper-sensitive environment, a fact of life to be accepted and accommodated, and the story just recounted is but one example. The following (incomplete) list of probable Black Zones is one that current and prospective directors ought to discuss with their boards, public or private.

- How do you satisfy yourself that the company observes the laws, rules and regulations governing the procurement of goods and services; how do you test to be sure that you are in compliance?

- How do you know that the company competes fairly and ethically for business opportunities? Under what circumstances would the company bid with an unusually low margin? Would it ever bid at a loss?

- Are there policies to guide personnel involved in the negotiation of contracts? Do you think they will ensure that statements, communications, and representations to customer representatives are accurate and truthful in detail, context and inference?

- Are there policies stating that employees may not attempt to obtain, from any source, information classified by government as sensitive or restricted?

- How does the company react to information regarding competitors' bids or proposals?

- Would the company accept a bid for services from a family member of an employee?

- Does an inspection of accounts show that the recording and charging of costs is scrupulous? The falsification of time, material or other cost records cannot be tolerated, but can you be sure that is the case? Are there policies making every supervisor personally responsible for assuring that such charges are recorded promptly and accurately?

- Is there a specific policy prohibiting fiction or fraud in claims, bids, proposals or any other documents of any kind? Do the policies extend to those who approve such documents after they have been submitted?

- How does the company handle the employment of family members of current employees? What does it do when two employees marry?

You might also wish to conduct a few well-placed interviews to determine if supervisors seem to be careful in words and conduct to avoid placing, or seeming to place, pressure that could cause subordinates to deviate from defined processes, policies, procedures and other acceptable norms of conduct. For directors of public companies, some of these issues should have been moved into the White Zone by the ICFR process that is a part of its CEO/CFO certification process, but further questions are always valuable.

Entertainment, Gifts and Payments

This batch of pitfalls should be met with the admonition at the edge of old maps, "Here live dragons", beyond the pale and in the dark. Generally difficult, this risk collective is squarely in the black cell when dealing with government of any kind. Federal, provincial, state and local government departments and agencies all have laws and policies concerning their employees' acceptance of virtually anything. The rules cover entertainment, meals, gifts, gratuities and other things of value when that seeming generosity comes from someone who wants to do business with them, or who falls under regulations over which they have authority. Many companies have similar rules, perhaps less strict, but they can still create issues where none need to be found. Simply finding out the relevant policies of your customer or supplier will tell you what to do as a minimum, with your own company's policies as an overlying and perhaps stricter regimen.

Chairs and Tables

One sensible practice is to define what can be given away, thus removing doubt and lowering the risk of an unguarded moment creating an issue. For example, Lockheed Martin prohibits its employees from giving things of value, as a generality, but permissible exceptions are defined as company advertising or promotional items of nominal value such as a coffee mug, calendar or similar item displaying the company logo. It is acceptable to provide modest refreshments such as soft drinks, coffee and doughnuts on an occasional basis in connection with business activities. By the way, "nominal value" is also defined — at $10.

Entertainment is even more treacherous. It probably occurs away from company premises, it is usually after hours and it is virtually impossible to describe in advance the specifics of any particular event. A strong compass is the best and probably the only guide. Another anecdote is illustrative.

During the first part of my journey through life, I was in the Royal Canadian Air Force (RCAF) and for a few years I was stationed in France, close to the city of Metz in the historic Moselle Valley. One of the younger men on my crew was a *bon vivant*, in fact, something of a party animal who loved to spend time in the many bars and clubs frequented by the Americans, Canadians and other militaries in NATO. At the start of an evening shift, he came to me in a state of shock, swore me to secrecy and revealed that he was being blackmailed. Apparently, he had been photographed on more than one occasion with a lady of the night draped around him in the back booth of "Willie's American Bar". He was adamant that "nothing happened" and that he was simply enjoying the moment.

This was 1961, the Cold War was very real, and so were constant attempts at various forms of espionage. The RCAF 61 Squadron operated a top secret, state-of-the-art radar installation just outside Air Division Headquarters, and our worthy opponents were more than a little curious about it. They had observed our ability to scramble a squadron almost as soon as their aircraft left the ground, so as to meet them for a long stare as each air force flew parallel tracks on either side of the border between East and West Germany. The young corporal in question had been informed that either certain operating characteristics and drawings were obtained or the incriminating photographs would find their way to his wife. There was a happy ending to the story, but it is recounted to illustrate the infallibility of Murphy's Law and its effect on risk. The young corporal would have been horrified had someone suggested that he was about to expose his country to any sort of risk when he entered Willie's Bar after work that day, but that is exactly what happened. He walked into a Black Zone and, in many ways, we let him do it.

The air force policy covering the situation was lodged in the "Queen's Rules and Regulations for the Air Force" (QR Air), which made references to "conduct unbecoming", but without explanation or specifics, preferring to focus on consequences. Assuming that the airman in question had read "QR Air", which his signature attested, it would have been unlikely that he would have seen the connection between the vague warning and his specific act. Most company policy manuals are little better. Have you ever seen one which explicitly forbids entertaining a customer in a strip club because there may be a risk to reputation? The usual rules and regulations are classic "inside the box" promulgations, and the risks are outside of it.

Humans being Humans

The breadth of experience inherent in moving into a directorship should prepare you for the especially complex Black Zone labelled "humans being humans". All but the most jaundiced are constantly astounded at the breathtaking imagination and virtuosity displayed as humans conduct themselves as humans. In this instance, the boundaries of the Black Zone will be formed or shift with how the organization, and the society in which it operates, defines morals and ethics. Selected specifics may be included or not, but there are behaviours that will affect your company whether you see them from a moralistic or ethical stance, or not. They are sufficiently persistent to be ubiquitous, and no doubt you have confronted them. Those that create the biggest headaches for the board are the ones likely to engender risk of some sort, often affecting the company's reputation, confidentiality and financial risk through lawsuits or penalties. Here is an example.

Several months ago, the *Toronto Star* carried an article by David Olive headlined "This time the boss got it". The article contrasted the reaction of the Boeing board, which had just sacked its CEO over his affair with a junior executive, with a 1980 parallel case at the Bendix Corporation, where the board decided that the appropriate response to a similar office romance was to fire the junior rather than the CEO. It was an insightful piece of reporting, highlighting our changing mores — but it was also simply another example of humans being humans.

It has taken far too many decades for the business world to conclude that drawing equally upon both genders would double the pool of talent available to it. One might argue that this is a work in process, but that is another matter. It is clear that when the proportion of males to females in the North American workplace was altered dramatically by the Second World War, a trend started, and it has continued. Business did not learn from history, another human tendency, so it did not draw on the accumulated wisdom of parents, teachers and assorted ecclesiastics and is, thus, still at a loss over how to deal with the inevitable implications of a lot of boys and girls together in the same place, for extended periods, working on common tasks. We have not done this well, although there are many hopeful signs. Beyond the rather commonplace events chronicled by the David Olive story, we are still wrestling with sexual harassment and its more malevolent cousins, and when an issue of that sort arises the board is likely to face a major risk.

What would you have done in the Boeing situation? The story in the *Toronto Star* had its roots in a previous scandal, which got rolling in May 2003 when the US Air Force announced its intention to lease a fleet of 100 Boeing KC-767 tankers as replacements for older planes. There was hot competition for the contract, which included an option to purchase the aircraft at the end of the 10-year lease. Boeing won over its rival Airbus, but within a few months critics were arguing that the lease was a lot more expensive than an outright purchase. The Department of Defence announced a revision to the contract then, and by December 2003, the Pentagon froze the project pending an investigation of allegations of corruption by one if its former procurement staffers, Darleen Druyun, who had moved to Boeing the previous January.

Druyun was fined and sent to jail for nine months for inflating the contract in favour of her future employer and for passing competitive information to Boeing. In the aftermath, then CEO Philip Condit resigned and CFO Michael Sears was fired. The board retrieved Harry Stonecipher, a retired COO of Boeing and a former CEO of McDonnell Douglas, as the interim CEO. Two years later, in March 2005, the Boeing board forced president and CEO Harry Stonecipher to resign because an internal investigation revealed a "consensual" relationship between Stonecipher and a female executive that was "inconsistent with Boeing's code of conduct" and "would impair his ability to lead the company". Another interim CEO bridged the company through to the appointment of James McNerney as the new chairman, president and CEO in June 2005.

To repeat, what would you have done? Was this sexual harassment, or simply bad judgment? If the latter, was it serious enough to dismiss someone, and if so, which one, or both? Why would an office romance "impair" the ability to lead the company"? Was the board attempting to send a signal that Boeing had cleaned up a culture that obviously had a few problems? Did it fire Stonecipher because he was an interim CEO? We will never know the answers to any of those questions, but the lesson to be drawn is, once more, the proclivity of the human species for sexual shenanigans, the fascination they hold for others and the havoc they can wreak on everyone around them.

Smaller companies seem especially prone to the risks inherent in the Black Zone. As the company grows from start-up to solid citizen status, it is likely to retain whatever passed for a policy manual on the day it opened its doors for business. At best, someone will do a cursory update, and that person is probably the sole occupant of the "human resources" function, having reached that position after passing through a stint in payroll or working as an executive assistant. Please do not misunderstand: these are valuable roles in and of themselves, but they simply do not afford the scope to develop the insights likely to prepare someone for the task of avoiding risk through well-conceived corporate policies. Those in the CEE Suite, now that the company has one, are more than a little preoccupied with issues of the moment, with little time for anything else, much less something as distant as the possibility of risk arising from a singular situation. Ergo, the company is exposed.

The purpose of tools like the Legitimacy Matrix is to identify possibilities which are not the norm and have, thus, been missed from explicit policies or standards of operation or where they might not seem to apply. Ignorance does not relieve directors of responsibility when lightning strikes, nor is it a defence after the fact. Corporate directors are expected to be constantly on the alert for risks of all sorts as a natural part of their DOC. Conflicts of interest, entertainment, and human foibles are three categories of what I have called Black Zone situations. It would be a wise practice to allocate some board time to the consideration of what the Black Zones contain for each individual company and the set of constraints peculiar to the environment in which it operates.

This book is not a "how to" on policy manuals, but it could be seen as an amber caution to a few danger zones. Here are some examples.

Other Danger Zones

There was a time when a warning about the checking the completeness and accuracy of financial records would have been *de rigueur*, but surely that time has passed. Today, directors get comfort from a thorough briefing on the ICFR process, or at least that should be the case for all public companies and all others that have their wits about them. Cautions remain for directors of private companies where the ICFR process is optional and the costs to establish it may be a barrier. This is especially applicable in the formative years of a new company, or after a merger brings unknown practices into the company. However, let us put most of the ICFR process risks aside and highlight a few others that seem to escape notice more often than they ought (although revenue recognition probably deserves its own chapter). Many such risks are ignored because the culture of the organization either does not see them or it deems them unimportant when they are detected.

> **The preservation of assets** is a director's responsibility, but they are in the employees' hands. How does the organization's culture treat company assets? Do employees seem to be cost conscious? No doubt the policy manual deals with the reimbursement of reasonable expenses incurred for travel on business or to company-sponsored events, as it ought to, but what is the attitude when selecting air carriers, vehicle rentals, accommodations and expenditures for meals? Are these viewed as a matter for conservation or as a perk of the job? For example, does the company encourage employees to use a hotel's complimentary transport from the airport, or a taxi or limousine? When you were being recruited, were you treated to a lavish, expensive dinner, one that you would question if you were approving the expense account?

> I recommend a review of the company's credit card policy. This is an insightful practice at any time, but it gains a special significance at the transition from private to public or at the point when a family-owned business brings in a major outside shareholder. Such events are demarcation lines in corporate governance practice and requirements, often accompanied by surprises and, occasionally, recrimination. Small, private companies view that which has been habitual as normal and hence acceptable, but "it ain't necessarily so" when the reality of the outside world intrudes.

Confidentiality about the company and its operations always appears in the policy manual in some manner and some companies have elaborate and specific rules on the topic. Well enough, but as a director how do you know that there is an atmosphere of discretion? Do employees understand their personal roles in maintaining confidentiality? There are occasions when important specifics about company activities have not been released and attitudes and mores are more reliable than prohibitions. For public companies it is illegal to purchase or sell securities using "material inside information" and this aspect is (usually) understood, but not always, especially in newly public companies. For example, employees might be scrupulous about safeguarding insider information from others, while assuming that their personal buying or selling is within bounds.

Antitrust laws may seem remote, but remoteness is one characteristic of a Grey Zone. Generally speaking, such laws prohibit agreements or actions "in restraint of trade", restrictive practices that may reduce competition without providing beneficial effects to consumers. Among those agreements and activities found to be clear violations are: agreements or understandings among competitors to fix or control prices; to boycott specified suppliers or customers; to allocate products, territories, or markets; or to limit the production or sale of products or product lines. Any and all variants of such agreements are against public policy and should be against the policy of your company, but wisdom suggests a step beyond the stated policies. Because they seem remote it is easy to transgress quite innocently, perhaps during a negotiation when the employee believes that he or she is simply attempting to get a better deal for the company. Directors are advised to review the orientation program for employees to ensure that training takes the issue beyond the policy manual. Employees need a practical understanding of the limits, ie, never discuss matters which are susceptible to misinterpretation by the representatives of other companies.

Be wary of Uncle Sam. The US extends its antitrust laws to apply to international operations and transactions related to imports to, or exports from, the US. If your company does a lot of business with the US, both it and its employees must be aware of the extent of those laws and where the difficulties start. Further, since the attacks on what was the World Trade Center in New York, the US has increased its vigilance to a variety of threats, all quite understandably, but regulations have increased in many areas and that includes business. For example, in some cases a US subsidiary must have a majority of US citizens resident in the US on its board of directors, and they are prescribed from co-operating with the parent company in the manner prior to September 11, 2001.

International trade is supported by most governments, but it comes with added risks. The international activities of your company could be subject to the antitrust laws of other nations or of organizations such as the European Economic Community. It is illegal to enter an agreement to refuse to deal with potential or actual customers or suppliers or otherwise engage in or support restrictive international trade practices. Since the mere receipt of a request to engage in such activity becomes a reportable event by law, all employees should immediately seek advice when the company receives a request that even seems to seek involvement in a restrictive trade practice. Again, employee programs such as orientation should cover the issue if the company is involved in international trade.

Political contributions are at least grey and they darken quickly into the Black Zone. The most prudent practice is for the company to avoid contributing, loaning or otherwise making available funds or assets to the party or the campaign of any candidate for a federal, provincial or municipal office. That should explicitly include direct or indirect employee time, when that person is presumed to be working on behalf of the company.

This is not to say that employees should not be involved in civic affairs, quite the contrary. Freedom depends upon, and thus demands, personal involvement and companies should encourage their employees to serve their communities and their country. But politics and business are awkward bedfellows, in spite of the frequency of their sojourns. In the language of the Legitimacy Matrix, their intersection is at least grey, and it could become as black as night faster than any sunset. It would be wise to be quite specific about employee involvement, to ensure that their participation is, at all times and in all ways, at their own expense. Further, when an employee speaks on public issues, it must be clear that their comments or statements are theirs alone and do not reflect the company.

Government contracts are prized for their duration and the financial soundness of the customer. Bidding, negotiating and performing such contracts are prized talents. So far, so good, but the reason for classifying anything to do with a government contract as code amber is that they are surrounded by a host of regulations and special conditions, and they are always subject to more scrutiny than is ever found in the private sector.

An especially tricky Grey Zone is the one reached through twin doors labelled "government employees" on the left, and "rules of engagement with government" on the right. On entry, know that perhaps no one is quite as sensitive to a real or imagined slight as the typical civil servant. Any hint that someone else has been treated exceptionally will awaken the green-eyed monster, while an unguarded remark is likely to be taken as an insult or a special request. If the circumstances are not clarified immediately, the rumour mill begins to grind and brown envelopes appear. The task of eradication is compounded by the persistence of this new belief once it establishes its place in the community mythology common to all government departments or entire agencies, boards or commissions.

The complexity of the interface with government employees is multiplied by the maze of unfamiliar and less than obvious rules and regulations. Federal, state or provincial, and local government departments and agencies have layers of regulations regarding employee acceptance of entertainment, meals and gifts from anyone with whom the departments and agencies do business or over whom they have regulatory authority. Employees may not give, or offer to give, virtually anything to government employees, including any form of entertainment, meals or gifts, loans or whatever, regardless of their value. Managing the interface is highly challenging, to say the least.

A variant is an employee who has family members working for the government. Paint this zone grey, too, and write clear guidance for one and all. While the company needs to avoid any semblance of interference with family life, it must be clear that entertainment, for example, cannot be related to the business of the company and is not reimbursable to the employee.

The Foreign Corrupt Practices Act received Royal Assent on December 10, 1998. It prohibits giving money or items of value to a foreign official for the purpose of influencing a foreign government. The Act further prohibits giving money or items of value to any person or firm when there is reason to believe that it will be passed on to a government official for this purpose. Many small companies do business in countries where customs and practices are quite different from what would be regarded as "ethical" in North America. In cases where their values are not sufficient guidance, they should scrupulously adhere to the letter and spirit of the Foreign Corrupt Practices Act.

Rumours carry a corrosive potential, and they often crop up in a director's in-basket. It places you in a dilemma, for you must now judge whether the message has validity, and determining that may invoke Heisenberg's Uncertainty Principle, that is, the process will influence the observation. An inconsequential notion could get a large dollop of perceived justification simply because a director asks about it. On the other hand, there is DOC, so you must do something. In my view, it is situations like these that support a belief that directors, especially chairs, ought to be close enough to the day-to-day operations that there is some possibility that the rumour might be placed in context at once or, if this cannot be done, at least you have the familiarity to know where to make discreet inquiries. My personal practice, with all companies where I am a director, is to appear regularly on the premises and establish habits that become the norm, such as stopping in the cafeteria and wandering about for casual conversations. As a result, when I need an insight it is at hand or easily found, and not through a "visit by a director".

When the rumour has substance, you have more work to do. An example along the lines of humans being humans led to a lot of gossip in a small Michigan town. One director was on the receiving end of a half-joking lob, "So, I gather things got pretty wild up at the plant last week". Only a week had passed, but the aftermath of a celebration had become a snowball of community gossip. It began innocently, with a bottle of champagne and some gourmet snacks served in the president's office to celebrate winning a major contract. Just as most of the celebrants were leaving for their homes, the vice president of marketing retrieved a couple of bottles of wine from his office, prizes in a raffle the previous Christmas. Only four people remained and they dwindled to two after one glass of wine. The company controller and the head of market research remained and, with spirits high and flowing, inhibitions — and judgment — went out the window. Unhappily, the inebriants were discovered by the cleaning staff whose entrance did not provide sufficient warning for the dishevelled couple on the president's chesterfield to retrieve their dignity.

This is not the forum to debate whether this liaison was a good idea in the grand scheme of things, but it was certainly not the right occasion for it. Aside from the personal difficulties confronting the participants, the company and its board faced some wonderfully salacious gossip, for which they were totally unprepared. Of course, it is impossible to have a specific answer to the shenanigans in question, but it is both possible and reasonable to conclude that gossip, in some form, will arise sooner or later, so have a "damage control" process ready and waiting.

A General Line of Defence

Obviously, the list of "other danger zones" is incomplete, but it will have done its job if the reader comes away with heightened wariness about issues which may appear innocent, but where dangers lurk. Presuming that your instincts are aroused and you suspect the presence of a danger zone, what then? What is a simple, practical means of checking the correctness of the path the board is considering, some means of knowing that both the spirit and letter of the law of the land and the company's code are the reasons for choosing this particular course of action? The following sequence of questions and comments is useful.

1. **Is the action legal?** For the most part, the answer will be obvious, since this is usually bimodal, but if there is any doubt, check with corporate counsel. All the following questions assume that the answer to this first question is "yes" since otherwise the ultimate resolution is obvious. Further questions will clarify the situation beyond the letter of the law.

2. **Does the action comply with your corporate values?** So, to repeat, there had to be a "yes" to the first question, but even if it is legal, does the contemplated act fit your values? It may be perfectly legal

to pour so much salt on the parking lot that it never needs to see a snow plow, but if an environmental conscience is part of your values the salt is probably a bad idea. Or, given the damaging effects of salt on concrete, its legal use would not fit a value of preservation of assets. It is assumed that your company's values are themselves appropriate, ie, they have not been distorted by the personal beliefs of the CEE Suite or otherwise placed themselves at odds with the community and the majority of your employees.

3. **If you do it, will you feel bad?** It is legal to apply the same payment process across all supplier accounts. However, the two-person design shop around the corner has only been in business for a few months and cash flow is tight, so making them wait for 45 days may hurt. How would you feel if the rigid application of an otherwise legal policy put them out of business? What effect would such a move have on employee opinions?

4. **How will it look in the newspaper?** How will the action look when taken out of context, or given a particular spin? This is where an issue can go from grey to black in short order. Here is an extreme example. In this instance, a well-intentioned company entered into a research agreement with a university, a two-year program fitting the interests of a couple of professors and the needs of the company. All went well until an activist website decided to ignore the research while describing the company sponsoring it as "baby killers". The company was a supplier of products to the military, but none were combat related. The reader may well wonder how even undergraduate naiveté could make the leap from the simple fact of a contract with the military to a horrible and very public accusation, but it happened. It took a lot of careful explanations to resolve this situation, and likely the only way to have avoided it would have required sufficient cynicism about campus values that the research grant was never made. Incidentally, in the situation just described, the research grant was withdrawn after the board evaluated the risk to the company's reputation versus the reward from the planned research, which was subsequently undertaken by company employees.

5. **If you know it is wrong, why do it?** This may seem self evident and most of the time it is, but from time to time, directors will be confronted with an issue such as a "strategic bid" (read: much lower than market) or a political contribution from company coffers or refusing to reduce effluent because of a "grandfather" provision for your plant because it is old. It may be that the company policy manual is silent on such topics, although it probably should not be, and these actions are legal within certain boundaries. These examples are not clever ideas, they are wrong. Why would any company risk a contract which will lose money and send the wrong signal to the marketplace? Why would a company choose political sides, a sure road to problems? And, why would anyone hide behind

a legal quirk that is sure to change at some point and allows an unsavoury practice in the interim?

6.   **If you or your board are not sure, keep talking.** Questionable ideas are like germs, they shy away from strong detergents, and thorough discussion on all sides of an issue will scrub it clean of misunderstanding and lack of information. It will allow an answer to emerge and it has a good chance of being one that the entire board can support.

You and your fellow directors should never doubt that the world now expects your board to monitor corporate compliance on a wide range of ethical issues. The issue becomes one of fulfilling this oversight responsibility and establishing appropriate diligence for doing so, and this implies that the company and its board have thought about it in advance, that there is an ethics program in place before the fact, rather than in reaction. For public companies, full compliance requires the board to develop and approve a code of ethics and corporate conduct and communicate them to the marketplace. Private organizations would be wise to take a similar tack and put a well-drafted and enforceable code in place. It should include elements like these:

- A "protected" mechanism for bringing complaints, concerns and code interpretation questions forward. Complainants should be assured about lack of retaliation, confidentiality to the extent possible and procedural fairness.

- An effective training and reinforcement program that seeks to communicate standards of proper business conduct.

- Agreement to comply with the code as a condition of initial and continued employment, with compliance incorporated into business objectives as well as individual performance appraisals.

- Accountability and reporting mechanisms, including proper measurement, auditing and feedback.

- Regular reporting to the board or a special committee on matters including compliance reviews, program effectiveness and risk assessment, as well as the establishment of regular opportunities for board input.

- Most importantly, a tangible commitment by senior management and leadership by the board in overseeing the corporate compliance program.

Integrating these into a coherent and effective ethics program creates and sustains an ethical corporate culture that guides decision making throughout the company. Second, it demonstrates to the public, government, regulators, employees, customers, suppliers, investors and competitors that the company's ethics program is alive and well and that the company is trustworthy. Third, it promotes high levels of individual and corporate performance and compliance. Fourth, an effective ethics program educates employees and management about the company's principles and values, and helps them determine appropriate business practices and behaviour. Lastly — and most significantly — an effective, comprehensive program helps to demonstrate that the directors are diligent in exercising their DOC.

7.   **The code of ethics must be enforceable** and to the extent that it is not, directors should worry and question the value of the code in the first place. Your company's code must have teeth. When you examine your company's response to a breach, you should find that failure to comply leads to disciplinary action. Depending on the severity of the breach, the discipline might include termination, referral for criminal prosecution and reimbursement to the company for any losses or damages resulting from the violation. The company should include those who authorize or participate directly in actions which are a violation of the code and those who deliberately fail to report a violation or who knowingly withhold relevant and material information concerning a violation of the code. Include the violator's manager to the extent that the circumstances of the violation reflect inadequate supervision or a lack of diligence and any supervisor who retaliates, directly or indirectly, or encourages others to do so. Finally, this is a good point to read the company's "Whistle Blower Policy", and if there isn't one, find out why not.

Stay with the Compass

Writing a summary for a chapter on ethics is more of a challenge than can be easily met. There is so much that could be said, but so little that really must be said. Every organization needs a compass. In a world of variables, of the unpredictable, directors are charged with charting the best course for their company in spite of uncertainty. For that reason, integrity, truth, courage, wisdom and the other fundamentals of a code of ethics are so very, very important. They clarify and illuminate strategy; they are Occam's razor to unresolved issues and impending risks. Your task is difficult and complex, and you can never learn all there is to know nor guess the intent of every regulation, but directors following an ethical compass have a degree of certainty on which to rely. That may be enough.

Chapter Five:

The Chair Wears Many Hats

Well, yes, and some fit better than others. If we are to believe the advice of the many governance and management gurus the successful chair of a board must embody an absolutely mind-boggling list of attributes and competencies. He or she might not walk on water but should easily navigate damp sand without leaving a trace. Such omnipotence may exist, and I for one am looking forward to meeting this paragon in person, but to-date, the "Caped Chair" has proven elusive. More seriously, and certainly more practically, every person who accepts the role of board chair for the first time or anytime, must immediately come to terms with the intersection of their own quite human capabilities and the fact that their new job is multi-faceted to a degree that was probably unsuspected prior to acceptance. In fact, I would extend this to every new directorship regardless of how much experience the new director may have.

The chair's first role is managing the home team, the board of directors. Their care and feeding, plus the particular issues generated by, and around, the standing committees and their respective chairs are clearly part of the job. Then there is the executive management team or CEE Suite and the interfaces with the members of that group, jointly and severally. There are all the stakeholder groups, led by the people who put you in the chair, but including customers, employees, suppliers, regulators, special interest groups, the media and the community at large. As if this litany were not enough, these players are both interconnected and interdependent in completely unsuspected and occasionally unfathomable ways, with each intersect *un aûtre chapeau*. To continue the apparel analogy, the person wearing those hats, the model on the runway if you will, is actually "on the carpet" much of the time, rather than taking a stroll along it. More will be said in a later chapter about this wonderfully rewarding role and how to manage the inventory of hats, but first there are some major tasks that never go away.

Setting the Tone

It is currently popular to talk about the "tone at the top" and this means the ethical and moral expectations and practices of the directors and senior team, especially those of the chair and of the CEO. Those crucial aspects were addressed in the previous chapter, and what I wish to do here is extend the concept of tone

It is absolutely consistent with the best practice of DOC for a director to have the broadest possible perspective on the company and its leadership. I believe that the chair should model this behaviour and thus "set the tone" for the board. A few of the majors require directors to visit customers, suppliers, sales offices and plants, including IBM, GE and Intel. It is an equally important practice for those on the boards of small companies, and the chair should lead by example. Directors who know what customers want from first-hand knowledge have a distinct advantage when the board considers a shift in strategy that affects them.

The same breadth of understanding should extend to the CEE Suite and this is more important in small companies, although it would be a close decision between small and large. The chair simply has to know every member of that group and know them well, as individuals as well as executives. Judging their performance other than through a mechanical process is impossible otherwise.

Managing the Board

The chair is directly responsible for managing the board, an opinion shared with Leblanc and Gillies on the first page of this book and worth repeating. You may recall that this was epitomized by the "first among equals" phrase which seemed so challenging to the writer of this book. Once past the stage fright, it was plain that, while all directors share common responsibilities and accountabilities, the role of the chair of the board clearly has other dimensions.

So, the gauntlet is down. The board is responsible for the business and the chair is the leader of that board. Strategic, financial and human performance will play out against risk management, and the chair must set the direction and ensure that ideas become actions that create value. It is daunting, even intimidating, but it is also an exhilarating challenge with rich personal rewards. Politics aside, how else is one to get the opportunity to be part of a group whose members volunteer to stand for election and are then entrusted to create jobs, wealth and prosperity?

Board Operations

While all boards have much in common, arguably the most onerous and sometimes the most mind-bending tasks lie before the directors of a publicly-listed company. This is so simply because of compliance rather than governance, those two being quite separate facets of director responsibility. To set the stage, let us assume that the organization in question is a small cap company on the TSX. It has annual revenues of less than $100 million, so the resources allocated to compliance are a significant item in its chart of accounts, but it is determined to do whatever is needed to be fully compliant. This implies that it almost certainly has three standing committees: audit, compensation and governance. Its external auditors conduct a quarterly review and the audit committee and the CFO poured a lot of time and effort into the design of an ICFR process, which they tested in 2007. Its compensation committee stays in tune with the market place, monitors the CEE Suite, worries about succession and wonders about the implications of the regulator's intended MD&A of compensation. The governance committee, which also handles board nominations, is constantly on the alert for disclosure issues. Putting these together, basic board operations might look like this.

1. **The First Quarter** is one of the two busiest, as the previous year is audited and reported while the new one gathers speed. The audit committee will meet at least a couple of times on the consolidated financial statements for the previous year and an extra meeting may creep in to accommodate the review and approval of the MD&A, annual information forms (AIFs) and other core documents. The compensation committee has to complete the CEE Suite performance reviews for the previous year in time for the resulting bonuses to be included in the audit and the financials for that year. The governance committee must attend to nominations in sufficient time to have the proposed slate of directors ready before the proxy is to be printed and mailed, all taking their cue from the date of the annual meeting, likely to occur sometime in the second quarter.

2. **The Second Quarter** may seem less busy because it likely has fewer meetings, but there are always the unexpected times when acquisitions are underway or new territories are opened. The audit committee meets at least twice and approves the first-quarter financial statements. If the governance committee did not have time in the previous quarter, it will now complete the board, committee and director assessment process for the previous year.

3. **The Third Quarter** sees more work for the board and the committees, with a half-year review of operations, mid-point performance reviews for the CEE Suite, and probably the start of the annual planning cycle. The audit committee has its usual slate of meetings while tending to the second-quarter financials.

4. **The Fourth Quarter** is another busy period, with year-end corporate reviews, business plan and budget approvals, CEE Suite goal setting for the coming year, and at least the first round of assessments of CEE Suite performance during the current year. The audit committee handles the third-quarter statements.

Chairs and Tables

Even without one of the major discontinuities mentioned in the DOC discussion, this brief overview suggests a substantial workload for the board and its committees. The board met face-to-face at least six times, perhaps as many as eight, plus several teleconferences for approvals or quick decisions. The audit committee met on at least eight and probably 10 occasions, most of them face-to-face. The compensation and governance committees each met four to six times. The entire board and the senior management team spent two days off-site for strategy and business planning. By any reckoning, a lot of people spent a lot of time on meetings and preparing for them.

A quick summary shows that any individual director had face-to-face meetings about a dozen times and the total could easily double if that director was on two standing committees and had perfect attendance. Add the teleconferences, interviews, smaller meetings, preparation, research and keeping abreast of regulatory changes, and the hours mount quickly. A US survey conducted in 2006 by the National Association of Corporate Directors (NACD) and Mercer Delta Consulting, found that directors on public boards spent an average of 209.7 hours per year on board-related matters, up from an average of 190 hours in 2005. Of course, those with committee or chair roles will spend more time than this, with committee work requiring another 75 to 100 hours, committee chairs a further 50 to 75 hours, and the chair of the board needing as much as 350 to 500 hours to manage an active board for a company that is undergoing a lot of changes. Little wonder that a friend of mine was heard to mutter, "We need to maximize DRIT" which I finally learned meant "directors return on invested time".

Co-ordinating the calendars of busy people is a challenge at best and it becomes a nightmare when the activities come from conflicting spheres, which, in the case of a director, includes at least family, work, play and directorship. Further, although the board of a small company may have one or two people who are in their first directorship the remainder will have other boards. The challenge of co-ordinating perennially busy people quickly assumes overtones of critical-path programming or solving simultaneous linear equations. Simply establishing an agreed calendar is a chore and, even as it is completed, its author knows that it will probably change and then the dominoes will fall. Further, the work of the committees and the board as a whole are interdependent and sequencing is often critical, eg, the governance and nominations committee (GNC) slate before the proxy mailing, or the MRC decisions on bonuses before closing the year. Finally, there are at least two and possibly more CEE Suite executives interacting with the board and all are busy people. Having said this, the board calendar is hardly an esoteric subject and, because it seems mundane, it is easily ignored except as a subject for complaints.

It is actually a lost opportunity. One of the hallmarks of an effective board is its discipline around its calendar, for the priority that an established calendar receives is a clear indication of the importance of corporate governance in its competition for time and attention. People like to be part of a success, and there is a sense of being part of a well-managed organization imparted by a carefully planned board calendar. There is security in that certainty, and it is an opportunity to foster group cohesion. The chair and the corporate secretary need to make this work whether their board is public, private or NFP.

Clearly, this hat must fit. As the chair you cannot expect kudos for planning the calendar, but you most certainly should expect a lot of grousing if individual calendars and company needs are not mutually accommodated. The only way this can occur is through the sort of advance planning that allows your directors to give the board calendar the priority it deserves. A calendar of five quarters will serve you well, so long as you keep rolling it forward so that there is always a year ahead. As chair, you can hope for help from the corporate secretary, but the responsibility is yours, simply part of managing the work of the board. There is an example of a one-year board calendar in Appendix Four of this book.

Meetings of the Board

A group of directors came to be called a "board" because they customarily met around a table or, as it was once called, a board. We still meet around a boardroom table, but we congregate as often by teleconference, over a table in a restaurant, by web conference and in all the ways that people can and do meet to discuss business. And meet they must, for meetings, virtual and real, are an important mechanism for the board as it does its job, whether that is discussion of strategy or routine housekeeping.

Given the responsibility of the chair to manage the board, it follows that said chair must take pains beyond scheduling to ensure that board meetings are not only efficient and effective, but enjoyable and stimulating. This is of particular importance in a smaller organization, where the intellectual stimulation and collegiality of the board are significant in the trade for the director's time and effort. Directors do not have an employee relationship, and they can simply disengage when the experience called a board meeting becomes objectionable. It is the job of the chair to add the extra layer that makes the board meeting more than a chore to be done. Here are a few recommendations.

1. **The agenda rules, up to a point.** There is a danger in agenda, of becoming rigid and inflexible, of delaying an important discussion simply because it is not on the agenda at the time it arises. But this is an instance when the end may justify the means; for without an agenda and its priority, meetings are liable to go "dancing with the daffodils", while the poor sod in the chair will be left to wander "lonely as a cloud". With apologies to the Great Romantic, that would not serve the shareholders well. It is up to the chair to ensure that the agenda is set, that it is complete and agreed, and that every item on it gets its due. Having said this, it is a valuable exercise to "put the agenda on the agenda" on occasion just to see if it is still viable or needs adjustment to suit changes.

Every board and every chair has a preferred format for the agenda, but the Wise suggest starting every meeting with a management update that is strategic in tone and content. Directors will always be interested in questions such as, "What has changed since the last meeting?" or "What developing issues concern you?" and it is important that the agenda facilitate that discussion because it is central to oversight. As the chair, you will wish to encourage an enquiring and wide-ranging discussion, and the agenda will aid in steering away from disproportionate time spent on operational issues.

2. **Allocate timing.** A useful habit is to estimate the approximate time for each item and indicate it on the agenda before it is sent out as part of the board package. Committee chairs, members of management and others on the agenda for the day will surely signal their needs for more time (give a prize to those who ask for less!) and priorities can be set during the agenda review at the start of the meeting. In the spirit of continuous improvement, have the secretary of the meeting record the time actually used for each item. Reviewing those notes may be a revelation as you discover the amount of time spent on housekeeping or presentations, as opposed to discussion and debate of issues facing the company.

    The agenda intersects a director's twin duties, and the challenge is to ensure that the time actually spent addressing the major responsibilities of the directors, the five jobs, is somewhere close to their level of importance. Operational issues always loom large for a small company, and it is easy to consume an entire meeting talking to management about their daily fare, while ignoring the oversight responsibilities that are the true task before the meeting.

    This table shows the percentages of time typically spent versus what some experts believe is the ideal.

Responsibilities of the Board	Percentage of Time Spent	
	Actual	Ideal
Strategy	10	40
Talent	5	20
Oversight (audit, risk, fiduciary)	25	30
Routine	60	10

Make it a custom to place routine matters at the end of the agenda, or perhaps deal with them in a "consent agenda" to free more time for strategic business issues.

Finally, deal with that ever-present time consumer, the PowerPoint presentation. Boards would do well to set some rules around these beasties, addressing their length, their ability to transmit the true message and whether they have a purpose beyond helping the person making the presentation organize what must be said. There are two cardinal rules. First, remember that PowerPoint is almost innocent of subtlety or nuance, and when those would make a difference this tool can spell disaster. Second, while the PowerPoint screens may provide a wonderfully descriptive package, the job of the board is to ensure that it is translated into prescriptive actions.

3.   **Allow time to prepare.** It is absolutely essential to the concept of the DOC that directors get all the information they need and that they get it far enough in advance of the board meeting. Surely it is endemic to the DOC process that directors have the time for thought and reflection, and to refer to information from other sources, to read previous minutes and to complete their personal analysis. Directors who have this opportunity are likely to contribute in a manner simply not possible for the less prepared.

Coach the CEE Suite to prepare board proposals that:

- set the context and bring the directors into the picture;
- describe the opportunity or risk behind the proposal;
- present the proposed solution in a simple and straightforward manner; and
- support the proposed action with three key arguments, no more, no less.

Set an expectation that major proposals ought to reach the directors' hands at least two weeks in advance. Gradually build the habit until no one would dream of coming forward with less rigour behind their proposition.

When the senior team is unfamiliar with benchmark practices and standards it is salutary to have the board chair or an experienced director edit all paperwork or presentations before they go to the directors.

4.   **Record the action items.** Any corporate secretary worthy of the name will capture resolutions and motions verbatim, record significant discussions and decisions and provide an account of what was considered and decided. It takes only a little more to note all actions, voluntary or directed, expected to flow from the meeting. It is quite likely that the context of the meeting created an expectation that the voluntary, "I'll get that information" will actually happen. Too often it is forgotten until the need becomes more critical, except that now the volunteer is absent and someone must scramble to fill the gap.

5.   **Let no director be silent.** Aside from those gregarious souls who always have something to say, it is a human foible for some to maintain an inexplicable silence even when the director in question has an opinion or a piece of information to contribute. The chair can easily offset this tendency by the simple expedient of going around the table and asking directly when the issue at hand merits the time taken, which should be the normal case, for otherwise the topic would not be before the board. Further, the moment taken to ensure inclusiveness has an automatic effect beyond the director's contribution in that the minutes will reflect a more robust and thorough contemplation of the issue, and that may be significant in the event that board process is ever examined.

6.   **In camera is informal.** Let us agree that an in camera session is always on the agenda so that the question becomes, "How should it be used?" A superficial "to have a discussion independent of management" sort of answer is not quite enough. One chair I know asks the directors at the start of every meeting to provide written items for the in camera agenda, which are read aloud at the start of that session. Another reminds the independent directors in advance of the actual board meeting, and asks that each circulate issues to the others. Both are useful ideas. I follow two other practices that I find helpful. First, although the in camera is conversational in style, formality is dropped. I keep notes and circulate them among the independent directors for their comments, much as one would for minutes of the whole board. This has the effect of ensuring agreement on what was decided and tracking any actions arising from the session. Two of the boards where I am a director attach a synopsis of the topics discussed to the minutes of the board. Another tactic is to use the in camera as an informal check on the health of the board, a sort of ongoing evaluation that becomes something of an early warning system.

7.   **Minutes are archaeological artefacts.** When a company is incorporated, its new owners receive a government charter plus a minute book and a corporate seal to commence keeping records. The importance attached to the formal deliberations and decisions of the board of directors would be difficult to over emphasize, for they are fundamental to so many business processes. But having agreed on their legal status and value, we ought also to realize their worth for other purposes. For example, read your latest board minutes for qualifying phrases such as "concerns were raised" and "extensive discussion followed" and take them as flags raised. Their appearance suggests that the meeting of record faced an issue that it found so difficult to contemplate that the record prefers to be obscure. Of course, neither is acceptable, for both the minutes and the process they recorded need to be transparent, but the point is that the minutes are themselves the artefact of the event for the chair seeking to improve it. A second purpose of the minutes is

that they record the directors doing their DOC, an invaluable asset in certain situations.

Following the advice in these seven points will not guarantee success, but it will get you close to it. I want to add a couple of other suggestions that are closer to personal style and practice. I avoid the use of "parliamentary procedure" in the sense of protocols like "Robert's Rules of Order". The agenda plus mutual respect should be sufficient and, if not, the board has larger issues than procedure to be concerned about. Also I favour taking personal notes at all meetings, a habit questioned by some on the basis that every word might have to be defended if a plaintiff's lawyer were to examine me on their meaning. I accept that risk as preferable to the vagaries of memory, and with respect to board minutes, I find my notes quite valuable when I review them after the fact. When I am in the role of chair I follow the practice of reviewing the minutes in their first draft, then asking the directors to review them, and finally asking one last time before they are approved.

Herding the Cats

Directors, whether collected one at a time or in a sea change, are a multi-faceted assemblage of intellects and egos, experiences and competencies, brought together in a group called a board. The word "group" was chosen deliberately, to go beyond the obvious and draw attention to group dynamics, the *bête noir* of every chair. This book has neither the space, nor its author the knowledge, to explore this topic, but its importance is such that at least an alert is in order.

While I toiled for a large consultancy, a senior partner in the firm provided a simple and somewhat humorous illustration when we were returning from a meeting which had been sabotaged by two of the people in attendance. I had expressed my surprise and frustration and my mentor said, "Think of it this way. The Bible says that as soon as God made the first individual he immediately made another. That made a pair and that was the first group. Those group members begat others and increased the size of the group. Group politics led to friction, the group disintegrated in conflict — and there has been trouble with groups ever since." We both laughed, but I never forgot the lesson.

There are always at least two very separate issues when people work in groups: the task that is the rationale for the group's existence and the processes through which the group accomplishes that task. It is the processes of a deliberately formed group that differentiate it from a miscellaneous collection, also called a rabble. Directors, and especially chairs, would be well advised to revisit or add to their reading some of the standard works on group process and the insights of Bruce Tuckman would be a good starting point (Bruce W. Tuckman developed the "forming — storming — norming — performing" model of team development in 1965, later adding a fifth stage, adjourning or transforming.)

The processes of the group are the means by which it acts; how it works as a unit rather than a loose assemblage. The mechanism of the group, its process, must accommodate norms, roles, relationships, status, power, the need to belong, social influence, individuals' behaviours and many more. Group dynamics are not simple and seldom easy to manage. Ignore them at your peril.

This is not to suggest that all directors ought to study group dynamics, nor that all chairs should try their hand at amateur psychology. But I do urge a heightened awareness that your board is like any group of people, meaning that while it may have the strengths of a group it will also have all its foibles. Knowing the dangers, here are a few simple precautions:

- **Get to know every director outside the boardroom.** As you find common ground respect for the other person builds almost automatically, and respect is an important lubricant of group process. Further, as we come to know more about an individual as a person we discover more of what motivates them and what constraints from their daily lives may be present in the boardroom. In one case, a director wanted to serve on the audit and disclosure committee (ADC) and, when I asked if he had discussed his interest with the governance and nominating committee, he replied that he had, but audit had three independent directors with either an accountancy or financial analyst designation and he had neither. He also revealed that his father was a chartered accountant and had expected him to follow in his footsteps. He had become a marketing specialist instead, but wanted to scratch an old itch. We increased the ADC to four members, enrolled the newest in a financial literacy course and a happy director was able to tell the story at dinner on Sunday.

- **The relationship with the CEO should not be a matter of chance.** It takes more than a few minutes at the onset of the board meeting to build and maintain the relationship with the CEO. It is absolutely crucial, to the point that it ought to be regarded as a risk factor. When the board-CEO relationship is an armed truce, it is a distraction standing in the way of the corporate issues that are the main responsibilities of both parties. This will be discussed again in this chapter.

- **Work on the process rather than the event.** The mechanics of the event are easy enough (see the previous section), but although their meetings are important, the best boards understand that oversight is continuous. DOC never ceases for them, and feeding it is an opportunity for the thoughtful chair. The process is a continuum of interaction with the management team, market or industry reports, media, casual meetings and a host of other inputs. The chair can colour this stream by supplying some of the information, sending a few extracts or web links from industry publications, this helps to maintain currency while simultaneously touching the directors regularly.

- **Be wary of conflicting commitments.** Company employees may ask for a promise of confidentiality, which may be impossible until you know if the issue might come between you and your first obligation. Directors, especially the chair, often receive unsolicited information accompanied by the admonition, "Please don't say anything, but... ". Thoughtfulness and sincerity are enhanced if you avoid this compromise in the first place, while integrity demands it in any event.

- **Review the agenda in advance** of every board meeting to ensure that the directors believe that the agenda covers the issues, that those issues are understood, and that questions have been answered. Simply circulating the agenda to the other directors will take care of this task, as long as it is sent out at least a week ahead of time to allow busy people to read, think and telephone if they need to talk about it. Consensus building rewards its architect with reduced friction and coherent board actions.

- **Be wary of "group think"**, the tendency to follow the herd and dwell in the comfort of its numbers, rather than putting forth a minority view. Humans are prone to accept statements at face value when they come from a trusted source, such as another director. This is positive and should be prized and cultivated. However, a "no questions asked" approach can also lead the group into a common opinion without anyone exposing the fatal flaw. One director related how information was passed through the "whistle blower" channel of his company and reached the board. The director responsible received the information and brought it to the governance committee, where at first is seemed to be a serious issue. Debate began and continued apace until one director asked, "Do all of us agree that this is a whistle blower issue?" There were a few moments of silence and then, a short discussion later, the group concluded that the complaint was a management issue that had no bearing on disclosure. It was classified as a misunderstanding and dispatched to the CEO as an item needing repair. It should never have reached the board in the first place, but a dollop of group think gave it an undeserved moment in the sun.

- **Spend the bulk of the board's time on the future.** That is where optimism lies, where there are deeds to do, and excitement to be generated. This is not a flippant or dismissive remark. Much can and should be learned from a missed bid, for example, but with the learning in hand, turn to resolution, which lies in the future not the past and is not encumbered by potential recriminations, which rarely contribute to team solidarity. The consolidated financial statements are historical documents; beyond their necessary treatment, ignore the past.

- **Be patient.** A basic feature of the board system is that while the legal power of directors is potentially total in certain situations, in practice it is limited by a complex set of checks and balances. Even the best directors, chairs and executives, who understand the board system well, can find change a slow process. Directors have several sources of power, such as their oversight of the CEE Suite, the combined strength of the board and its members, access to the other directors as a means to sway opinion, and the emphasis on independence that ensures a hearing for individual views — if there is the patience to allow the process to mature.

One of the Wise offered a wonderful simile during our conversation. In response to the question about the role of the chair of the board she said, "The chair is an orchestra conductor". She went on to explain that a conductor must subjugate personal ego to allow the full expression of each talent in the orchestra, and that "when the music is beautiful, the board is performing well and you know the answer about assessment". I learned something from that remark and I hope you do, too. Herding cats, conducting orchestras, the parallels with the group dynamics of a board are irresistible.

Relating to the CEE Suite

Francis Fukuyama brings a superior mind to bear and writes persuasively on the interconnectedness of economic life with cultural life in *Trust: The Social Virtues and the Creation of Prosperity* (Simon & Schuster, 1995): Fukuyama argues most persuasively that almost every form of economic activity relies on what he defines as "the social collaboration of human beings", which is one definition of trust. In his view, in an era when social capital may be as important as physical capital, the level of trust in a society will far outweigh the tenets of the left or the right. It is a great read and I recommend it highly, but if you want the summary, here it is: play nicely with the other children.

When the board and the inhabitants of the CEE Suite successfully form a "community based on mutual trust" two great benefits roll into place. First, those two groups are together responsible for corporate success and that is much more likely in an atmosphere of trust and the co-operation that goes with it. Second, there is a likelihood that the atmosphere will spread to encompass others, or at least to those stakeholders who find confidence in trust they can observe in practice.

Not long ago, most boards saw their major intersects with management as "approval times", meaning they said grace over the strategic plan, budgets and capital expenditures and then spent time talking about the performance of the CEO. If a director was a quick study he or she could get by on a scan of the board package while the chair made a few remarks or, at most, some reading over breakfast. Today, a director must absorb a flood of information, place it in the context of the company, its industry and its chosen strategy, and then become part of the team while it addresses its responsibilities. All this while regulations proliferate and become more abstract and personal risks multiply. Continuous learning is the order of the day and to those who cavil at it, there is an old adage which says, "If you can't stand the heat, get out of the kitchen".

Supporting the CEO

Wisdom and governance alike dictate the separation of the chairman and CEO jobs, but that very separation creates a relationship between two powerful roles with differing goals. For the most part, those objectives should be quite similar, for if they are not, then the board has a different problem. However, even the common goals are likely to be approached from separate points of the compass, in turn originating from the degree of coherence on corporate strategy. An easy example is targeting a dramatic increase in revenue, but one party believes in organic sales and marketing while the other prefers growth through acquisition. Such differing views often lead to friction around metrics and their application, especially when the issue is the CEO's bonus. The board and the CEO would surely agree that boosting shareholder value carries a lot of weight, but one might like the longer term effects of a backlog of contracted revenue, while the other prefers the more immediate metric of share price.

It is no wonder that the board-CEO relationship predicts much about the creation of enduring value as well as effective governance. Like most relationships, it is all about chemistry, communication, collaboration and focus. When the right people are in the right place at the right time, the chairman and the CEO can spend their time getting the mix right. Those accustomed to an open, transparent working style based on mutual respect, trust and confidence in each other will embed this style in the company and the board. In these happy circumstances, the question of supporting the CEO is "asked and answered" for none of the participants could imagine it any other way.

In many small companies, the chair will be fortunate to encounter this ideal. The CEO may not have a lot of experience; this could be his or her first time in the position. A first-time CEO, leading a rapidly growing company, has a daily encounter with the biggest job ever experienced, ie, bigger than yesterday. Similarly, this CEO may never have worked with a board before, and if the company is public there is an additional layer of challenges. In such cases, support for the CEO might include coaching and mentoring, often an undertaking for the chair. In the belief that good ideas will surface — especially when they have been carefully embedded at some point — here are a few guidelines to proffer as counsel to the CEO of public or private companies, or for that matter to the executive director of a charity.

- Be visible to the board and the directors and get to know them as individuals. In this case absence does not make the heart grow fonder, but it can easily lead to questions and misunderstanding.

- Learn what the board wants, what it needs to do its job, and then provide it. If the board is less than certain, help them figure it out.

- Build the plan for the business and share it with the board. The CEO is expected to make things happen, so tell the story and how you will make it come true.

- Display your prudence by having a contingency plan and telling everyone what it is.

- The surest way to success is through results for the company and for you, so make them happen. Lead by example.

- Treat the board with respect. Never forget that you report to those chosen by the owners to oversee their investment – which was the basis and prime mover that created your job and provided you with this opportunity.

- Compromising on people is a very bad idea. You cannot possibly do everything and grow at the same time, so recruit a team of high performers. Never forget that good people really help, while bad people really hurt.

- Manage performance at the top, in the CEE Suite, and it will flow down from there. Set clear expectations and stick with them.

- Be consistent and you will inspire confidence and a sense of security. Beware of the off-the-cuff remark that can be taken out of context and become a roadblock to progress.

- Never hesitate to make the tough call and take strong action. The board expects you to make decisions, not seek them from the directors.

Herein lies a grave danger. The (presumably younger) CEO needs supportive counsel and the chair of the board may be the best source — but — that individual must also oversee the performance of the same person to whom the advice has been given. If the chair really does wear many hats it would be worth a glance in the mirror to check which one is atop the dome, especially after adding coaching to all the rest.

Of Phone Booths and Capes

An earlier section positioned the chair as *primus inter pares* — first among equals — and, thus, not quite like other directors; in fact, not even like the chairs of the standing committees. In addition to the responsibilities attendant with managing the board, the chair is certainly first in line for telephone calls from directors with an agenda, first to be called when members of the CEE Suite are playing games, first to get emails — but you get the idea and I want to avoid sounding defensive or prone to self pity. I do want to make two points and I will start with the line first delivered by the immortal Pogo, the prognosticator from Okefenokee, who famously said, "We have met the enemy, and he is us." (The Pogo strip from Earth Day, 1971 — with thanks to Walt Kelly.) I cannot think of anything more important for the chair of a board, and especially a newly-minted version, than to take a long, hard stare in that mirror. That suggests that we know and understand the "what we have" part, and possess the wit to see how our talents may be deployed in the role of professional director and chair. Let us look at one way to do this.

1. **Describe yourself, part one.** Start the process by putting together an inventory of your competencies, restricting them in this first pass to specific skills, knowledge and qualifications. Remember that the "job description" to be filled is director and chair (the examples in the appendices may be useful). Since parallel processing can be quite efficient, you might consider writing a "board resume" during the mirror-staring process. Consider using the competency matrix found in Chapter Six, *Advanced Carpentry*. This step is intended to identify your specific competencies so that they can be compared with the minimums for the job, which is the next step.

2. **Compare the results with the job at hand.** The board you have just joined, or are about to join, should have thought about what was needed before the nominating committee recruited you; in fact that thinking should have been at least one reason for contacting you in the first place. There may be a matrix of essential competencies versus corporate strategy and plans, in which case comparing your self assessment with the company's needs will be easier and you already have the nominating committee's opinion. What is needed is your personal — and scrupulously honest — assessment of whether the committee is correct. Consider aspects like these:

    i. The board is seeking some minimum number of years of experience in a given sector, and you have those years, but you also realize that they were early in your career and the industry has changed. Do you still have the expected depth in this sector and, if not, are you willing to go out and get it?

    ii. The board is asking for a professional qualification and again you possess it, but you have not been active in that arena for many years and are quite out of date. Those of us who wear the engineer's ring are painfully aware of how quickly such knowledge outdates.

    iii. The board has asked if you have the time and are prepared to commit it to the company. You sit on a couple of not-for-profit boards and two private companies already and you are eager for a spot on a public board. You also have a rich and rewarding family life. Do you actually have time that you can allocate to this new role?

3.   **Describe yourself, part two.** To the specific competencies of part one add the less tangible, but equally important, personal qualities and characteristics that will shape the way you carry out the role of director and chair, especially the latter. For example, you might be a skillful executive with many successful years behind you, but what is your personal style? If you have succeeded by using a "command and control" style, will you be able to guide a diverse group to consensus? Are you impatient when people ask a lot of questions – and how will that sit opposite a careful former auditor who happens to chair an important standing committee? This is a tough one, but current or former colleagues will be able and perhaps willing to describe how they think you will perform as a chair, based on their first-hand knowledge of your working style. When working your way through this exercise, remember that your spouse or a sibling know you better than most and could be an important coach for the role.

4.   **Check for blind spots.** Perhaps this should be called, "the really big lies I tell myself". For most of us, these are a product of the years, the habits, quirks and foibles that are now second nature. For the most part, they take the form of assumptions, things we take for granted about ourselves, but perhaps should not.

   i.   "I am good at judging people; I know which ones are honest, smart, and hard-working". Right, and do you remember Andy Fastow? A universal fallacy seems to be the rather quaint belief that, because we are humans, we therefore understand and can assess others in the species. A currently fashionable response would be, "Not so much". We are notoriously bad at judging others, tending to remember the best decisions while forgetting all others. As directors, one of our most important tasks is choosing and evaluating the CEO, but how effective are we at that task?

   ii.   "If we work hard enough we can solve this", or its close counterpart, "I am sure there is a solution, in spite of the odds". Horatio Alger Jr., a popular eighteenth century American writer, wrote dozens of "dime novels" extolling the virtues of hard work, pluck and determination, and how success would follow if all were applied. Horatio was right in the context of his simple stories of struggle and success, but a CEO who works ninety hours a week may not be especially successful, though he or she is working like a slave. Such was the popularity of the Alger books that their message became woven into the fabric of North American business and when we encounter hard work we tend to see it as an end in itself and forget to ask what it produced and how it added value.

iii.   "This a great deal — we'll all get rich." Especially enthusiastic investment bankers are sometimes described by the phrase, "He never met a deal he didn't like", which may be a useful outlook — but not for a corporate director. A discriminating taste around opportunity is an invaluable trait, but if the new director has never been involved in the excitement surrounding a merger or an acquisition this competency is certain to be undeveloped.

Once we have examined our navel, we should know what we have to work with, or at least we will if we have been honest throughout. Given that the availability of a magical cape and a phone booth for a changing room are rather limited we must do the best we can with what we have.

5.   **Define your personal development plan.** Item one in your plan, if you have not yet done so, is to consider joining the Institute for Corporate Directors (ICD) and taking the Director's Education Program. A workable alternative, if you have the personal discipline, is a concentrated reading program supplemented by attendance at a selection of the very good seminars offered by the accounting and legal firms as a service to their clients and the community (see Appendix Seven). Some will assume that a few years of experience is all that is needed to be a competent director. Perhaps, but consider the many people with truly significant years in business who know that further education is worth the time and effort. Follow their example. Consider as well that acquiring further knowledge and learning are simply the first steps in DOC. (Do I really need to make the argument about life-long learning? If so, put this book aside and think about whether directorships are for you.)

In addition to corporate governance *per se*, how much do you know — really know and understand — about each of the corporate functions? Most of us climbed the ladder through one of them, or perhaps we branched out and learned about two of them, but a director is expected to know something of all of them. Certainly, management reports to the board will assume that you do, and the boardroom table is not the forum for beginners. As an executive, you are able to call on a functional leader to brief you on some aspect of how that group fits into the overall organization. As a director, that is much less likely, as a director of a small company it is quite unlikely.

Read the assumptions about what a director should have as baseline knowledge (see Chapter Two). Look into the nearest mirror and ask, "Do you have it and is it current?" If there is the shadow of a doubt as you gauge your baseline competencies, do something about it, because you and the company on whose board you sit will be exposed to a serious risk otherwise.

Finally, review your reading habits. Become an omnivorous reader or find an alchemist with a learning pill designed to contribute everything needed with an occasional glass of water and a swallow.

To Thine Own Self

Those who sit as a chair should expect more of themselves, capes and phone booths aside. The board assessment process will provide feedback on how the team functioned for the past year, but unless your reviews are better than most, an additional step is recommended. You are responsible for managing the board, so it is useful to have a few measures that tell you how that is going, and they may not be part of the evaluation that your board has chosen. Introspection will prove to be invaluable, assuming frankness and clarity in the self portrait. Painting that picture is up to you. My personal attempt to reduce self-delusion is to apply yardsticks that accumulate information through the year and become the topics of a conversation that I have with myself. This process relies on my willingness to assume responsibility for four goals that can each be measured objectively, thus reducing any tendency to find excuses. You will know what works for you, but here is what I do.

1. **Director attendance at meetings is a good indicator.** I accept it as a personal responsibility, generally speaking, and anything less than 95%, barring bad weather and personal problems, indicates that there is a problem. Since I like to stay in close touch with the board, if someone misses a meeting without a practical reason I take that as an omen and move directly into "find and fix" mode. Sensitivity is the order of the day — recall that directors expect to be led, but they do NOT expect to be managed. Your ability to discover the source of the problem through a casual intervention such as a coffee or a quick telephone chat depends on an established rapport and a familiar pattern of discourse.

2. **The minutes of the board are revealing.** I scan the record to see if each director spoke at least once, on a non-procedural item, at the most recent meeting. If someone's name is absent, I refer to my personal notes and speak to the corporate secretary to see if we missed anything. At the next meeting, I observe carefully to see if the director in question is more engaged this time out. Body language, facial expression, tone of voice and question content are prime indicators. It is usually apparent if the director was prepared for the meeting. If the director was unusually quiet, seemed distracted or asked questions that seemed to be out of context, it is time to go for a coffee or lunch. I bring the conversation around to those things keeping us busy, and listen carefully for signs that the director is becoming overloaded and if this is temporary, ie, a bulge in the schedule, or likely to persist. Again, sensitivity is the watchword and success depends on a working relationship established in advance.

3. **An unknown vote on a divisive issue is a bad omen.** If we need to tally the votes for anything other than housekeeping purposes, I assume that I have failed to manage the issue in question. We hold the vote, of course, but the chair should now be able to guess the results in advance. This may not be the case but it is a prudent assumption and likely to lead to more careful preparation in the future. This is not to say that the board will always be unanimous; if it were, we may have fallen into another trap. My point is that the views of the directors should be relatively transparent to an observant chair and the probable outcome is an important guide to continuing the dialogue or moving to a decision. My notes track the predictions and hint at what I should do to improve the consensus process.

4. **Unplanned director turnover is my responsibility,** and the goal is zero. It seems obvious that, if I have kept in touch with the directors, any unforeseen defections indicate an issue of a personal nature. Directors rarely leave a board before the end of their term or their retirement, and when one does, it needs scrutiny.

These are simple metrics that are easy to apply, they are objective, and they are good indicators of how I am doing my job as the chair of the board. In my view, the board assessment process is necessary but not sufficient, and as a once- or even twice-a-year exercise it is not sufficiently proactive in addressing issues and resolving them before they solidify into a massive problem.

Bareheaded?

Rather than try to wear all those hats, perhaps the chair should be bareheaded. Certainly, he or she must be clearheaded. I remember listening to Paul Cantor speaking after a dinner and, while I cannot recall the exact words and when he said them, they were something like this:

> "At first I thought of myself as the CEO of the board, but that passed and I considered myself first among equals. That was better, but I finally concluded that I am the last among equals".

My apologies for not writing that down the moment I heard it, but thinking about his conclusion I have decided that "last among equals" is the right hat to wear, a fungible one allowing the chair to assume many roles and many responsibilities. That is the secret of getting the job done.

Chapter Six:

Advanced Carpentry — Building a Better Board

One long-term director told me that the well-crafted board is one where, no matter the issue or threat, at least one director has the tee shirt. While that may not be impossible for the board of a small organization, it would be a tall order for most. Few boards would claim to be perfect, and given that new companies and their boards are created everyday there simply are not enough tee shirts to go around. But whether you sit on an existing board or you are building from scratch, fashioning a great board of directors is a tough task. On the other hand, you do have the opportunity of "doing the right things the right way" to quote a slogan from the world of total quality. Perhaps this chapter will help.

Start with a Plan

Consistent with the principals of an ethical compass, building a better board needs the guidance of a thoughtful blueprint, a statement of "what we need on this board". The more you know or can learn about that "what" the better your chances of success. Well, to start from that most logical of places, the beginning, the board ought to be created with the purposes of the company in mind and these can be seen rather clearly in a well-written business plan. The suggestion here is that since the board is to be responsible for strategic oversight, for selecting and monitoring the CEO and so on, perhaps its chances would be improved if the directors were chosen so as to bring the appropriate competencies to bear on those responsibilities.

For example, consider what you would do if you were part of a special committee struck to manage the merger of two quite similar companies. Assume this to be a merger of equals with roughly equivalent revenues and similar capitalizations. One company has a 17-year history; the other was incorporated only three years ago. The management teams working on the project have agreed on the structure of the merged entity and how it should be populated. Key aspects of the business case are the expectation of synergistic cross selling, since the customer bases do not overlap, and a major improvement at the bottom line since there are significant economies of scale. This combination will be accretive for the shareholders of both companies, since revenues will rise while costs are reduced proportionately. The current boards each have seven directors and part of your committee's remit is to create a new board of directors. What approach to fashioning a new board should you and your committee take?

As an experiment prior to writing this book I posed this fanciful situation for a dozen or so small groups of three or four people and asked for their solutions. Each group is currently busy running a small enterprise and would match one of the management styles to be found on the left side of the diagram below. There were only a few individuals with any sort of board experience among the approximately 60 entrepreneurs involved in this small and distinctively unscientific study. I expected to see significant differences depending on their supposed styles, while allowing for my likely errors in classifying the groups and those in them. To my surprise there was very little difference in their thoughts as to the best way of creating the board of the merged entity. Before we look at that more closely, here is a simple diagram of the situation faced by the "special committee". It reflects the committee's concerns about the perceived differences in the management styles in the original companies on the one hand, and on the other, the adaptations likely to be needed from the day the deal closes to the point when the company reaches stability.

		Formative	Transitive	Stable
LEADERSHIP	CEE Level	Act like an issuer from day one; recruit for independence and future needs.	Adopt best practices; fill gaps; build depth, special competencies.	Grow company with benchmark class governance standards.
	Business Builders	Board supports BB as company grows; attract a chair for the future.	Momentum and direction dictate board needs — strategy and sector crucial.	Will company growth demand CEE Level competencies?
	The A Team	Founders/ shareholders as directors and management; cover legal essentials and help management.	Where are we going? Will the A Team grow and stay — will the company grow and succeed or wither?	Probably not applicable

CORPORATE CULTURE AND OPERATING STYLE

The chart portrays the interplay between the culture or operating style of the company and a simple characterization of its leadership team. The special committee can treat the horizontal axis as a rough estimate of the time needed, while the merged company forms and then develops into an integrated and stable operation. Similarly, the leadership style axis will depend on the makeup of the management team chosen from those in place before the merger, plus new hires as appropriate. The expected interplay should say a lot about the board and the people on it. Management teams and the companies they lead share a dynamic that shifts and adapts. The CEE Suite may be moving from entrepreneurs to operators even as they grapple with the phase or state (in the chemistry sense) of the company. Boards oversee both, and the stage and speed of the evolution of each will influence the qualities demanded of that oversight and, thus, the specific competencies needed in the board's makeup.

The horizontal axis presents three stages, generalizations one and all, but useful as an aide to thinking. Companies in the formative state are newly minted or they have been formed through one or more mergers, as in the case posed in my mini survey. They may have unusual circumstances such as Crown Life Insurance when it moved to Regina and shifted substantially all of the company to a new location in a new economy within a new culture. A risk factor at the moment of a merger or a other major change is that systems, processes and other support may be weak or untested. Companies in transition have likely passed through the formative stage but if they now face a transformational event such as a merger, a financial re-structuring, a major acquisition or perhaps an initial public offering, they will be sorely tested. The board is faced with substantive change, including the creation or acceptance of a new governance regime. Finally, those with a CEE Level team are likely larger and more secure, even when they have just been formed from a relatively massive merger. In any event, the directors can count on the experience and talents of a larger team and its added knowledge and acceptance of good governance practices.

Companies led by an A Team. In this situation, the "A Team" probably started one of the companies three years ago, or perhaps they are the dominant group that took control of an existing company. These people are likely to be a small group of specialists or technologists with a charismatic leader, who may have done this before but who has not necessarily had a lot of experience operating at this level. They are all risk takers, and while they will stay inside the strict legal limits, some of them are ready to rationalize the means to an end. In a start-up, those who incorporate the company become its directors, and A Team members may see governance as a necessary evil and minimize it. While the company is private and small this is a matter of choice, but with growth, and certainly when it goes public, matters must change.

You may be asked to join such a board, perhaps become its chair or to lead one of its committees. Your presence may add legitimacy or contacts or both. It is highly likely that those asking you to come aboard have done little or no thinking about the qualities the company needs in a director (sorry about that) and your nomination was almost certainly through a personal connection. Fair enough, and since you are reading a book on governance we know your heart is pure, so accept the offer, but make it a condition of acceptance that the next director and the one after that will be chosen primarily because they bring needed competencies to the mix at the interface between the A Team and a board with growing strength in corporate governance.

The "Business Builders" are often a group of competent entrepreneurs that includes one or two functional experts, perhaps marketing, finance or technology. Typically, they have solid middle management experience or time in a senior role with a mid-sized company. The group may include a senior executive, but as a whole, the Business Builders are not quite ready for the corner office. Some of the Business Builders will be comfortable with governance, likely the finance or accounting people, and one or two may have been part of a reporting issuer in the past. They might do well leading a small private company, but they will be challenged as growth accelerates, a merger looms, or a liquidity strategy forms.

If you are being asked to join the board of a company led by a Business Builder team, there is a reasonable probability that someone thought about it and you have been asked for the best reasons. The rationale for director selection may have been well crafted and has been or could be applied when choosing the other directors. If that is the case, accept, for you have just found an excellent reason to become part of a thoughtful team.

Here is a quick thought about the boards of newly-formed companies. Please be aware that when such organizations are still in the formative stage, the board often includes more than one member of the senior team. This is normal and to be expected. Those same senior employees may also be founders and they will undoubtedly have strong views about "their company" even when they are no longer own the majority of its shares. Given that the best boards seek consensus on most issues, these opinions may be difficult to meld into a board decision. It is a point worth talking about at the time that you are being wooed as a director — if your voice is to be heard.

The CEE Level team are professionals with successful track records and a lot of depth in at least one function and possibly two, plus solid credentials in the company's industrial sector. They have likely been part of a public company before and are more at ease with corporate governance and working with a board of directors. With a CEE Level team running the show the passage from formation to stability is likely to be guided by their clear articulation of how to follow the path. The board may be able to spend less time on counselling and more on strategic oversight. This might imply a slate of directors who want to "do it right from the start".

Let us return to the question: what should the special committee do to create the new board? One way to focus the committee's thinking is to create a diagram such as the one a couple of pages back. The obvious implications are likely to spark a debate, which I hope will be intensive, about the board competencies needed as the newly merged organization moves through the three phases or the next few years or however you style the future. The goal for you and your committee is to design a "competency matrix", a map of those competencies essential to the board over the ensuing years (see the following section). Whether you are filling a vacancy or creating an entirely new board, the first step is the same. If the business case for the merger was done well, it included at least the outline of a business plan for the new company, so the special committee knows the answer to, "Where are we going?"

Part of the challenge in real life is the politics and/or deal making in the situation, which may contrive to constrain the best solution. A company with 17 years of history will likely have some executives with tenures of the same length, and perhaps some are directors. The other company will be a different situation, but its people will have equally strong views. It is tempting to avoid the issue of choice by simply merging the two boards as well as their companies. That would be a very bad decision, for while it will place the two boards in one room, it will not create a single, focused group of directors doing their duty to the company. Two armed camps intent on sabotaging each other is a more likely scenario.

In another part of this book, one of the Wise says, "You cannot teach courage". True, and this is a case where it is needed. The special committee should develop the competency matrix regardless of the deal contingencies, because then it will know what is being relinquished when a choice is forced because of the deal. It will know the concomitant risks when it accepts the optimum rather than the perfect, the lesser of two weak directors rather than opting to go outside and recruit. The results can be bizarre. For example, imagine a rather large board, nine or so directors, but four or five were forced choices from the previous boards, and they also happen to be insiders. Suddenly, the seats available for independent directors, the folks who fill the ranks of the mandatory standing committees, are reduced such that any one committee is remarkably similar or even identical to the others. Group thinkers unite!

A well-considered competency matrix will reveal the pattern of competencies that will evolve along the axis of culture and operating style. That terrific director for the formative phase may not have the appropriate skills or personality when operations are stable. On the other hand, if this merger is the first of several, perhaps such a package of competencies is valuable because there will always be a part of the company that is in the formative stage.

The special committee might prize independence of thought, but find that it is tough to find unless it accepts candidates with less industry knowledge than it would wish. A new director, a recruit, might supply some of the industry knowledge, but would obviously have no company knowledge, which might be crucial during the formative and transitive phases. It is not simple — but you must decide — and the decision must be reasonable in the circumstances.

One final thing: do everyone a favour and have a good argument about the map, its components and how it is to be used. It is to the advantage of one and all to get coherence at this stage, for it predicts later success. The time spent will contribute to writing or modifying the board charter, it will provide key thoughts around the director profile, and the process of debating it is a salutary experience for management and directors alike. If the discussion is truly thorough it will become an abbreviated orientation for the new leaders of the merged entity.

Before we leave this section, let us return to my informal survey. The dozen or so groups that were asked to opine on how they would resolve the issue of board formation were remarkably unimaginative and more traditional than I expected. Only a few individuals suggested that competencies tied to the business plan was the logical starting point and those worthies were, I understand, shouted down by their compatriots in whatever group they were in on the basis that the deal was the prime mover, not the business plan. One group suggested a 14-person board composed of, you guessed it, the entirety of the two original boards. What was learned? The appreciation for, and understanding of, the role of corporate governance is thin on the ground, so when you find yourself in a situation with any resemblance to the case used in the mini survey, keep your expectations in check and you will be less likely to be disappointed.

Finding Them; Recruiting Them

The person responsible for finding board candidates is often the chair, especially in small companies. Some recalcitrant organizations still leave this to the CEO, but this habit seems to be fading, to the benefit of all. More established boards spread the workload through a standing committee, a tactic that will broaden the pool of known candidates, too. Since this is a situational issue, this book will be content with offering a few pointers rather than a prescription.

The Competency Matrix

In the manner of all job descriptions, the board charter states what the directors must do to fulfill their responsibilities. Unlike the "right person for the job", the focus when hiring an employee, here there is the freedom to split the overall job into several parts and distribute those accountabilities among the several directors composing the board. It is instructive to think of the board as organic, a "body politic" which has directors as its members. That ought to make the task easier, but it does not, for reasons that will appear. A common and useful tool is a map of the job of the board, often in the form of a matrix composed of the current or future directors and their fit with a set of competencies chosen for their expected accomplishment of the twin purposes of duty to the company and board effectiveness. A director matrix is an applied process and the following table explains how it comes together.

Directors' Names	Key Competencies and Weightings							
	A	B	C	D	E	F	G	Σ
Ideal	15	10	15	20	20	10	10	100
Tom	12	8	11	13	18	9	7	78
Dick								
Harry								

First, choose the core and situational competencies needed to fulfill the mandate and responsibilities stated in the board charter and in the company's business plan. Typical choices might be "industry experience" or "team player" or "corporate governance" (discussed previously). Stay with seven or fewer, since the research on human ability to grade people on more than about that number says that the law of diminishing returns sets in and the value of additional factors drops off or even becomes negative. As in Chapter Two, there is an underlying assumption of the prerequisite capabilities and knowledge that are in place, or a new candidate would not be considered in the first place, so those need not appear at the head of a column. Engage all stakeholders in a serious discussion when choosing these competencies, for this is not trivial and the choices are not always obvious.

Next, establish the scores for an ideal director, which are really the weightings assigned to those competencies beyond the prerequisites but agreed as essential to board success. Discussing the assignment of these weights will be another valuable step and a guide to the culture of the board. Be aware that the emphasis may well evolve much as the director's allocation of time between operational and board issues shifts with the maturity of the company. Avoid invidious comparisons, ie, talking about a specific person. If your board can successfully establish the profile of the ideal director then it will be able to see clearly what it must give up as it selects a specific individual, the price to be paid for that person, unless of course there is an abundance of perfect people in your Rolodex.

It is important to predetermine how to grade each person against the ideal. A common approach is an applied behavioural scale, with seven- and nine-point scales the most prevalent. The behaviour which describes each point on the scale is agreed in advance, thus determining the metrics to be used later when comparing anyone with the ideal. For example, assuming a nine-point scale to assess experience, the low end could be nil experience, the middle at five to seven years and the top end at 15 years or more.

Directors' Names	Key Competencies and Weightings							
	A	B	C	D	E	F	G	Σ
The Ideal Director	15	10	15	20	20	10	10	100
Chair	13	4	10	15	18	8	9	80
Mary-Ann (Chair, MRC)	14	5	12	16	12	8	7	74
Tom (ADC, GNC)	12	6	11	13	18	9	7	76
Katherine (ADC; MRC)	11	4	9	18	17	8	8	75
Sarah (GNC; MRC)	14	8	12	12	15	9	6	76
Richard (Chair, ADC)	11	6	9	20	15	9	9	79
Harry (Chair, GNC)	12	5	9	16	16	8	7	78
Averages	12.4	5.0	10.3	15.7	15.9	8.4	7.6	76.9

The board is now ready to tackle the most difficult part: placing real people into the matrix. As a demonstration, here is the matrix for a board of seven, and Richard has announced that he is about to become the CFO of a major supplier to the company. The directors have assessed their peers and themselves on each competency and the table shows the average of all seven scores, which we will assume are reasonably accurate. The Ideal Director has, of course, a perfect score on each competency, where the target scores reflect their relative weight or importance.

As it happens, there are actually two issues that need board attention: the departure of Richard, who is the chair of ADC, is an immediate problem, but there is the longer-term weakness of everyone except Sarah on competency "B". The total scores for the directors remaining on the board average 76.5, and the individual scores cluster about that mean. This is not a re-building exercise, as it might be following a dramatic shift in strategy, so the sole discrepancy is competency "B". Everyone on the board is financially competent, but Richard led the audit team and is a chartered accountant, so that will be a factor in replacing him. Beyond finding a replacement for Richard, the board needs to improve its average on competency "B". The search, therefore, will focus on chartered accountants with a balanced rating across the matrix, added strength on competency "B", availability, time and interest. Then the board will be left to decide on chemistry. It is important to emphasize the matrix at this juncture, for there will be a tendency to be overly impressed with those easily available rather than stress what is needed.

Some readers will no doubt be muttering, "All very well for you, but when we were in Waterloo we had to…" That is a fair comment, and without delving into specifics, it is impossible to say much more. What can be stated is that boards with the discipline and maturity to focus on the competency matrix as a specific manifestation of the best strategy for the company will have success. Real situations are always much messier, much more complex than the tidiness of the example, but with focus and effort they can be reduced to their elements and fitted into a matrix. There are some provisos. The future value of the matrix rests on the frankness and thoroughness of the argument about the competencies; otherwise, second guessing will appear when discussing the candidacy of an individual. For the same reason, agreement on the weights assigned to the Ideal Director should be close to unanimous. Obviously, this takes work, but the effort will be repaid with a selection method that is aligned with the business and its strategy, and it will be as close to objective as you are likely to get.

Emulate the Recruiters

When professional recruiters accept a mandate from their client, they create the largest feasible pool of candidates who are a reasonable match with an idealized profile. They follow the impeccable logic that their chances of satisfying their client increase with the numbers of people in that pool. Boards should emulate their example. Consider whether you and your colleagues have access to a suitably large pool of candidates and if they present a diverse set of backgrounds and experiences to bring to the table. Professional recruiters are expensive and may be out of the question for a small company, but you should consider the costs of making a mistake, since once a director is in place, he or she cannot be fired and so might be an issue until at least the next AGM.

Since you are probably familiar with the executive recruiters' approach why not imitate their methods? This is not rocket science, it is a pattern of steps that, when carried out competently, produces a pool of candidates from which a short list can be drawn and then a finalist selected. The advantage held by the search firms lies in their familiarity with the process, the fact that candidates make themselves known to them and they are a third party. You and your committee can do everything that the search firm does – but do not omit any steps, an all too common error in employee recruiting. In other words, do not do what most people do when hiring, instead, stick to a process along these lines:

- **Describe what is needed** — by developing a competency matrix based on the company's plans and intentions for the next few years. Be especially thoughtful about aspects of the board that may evolve quickly as the business grows or shifts strategy, and consider tactics such as limited-term appointments to improve the ability of the board to match the changes in the company.

- **Create a pool of candidates** — augment your Rolodex with those of a few directors from other boards, those who will be glad to help broaden your pool, because you may help with theirs. At the 10th Annual ICD Awards Banquet, May 31, 2007, the Honourable Paule Gauthier said in her acceptance speech, "Diversity of background and experience are essential — good business sense transcends all definitional independence of thought..." Importantly, consider any source which might supply a candidate who has all of the competencies inherent to the individual, though lacking one which could be acquired quickly. For example, there are directors from the not-for-profit world who may have excellent credentials in all aspects except industry knowledge — and someone with a short learning curve could move past that very quickly.

- **Select a short list** — of those who have the best fit with the matrix. If your net was cast widely you should have three or four candidates with relatively close matches with the board's needs.

- **Qualify the short list candidates very carefully** by screening for personal chemistry and characteristics beyond the essentials. This is an opportune stage to have the candidates meet the CEE Team to check that interface. I suggest that you ask each candidate to complete a personal information form (PIF) at this stage. It asks questions that you cannot, but is standard practice for public directors. There is an electronic version on the TSX website.

- **Do the due diligence** — and complete background checks to ensure that there will not be any surprises. Check the online versions of the newspapers in each city where the candidate has worked (I use Google, but any search engine will do) and the websites of the companies for press releases or announcements.

- **Make the offer** — in the comfort that the finalist will have the basics, fits the board's personality and will accept because there is a match.

The first time that I was asked to sit on a board the "selection process" was akin to the current television commercial wherein a job applicant succeeds because his freshly-laundered shirt smells like the sponsor's soap powder. Yes, it is quite silly, but so was my selection to the board of a large charity many years ago. I was immature enough to be flattered when asked, while the chair doing the recruiting talked about the charity but never the expectations of the role, not even the time demands. We met and agreed over lunch, end of story. Lessons were learned.

When an organization wants to hire a new employee it is, in effect, attempting to predict the future. In other words, it wishes to select and then hire the person most likely to do the job well and keep at it for an extended period of time. It is a very tall order and many companies do it very badly, with costly results. Most organizations are no better when they select directors for their boards.

Some companies use a process calculated to ensure success at hiring and retaining the best talent available, and the board process can learn from it. These companies are unusually thorough, with a focus on ensuring consistency, fairness and as much accuracy as possible, given the difficulties inherent to a human process based largely on personal observation and judgment. The three elements essential to success are knowledge of the requirements, accountability for the process and understanding that human judgment is fallible.

1. **One more time: know what is needed.** Express the need as a job description, and then specify the kind of candidate that the company wants to fill that need. The company does this by writing a competency profile to match the demands of the job, and it is rigorous in its insistence that this step be completed before any individual is actually considered for the job. Applying the lessons to the board process, the job description should be an appendix to the board charter while the competency matrix leads to the candidate profile.

2. **The chair is accountable.** In a company, the person to whom the new hire will report should be accountable for the recruiting process. Human resources will help and an external recruiter or agency may be involved, but accountability is vital and the best choice is the person with oversight of the function where the need is being felt. At the level of the board the "person with the need" is the company and its board, as personified by the chair of the board, the person responsible for the "function" called corporate governance. The nominating committee may take a leading role, but the final responsibility lies at the head of the table.

3. **Go well beyond interviews.** Use as many tools as possible to choose the successful candidate. Research has proven repeatedly that while single interviews are notoriously unreliable, the same research shows that multiple interviews combined with at least two other selection tools improve the chances a lot. As more selection devices are added, within reason, the success rate continues to improve.

You might expand upon the thought of enlisting the aid of a few directors on the boards of other small companies and trade favours, somewhat on the lines of a co-operative. When four or five directors (each from a different board) form such a circle, any individual director can ask the others to act as a third party, a momentary but independent committee working to not only throw names into the pool, but also to comment on the competency matrix or even interview finalists.

Choosing directors solely because they are your friends might not be the best idea, but you should not avoid them either, and here are two good reasons. First, finding a person who will tell you the unpleasant facts of life regardless of circumstances is surely valuable. If a friend has such a trait, known from personal experience, plus a fit with the needed competency profile, you may have a bonus. Second, the best boards operate with much mutual respect and trust, and with a friend this is in place even before he or she agrees to serve. The prerequisite is the slate of competencies to do the job, but with those in place, the rationale to avoid friends as directors is thin, while there are a couple of points in their favour. There is a final caution about turning to friends while recruiting: do it once per friend. Interlocking directorships are an independence issue at the best of times and asking close friends to sit on several boards will come back to haunt. One of the Wise noted that the proximity of cottages at Lake Muskoka is often highly correlated with the degree of inbreeding between the boards of companies with head offices in Toronto. I have yet to test that thesis, but it might be an interesting insight.

One issue garnering much attention is variously presented under "diversity" or "minority representation" or similar headings. Given the history of boards in North America, this generally means the consideration of women or visible minorities for a director's role. Some large enterprises trumpet their instant diversity the moment they recruit the first representative of either to their board, but let us put that aside in favour of recognising that there is an opportunity available, which emerges as we walk through the recruiting process. Nominating committees have a responsibility to secure the essential ingredients to satisfy their competency mix. They assemble a talent pool with recommendations from other directors, recruiters, executives or any source that seems promising. The committee members naturally wish to ensure that the pool is well stocked and that the sought after competencies are present in large measure in every candidate. The twin demands of efficiency and effectiveness should encourage the realization that it is thus in their interest to populate the candidate pool from as many sources as possible.

So far, so good, and with that logic in mind, this author proposes two important considerations. One, before stocking the pool, study the director competency matrix and ask, "Would ethnic origin or gender hinder a director's ability to add any given competency to the pool?" I am certain that when you pose and answer that question you will discover that the potential pool of candidates has just become satisfyingly larger and your task easier. Here is a case from a different venue. In the early seventies, the business school at York University struggled to attract its share of top-ranked MBA applicants. This was before the Schulich School and its international reputation could be proclaimed. We were the Faculty of Administrative Studies on the plains of Downsview and nobody had ever heard of us. As the Assistant Dean I was responsible for admissions, which included attracting the best and brightest, and Jim Gillies, the school's founding Dean, agreed that my staff and I would deliberately seek female applicants. We did not do this to redress the gender imbalance in business studies, which was quite significant at the time. We did it because it was apparent that there were many women who were straight "A" grads and who might be recruited from under the noses of our worthy competitors. Our pool of applicants suddenly grew and, more importantly, the grade point average soared.

Given that the answer to question one cannot be negative in any rational world, you can move easily to the next question, "Are there important factors beyond the essential competencies that might aid our choice, all other considerations aside?" In other words, with the pool now assembled, if the competencies to match the company's needs are common to two or more candidates, are there other ways to choose? In such a case, the board might deliberately choose a woman from an otherwise equally matched male-female candidacy, for example, because it is able to address a broad community or societal consideration at absolutely no cost. And remember, it had that choice because it created a bigger pool of candidates, in its own interests, in the first place. While I am adamantly opposed to choices that emphasize race, gender or similar discriminators over job requirements, as one maven is wont to say, "This is a good thing".

You might be interested in a 2004 article by Carol Stephenson, Dean of the Ivey School of Business, "Leveraging Diversity to Maximum Advantage: The Business Case for Appointing More Women to Boards", in that school's journal. Dean Stephenson's article reviewed research on the value of women on boards and concluded that there is a favourable business case. Research shows that the boards with the highest numbers of women on their boards have a 35% better return on investment. A rational person might suggest that choosing a higher proportion of female directors could be correlated with being able to direct the company so as to outperform its peers. Finally, the words of one of the Wise:

"Building a board is like weaving a tapestry. It gains vitality and depth when threads of many textures and colours create the pattern."

One fertile ground for sourcing candidates is the graduating ranks of professional certification programs, people who have demonstrated their commitment to learning about corporate governance through the investment of their time, effort and dollars, and where the recruiter can take comfort that the prospect has at least knowledge, if not directly applicable experience. Another source is the considerable number who sit on volunteer boards of one sort or another. Many have jobs in the corporate world and when functional expertise is combined with their board experience in a charity, you may discover a gem.

Try to avoid the "expectancy problem". Custom and practice created this problem, meaning that once a board candidate is approached, he or she is likely to operate under the assumption that selection is complete and they have the choice of agreeing to be recruited or not. For very large boards, those with a market cap of a billion dollars or so, the selection process is likely to be more involved, but can you imagine the former president and

CEO of a chartered bank agreeing to be compared against other candidates? Even for smaller companies there is a clear presumption that when someone has been approached they have been selected.

It need not be so. The crucial point is the first direct contact with the prospective director. When approaching a prospective full-time employee, there is an unspoken understanding that there is a competition and that recruiting may have many steps. Since this does not seem to be the case in most director recruiting processes, care is needed to send the right message. Assuming that a reasonably large pool of prospects has been assembled, careful pre-screening will ensure that each candidate has the qualifications so that worry is avoided. You can have confidence in the quality of everybody on the short list, but you would not want to be constrained by inappropriate expectations on the part of each person approached.

The multiple opinions of the nominating committee members provide different slants on the candidate's background, personality and working style. When this is extended by discreet inquiries, a sort of reference checking in advance, you begin to understand how to deal with each candidate individually. Finally, the first meeting to discuss the board and its needs must be orchestrated as a two-way exchange of information, with no commitments on either side, and it ought to be with two or more directors in attendance. Make it clear that there are several steps, including meetings with the CEO and the CFO, a third-party interview and possibly a one-on-one with the chair of the board. Assign a couple of key questions to each interviewer, with each responsible for checking two or three competencies. Confirm the previously agreed metrics, ie, the minimums for this particular director and the needs at this particular time.

It is appropriate during this first meeting to announce that the company expects to complete its due diligence by requiring the candidate to complete and sign the PIF required by one of the stock exchanges or securities administrators, even if the company is privately held. This is an excellent screening device with the virtue of eliciting some tricky personal history without interrogation. It can be embarrassing for all concerned if the candidate's history includes situations, even though now well in the past, that may have a bearing on his or her suitability to be a director.

Finally, call it as you see it. Do not hesitate to decide that the potential director does not fit, even if the process is at an advanced stage. In the extreme, employees can be fired, but a director is elected by the shareholders, not hired, and cannot be removed until the next shareholders' meeting.

Orientation

Orientation for new directors is really part of DOC, a natural extension of the due diligence that the nominee conducted on the way in. Returning to selection for a moment, if he or she does not carry out more than a cursory due diligence, the nominating committee should reconsider its choice.

Orientation gets the new director off on the right foot, and it demonstrates a culture and expectation of DOC in action. It is such basic common sense that a further rationale is not needed. Instead, time spent on how to do it is more useful.

There are many ways to spend time or money when neither is an issue, but thrift is a virtue and, in small companies, not a matter of choice in any event. Fortunately, an effective orientation can be supported with only a few inexpensive tools and processes chosen to deliver the "director information package" (DIP). The DIP has three essential features:

- **The DIP must be comprehensive** with respect to the company and everything about it. The DIP is not a marketing brochure; it is an operating manual, describing how the board runs day-by-day. As such, its table of contents should be extensive, and it should be a hefty tome as a single volume. It probably is not, and should not be, a "volume" as that term is usually understood. It could just as easily be a portal on a website. It must, however, cover all the bases and, in that regard, it will bear a strong resemblance to the information assembled for the due diligence expected when a merger or an acquisition is contemplated. It may be less comprehensive, but the goals of orientation and due diligence overlap and much of the former can be found in the latter.

- **The DIP has to be current.** If there is a paper version it should be a "loose-leaf binder" because parts of it must change frequently and the remainder evolves constantly. Careful planning can ensure that certain databases automatically feed documents, electronic or otherwise, that are then forwarded into the DIP. As a website the DIP is easily updated, so long as being current has enough priority that the site is maintained.

- **The DIP has to be accessible.** Certainly it is the common body of knowledge for the orientation process and it is a reference for the board and the CEE Suite, but its value goes beyond the obvious. For example, the DIP could be a starting point for the annual business planning and strategy process. Several parts are not confidential, but some are documents that would normally be constrained by a non-disclosure agreement (NDA). The DIP is a window into corporate governance for the company, and parts could inform investors, analysts and others, but some parts are for insiders only.

It is useful to sort the DIP into three parts or layers, where the outer layer is composed of the documents likely to be requested by the due diligence process of a potential director or executive level hire, the second layer addresses the more detailed questions that will arise after a candidate is content with the outer layer and, finally, the inner core is information for someone now on the board or committed to it. Here is a list of the items that might be found in a well-considered DIP, sorted in the manner just described.

The list is meant to cover both public and private companies, and many items will be germane to charities and not-for-profit (NFP) entities.

The basics are those documents that all directors or senior new hires will request and, as noted, if they do not ask for them you might consider what that means. The basics are:

- the company's articles of incorporation and bylaws, with all amendments to date;
- a brief history of the company;
- the company's legal and operating structure;
- the company's mission and vision;
- the company's business and strategic plans for the next three years;
- corporate organization chart;
- an industry overview, including the major competitors;
- annual reports for the past three years, plus the quarterly MD&A;
- AIFs and all press releases;
- the report from the external auditors for the previous three years;
- any analysts' reports; and
- a copy of the current presentation to the investment community and the most recent annual general meeting.

All of the items above are or should be available to the public.

The middle ground includes information that might be in either the first or second layer, but will definitely be of interest at some point. Note that some of this is public information and some private. The middle ground should include:

- a copy of the D&O insurance policy;
- director independence questionnaire or PIF;
- the minutes of the board and of all committees for at least the previous year;
- management and consultant reports or presentations for the past year;
- the board, committee, director and CEE Suite evaluations for the past three years;
- the board compensation plan;
- director indemnification; and
- biographies and contact information for all directors, senior executives, divisional heads and other key personnel.

The second layer is for the second orientation session and the recruit who is becoming serious. This layer includes:

- the code of ethics;
- the charter of the board of directors and for each standing committee;

- position descriptions for directors, committee chairs and the chair of the board;
- job descriptions for at least the CEO, better for all members of the CEE Suite;
- major industry studies, especially those of respected economists, academics and consultancies;
- the board calendar for the past year and for the next twelve months, with important events such as the annual general meeting, board and management retreats and planning sessions; and
- an overview of the ICFR process and how it is monitored.

The inner layer and the final stage in the DIP or in the due diligence of a new director includes at least:

- the operational results for the past year, and during the orientation the directors need a briefing on how to interpret this information as it is understood and used by management to run the business, ie, this might be called the "dashboard";
- a description of enterprise risk management;
- the employee stock option plan;
- a copy of the company's disclosure policy, especially the black-out policy and insider trading rules as they affect the director;
- a copy of the whistleblower policy;
- co-ordinates for the external auditors and corporate counsel;
- copies of recent issues of trade publications and subscriptions to the major ones;
- an index to the corporate policy manual and the text of those policies of particular pertinence to the board and its oversight role, eg, conflict of interest, human resources, expense reimbursement, budgeting and expenditure, etc; and
- a glossary of terms, in particular all the acronyms, slang and technical terms peculiar to the industry and the company.

Well, this is an imposing list, perhaps an intimidating one, so two comments are in order. First, the new director should work through the layers with personal due diligence, then on to orientation and finally to ongoing DOC. Second, there are great efficiencies to be had if the company handles all the items in the DIP as part of its knowledge management process, ie, every item is part of a managed database. In this way, updating the various items is part of one or more standard jobs, embedded routines being accomplished for another purpose, and each item can be extracted and compiled at will to produce the DIP or some other combination if needed by the company

Orientation does not need to be an expensive process, although it will consume some time. My personal experience suggests that a couple of half-day sessions with two or three longer-term directors, after the new arrival has had ample time to read and digest the DIP, is quite effective. If the board is split into groups of two or three and the new director has a session with each, there are benefits beyond helping the newbie understand his or her new role. Once this has been done the new director should spend time with management, taking a walk through the business plan, being briefed on the market sector and its customers and competitors, digging into the operations side and so forth.

Finally, if the board has just been formed from scratch and the next orientation session will be the first ever held at the company, simply bring the directors and the team together for a few concentrated question-and-answer sessions centred on the DIP. Ensure that every item is explained — somebody will know the answers to most questions — and the ensuing discussion will address what is missing.

Performance Management for the Board

There are many opinions, but no thoroughly validated arguments for or against evaluating the performance of any person or group of persons accountable in some way to both the company and its shareholders, and that certainly includes the board of directors. One side of the discussion about board performance might go something like this:

> *"If ever there was a situation where the maxim 'physician, heal thyself' might apply, performance management for the board is it. In what world would it make sense that the directors who perform these two tasks never have their own performance reviewed, much less called into account? It seems so obvious. Directors are charged with increasing the value of the company entrusted to their care, and those same directors expect to assess the performance of the CEO as part of their oversight of the company. Start with what is wanted and state the goals of the evaluation process. These should be embodied in the charter of the relevant board committee, likely the corporate governance and nominating committee, or they should be stated in a resolution passed by the board, preferably with unanimous support."*

Many directors find such thinking acceptable, even compelling, and in the scurry to check all the compliance boxes, many North American boards now have some version of assessment. Few have a clear understanding of how to accomplish the task, and the usual proliferation of consultants has arrived to provide their "proprietary" solutions. The fact is that few board assessment processes have been in place long enough for their effectiveness to be judged, and several of the Wise reported their concerns about measurement that seems to lead to Neverland. We are not even certain that we are testing what ought to be tested, for research to show the correlation of individual metrics of effectiveness with corporate performance is scarce. In cases where it seems to have been very worthwhile it is unclear if the method used can be separated from the person carrying it out, ie, it is operator dependent. Certainly the dominant method, some version of a paper-based questionnaire, is often so devoid of subtlety and nuance that it is severely hampered. The over-arching problem is that performance assessment is not well done as a generality, and applying methods borrowed from human resource management may not lead to acceptable or useful results.

As a director you might ask questions like these:

- Does board assessment mean simply that, or does it extend to committee and individual director assessment? Again, why or why not — what is to be accomplished and what will it contribute to the job of the board? What will, or should, change after the assessment is complete?

- What is the job of the board for your particular company? Are there two or three tasks that are indispensable? How do they relate to, and support, the board's mandate? If a SWOT analysis was performed, what competencies would be crucial to a given board, and which would be missing?

- Should the board have performance targets and, if so, what would they be? Would the responsibility to increase shareholder value be captured in a goal? What about good governance, as opposed to compliance, how is that measured?

- Who will bell the cat? Everyone will participate, but who ensures that assessment gets done and then communicated? Once upon a time, it was left to the chair, or to the entire board. Today, it is likely to be a standing committee of the board, usually the one with a mandate that includes both governance and nominations. None can claim complete objectivity, so should board assessment be in the hands of an external party, somewhat like the audit?

- How will the board, committees or directors be assessed, and when will it be done? Some boards use rating scales and a series of statements or questions chosen to reflect the needs of the company (and thus the board) while others turn to outside facilitators or "governance consultants". Is the timing of assessment co-ordinated with input to the board slated to be proposed at the AGM?

- Once the results of the assessment are at hand, how will they be used? For example, will they be part of the nomination process and, thus, affect the slate of directors in the proxy mailing? Will they have an effect on governance procedures or on director compensation?

- How will the board change the assessment process and methods if board performance does not improve despite the insights gained?

- Finally, what is the correlation between compliance and corporate results? Are compliance and governance consonant? Is there a positive relationship between board performance, however measured, and corporate performance?

These can be tough questions, but the road to discovering their answers is worth travelling. The issue facing a small company, especially when it is in transition, is giving board assessment serious consideration among competing demands for director time. It is logical to evaluate the effectiveness of every process and that should include corporate governance, but given the uncertainty of an immediate return and the limitations on time and resources, smaller companies will likely direct attention to issues of revenue, customers and the like. It is practical to "do what can be done" and approach governance evaluation in stages, starting with an "assessment-lite" approach. This might entail a few easy targets, such as putting a charter and job descriptions in place and taking attendance. As the company and its systems mature, and the urgencies of "the next big contract" subside, the board could move to a more rigorous assessment, perhaps involving questionnaires or a third-party "visitor", or consultant. Answering the questions preceding this paragraph would help determine those choices.

Jack Welch, no shrinking violet in the opinions department, is known for his bluntness about directors and how they perform. If you vote to retain those whom Welch might describe as "seat warmers" then you have taken part in maintaining a situation that is less than optimal. You could reassure yourself that you are by no measure the first director to endure a dysfunctional peer, and you would be quite correct. Perhaps you thought it over and concluded that it would take more time and effort to remove the offender than the surgery is worth. You would be wrong.

It really does not matter if you are on the board of a large company or a start-up, a reporting issuer or a charity. Directors who do not do their job are a risk and a liability to the company, and to the other directors. I suggest that addressing the issue of the problem director is part of DOC, itself the foundation of good governance and, thus, there are two actions indicated when there is a "problem director". First and foremost, assessment or not, this is a responsibility of the chair. He or she is responsible for managing the board and its work; if that work is impeded, then the obstacle gets attention from the board leader. He or she should take the appropriate action and help the offender find something else to occupy their time. Second, as a director other than the chair, consider how the overall board, and you individually, are affected by the problem director. It will take courage to speak up, but DOC says you must.

We might consider borrowing an idea from the so-called "comprehensive audit" used by the Auditor General to inspect crown corporations. Canada and its provinces have hundreds of these entities, from the Canadian Broadcasting Corporation to the tiny and obscure. Each has a board and a mandate, and they file annual financial audits available to us as public documents.

Unlike their private sector cousins, these corporations are subject every five years to the additional scrutiny of the special audit, sometimes called an "effectiveness audit", and it is this thought that we might consider for corporate governance. I hasten to say that I am not proposing anything approaching the scope and scale of a comprehensive audit, but the idea of examining the effectiveness of corporate governance every few years bears consideration.

As a final note, it seems apparent that much of the attention given to board assessment originated with a few directors on a few boards. As noted at the opening of this section, one cannot really object to an evaluation of performance, but it would be terrific if we could avoid the airport security check approach. This is where everyone goes through an enormous amount of frustration by means of a process with dubious efficacy, at least if we are to believe the scary stories created by the media's deliberate and all too successful attempts to foil security at the various major airports. In spite of the headlines, we consider that security is good, just as we check the compliance box and believe that board assessment improves governance. The real issue is the problem director not the entire board. The ongoing work of the board is easily and simply checked: ask questions during the in camera sessions — do it frequently — and put the results in the minutes so that action items can be brought forward to make improvements. Do that and you are the epitome of DOC in action.

The Standing Committees of the Board

Dividing the governance farm into fields for cultivation is a subjective and situational task, and there are many ways to do it. Modest-sized companies might content themselves with three divisions. These standing committees, as noted earlier, might be:

- the Audit and Disclosure Committee (ADC);
- the Management, Resources and Compensation Committee (MRC); and
- the Governance and Nominations Committee (GNC).

Accepting a role on a committee adds to the work of the individual director, but the focus and specialization of the standing committees will improve the efficiency of the overall board. Each committee has a working relationship with that part of company operations lying more particularly within the purview of its mandate, somewhat like the "dotted lines" in some organization charts. In smaller companies these lines will be well travelled as directors with functional experience and standing committee responsibilities are drawn into advisory or mentoring roles with management. And, while the chair of the board should always know what is going on, these interchanges can and should hum along without worries about hierarchical issues, which will slow the process and clog communications unnecessarily. The following graphic illustrates some common links, but certainly not all the possibilities.

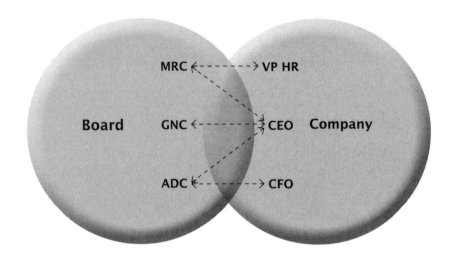

Before reviewing the general roles and responsibilities of standing committees I offer a hint drawn from experience and that is the practice of the "visitor". The visitor is a director who is not a member of the committee in question, but who agrees to attend its meetings, observe its methods and their results, and report them to the committee chair, or perhaps to the board assessment process. There are several ways of embedding this practice. The visitor could be the board chair or any other director, or committee chairs could alternate among the other committees as visitor. It is a great orientation for a new director to be the visitor for his or her first six months or year on the board and, while still somewhat objective, could offer thoughts about the effectiveness of the board. The role could be undertaken by someone who is an external advisor or, while not a director of this company, sits on other boards and, perhaps, is part of a "mutual visiting" arrangement between chairs.

I want to offer some thoughts about the three standing committees just proposed, but first, a couple of comments. As noted elsewhere, I expect readers to use the material in the appendices as freely as they wish, so please copy to your heart's content. Examples of standing committee charters have been included in Appendix Five for that purpose. My second point is that the next few paragraphs are simply a few personal comments and ideas, based on experience, about aspects not found in most charters that I have read.

The Audit and Disclosure Committee

The chair of the ADC is one of the two busiest people on any board of directors and for that reason should be unencumbered by other standing committee work (see *Balancing the Load*, below). In recruiting an ADC chair, look for someone who is prepared to work hard, who carries an accounting designation, and who is current on the body of knowledge behind that designation. On this latter attribute, my personal bias is towards someone with a chartered accountancy designation, but clearly there are many well-qualified directors and audit chairs with other backgrounds.

Audit committees are currently (2008) drinking from a fire hose of hot topics or issues, a steady, voluminous and relentless gusher. Two sources contribute the bulk of the flow: the regulators and the ongoing changes in GAAP. On the regulatory side, it is clear that the regulators are all conducting more normal course reviews than in the past, and they are inclined to be rigorous in those examinations. It seems that audit committees and thus the boards of which they are a part, should be prepared to defend their stance on revenue recognition, reserves and contingencies, hedge accounting and so forth. The increased regulatory scrutiny is leading to more enforcement actions, more re-statements of financials and increasing private litigation. And just over the horizon lie the International Financial Reporting Standards (IFRS), due for implementation in Canada by 2011.

In April 2006, the Accounting Standards Board of Canada (AcSB) announced that Canadian GAAP will be replaced with IFRS for publicly-listed companies. These standards, which were developed by the International Accounting Standards Board (IASB), will replace Canadian GAAP by 2011. The announcement advised that "Boards of directors of public companies should ensure that a member of management, or an advisor, is responsible for reporting on a regular basis on the implications of IFRS conversion". We learned from the Y2K, SOX and Bill 198 projects that early effort pays in the long run, and European companies found this to be true during their transition to IFRS in 2005. Start now, develop detailed transition plans, ready the resources needed and do the job on your timetable, rather than experience the loss of control likely when the task becomes a last minute dash for compliance. The entire transition is expected to be complete by 2011, and public companies must prepare and disclose their IFRS convergence plans in 2008.

A lesser issue, at least for now, is the XBRL Filing Program. XBRL (eXtensible Business Reporting Language) is an XML-based, royalty-free, open standard for business reporting. XBRL was developed by XBRL International, a not-for-profit consortium of over 400 leading companies and organizations around the world.

XBRL Canada's role is "to create and maintain XBRL taxonomies based on Canadian reporting standards, to increase the awareness, knowledge and understanding of XBRL and its uses in Canada, and to stimulate and promote the adoption of XBRL in Canada". The CSA have established a voluntary program to help the Canadian marketplace gain practical knowledge in preparing, filing and using XBRL information and to help the CSA test and assess the usefulness of XBRL as it considers whether to make filing in XBRL format a requirement.

Clearly, there will a lot of work for the members of the ADC, but what of other directors? The answer goes back to that list of competencies for people who sit on boards and the expectation of financial understanding on the part of one and all. To ask the questions and judge the answers, to really

Chairs and Tables

take advantage of DOC, directors have to have a reasonable understanding of the basics, what has taken place through ICFR, how the coming changes affect them and how they will discharge their responsibilities.

The Management, Resources and Compensation Committee

Boards successfully ignored any really serious contemplation of executive compensation from colonial times until a few years ago, but then the plates shifted and small waves of concern and/or outrage built into a tsunami. Now everyone has a favourite horror story about excessive pay packets, outlandish option grants or some other manoeuvre at the corporate trough. Suddenly, the committee responsible for pay and performance is much in vogue.

Two major events for this committee occurred in 2007. First, on March 29, 2007, the CSA issued a press release seeking comments on their joint intentions to improve disclosure on executive compensation.

> *The Canadian Securities Administrators (CSA) announced today they are seeking comments on Proposed Form 51-102F6* Statement of Executive Compensation, *designed to improve existing disclosure rules for executive compensation by all reporting issuers.*
>
> *The proposed Form will require companies to clearly define their compensation policies and objectives, and will provide the total compensation, in tabular form, for each named executive officer and director. In addition, the Form will require disclosure of key aspects of executive compensation such as salary, bonus, stock and option awards, payments upon termination or change in control, and pension entitlements.*

It seems that the CSA is considering a "compensation discussion and analysis" (CD&A), a sort of "MD&A for compensation" and in its request for commentary the OSC included the phrase "to improve the quality and transparency of executive compensation disclosure". While this is a great goal, if one recognizes that "pay and allowances" is often (always?) more than a base salary and a benefits package with a bonus in good years, it is not as simple as it first appears. As a result, it is likely that the "quality" of disclosure will be improved with more alacrity than its "transparency", meaning that companies will respond with answers to a CD&A requirement, should it come to pass, but there will still be gaps.

I was one of those who responded to the request for comments, and when I did, it was with small companies, public and private, at the front of my mind. Drawing on a few years of experience and some modest understanding — and having made the requisite mistakes along the way — I suggested that the word "compensation" is often too narrow, or at least it is as it is commonly used. Directors need to be aware of everything that motivates performance at the top. That almost certainly includes intangibles, such as being the largest fish in the goldfish bowl, an equity stake is compelling for many and the list probably omits a few items that may not be identified as motivators and, thus, compensation. I suggested that when we look at a company to analyze overall and specific performance, we ought to be interested in every item in a list that might be called "Things I Like" (TIL). That TIL list is different for each person, and it is usually invisible, because it is beyond what is typically considered to be compensation.

The TIL list is not fanciful and it is not necessarily inexpensive. Further, it is not innocent of manipulation, possibly by its owner, who may be blissfully unaware of complicity. TIL lists reflect personalities, operating styles, ego, personal likes and dislikes, and on through as many motivators as there are residents of the CEE Suite. Some favourites cost more than automobiles, and they migrate onto the TIL list in wonderfully assorted ways. An example is illustrative.

Office furnishings may be company property, but when they are there just because someone likes them, they qualify for the TIL list. In one situation, the CEO loved antiques with the result that his office was glorious, somewhat rococo and incredibly expensive. The costs to the company did not end when the office was finally completed (to the tune of about $250,000) because there was a hefty insurance premium, then there was additional security and surveillance and, later, some tricky manoeuvring to bring the digital age into the office without destroying the value of the antiques. While this particular CEO was in place, the furnishings were either amusing or a sore point for other executives. When he departed, there was the cost of selling the furniture at Sotheby's and refitting the office along more conventional lines.

I want to emphasise that this CEO performed well and left only when he reached retirement. The company grew and prospered under his direction, so perhaps the antique show was worth it. That is not the point. The challenge would be to identify the antiques, which were company property, as a form of compensation and reveal it to improve "the quality and transparency of executive compensation disclosure". I wonder what the effects would be on corporate jets, corporate art collections, unusually strong support for favourite causes and the like if they were seen as "TIL". If they motivate an individual, they are part of the compensation for that person.

This was certainly an unusual case, but it is recounted to help make the point that compensation is far more complex than has been suggested in the past. Knowing this it is hard to reconcile why so few boards recruit those who are seriously competent in the various aspects of human resource management generally, and the field of compensation in particular. The argument is not whether an art collection or an antique desk is part of compensation. What is needed is a deeper understanding that Frederick Herzberg was right and that once the hygiene factors have been covered, then the list of motivators is wide open ("One More Time, How Do You Motivate Employees?" *Harvard Business Review*, September/October, 1987). If we are going to be serious about designing compensation or disclosing it, we need a lot more knowledge and insight on, or available to, the board. If "financial literacy" is *de rigueur* for the audit committee, then the compensation committee needs a parallel competency to pass on "management's discussion and analysis of executive compensation".

The second major event for the MRC was in June 2007, when the ICD Blue Ribbon Commission on the Governance of Executive Compensation in Canada delivered its final report. It is worth reading, albeit a bit short of directly applicable advice on the key question of how much to pay. As an aside, the report agrees with a change in the name of the relevant standing committee, that is

> *"We have used the term human resources committee rather than compensation committee because it more accurately reflects the role that the committee should play in addressing strategic human resource issues and in determining executive compensation".*

Those interviewed by the Blue Ribbon Commission stressed greater depth in the human resource management field for directors on the MRC committee.

> *Adequately monitoring and evaluating performance is not an easy task. Consequently, interview participants suggested that at least one member of a human resources committee possess financial expertise and another human resources expertise. Some interview participants suggested that in addition to a thorough understanding of the business, this would include an understanding of compensation approaches and issues as well as formal human resources credentials such as the Certified Human Resources Professional (CHRP) designation.*

All stakeholders unite to laud pay-for-performance as the force that can align the goals and objectives of the company with those of the CEE Suite. It is simple when the relationship between pay and reward is straight forward, as it is for pure commissions paid on revenues booked, but the problem is that the executive team has a much more complex set of targets, which can be achieved only by simultaneously manipulating an interactive set of variables, many of which are beyond the reach of even the influence of the executive. The MRC charter likely says that performance systems are to be developed by management for approval by the committee, but small companies may not have much depth in the HR function, so systems design is likely to be an issue. The board will wish to see a strong correlation between pay and performance, but it may find that it has to roll up its sleeves to accomplish it.

A comment by Ron Osborne (Chairman of the Sun Life companies and a director of several other companies) is irresistible. He suggests the parable of the farmer and his cat. The farmer feeds his cat, but only enough for subsistence. If the cat wants to grow fat, it has to catch mice.

Another issue before the MRC committee is the growing tendency of senior people to seek employment contracts. There are many reasons. There is a lot more uncertainty in the CEE Suite. Boards have become more demanding, and they are more prepared to make changes and to make them more quickly. The certification process has placed an added strain on the relationship with the board. We should not be surprised that all of this has moved the formality of an executive's relationship with the company well beyond a letter of appointment or, as it once was, a simple handshake. Employment contracts for the president and CEO are common, and formal agreements for all members of the CEE Suite are no longer unusual. There are as many arguments in favour as there are against, but you can be certain that the trend is towards an increasingly formal interface, often negotiated by lawyers for each party. Given that employment agreements are a fact of life even in small companies, what is the advice for the MRC committee?

1. **Take charge of the process.** The board, through the MRC committee, should control the mechanics of the employment agreements. The contracts may have been in place when you came onto the board or the MRC, in which case you will need to be patient until such time as there is sufficient leverage for the company to change its senior agreements, but it is essential that this happen. If yours is a public company the MRC should retain advisors, otherwise the company's representative should draft the contracts. In either case, the MRC must have oversight of the terms of an agreement and everything that flows from those terms. Only in that manner can the MRC committee be in a position of ready disclosure and full transparency of all terms and conditions of employment contracts.

2. **Beware of terms and definitions.** If you are about to step onto a board or onto an MRC committee, take a hard look at some of the items in the employment contract. For example, many contracts include a change of control clause and all of them cover dismissal with cause or severance without reason. If these and similar clauses are not worded with care, they become a very expensive boomerang when they come into effect. If the board and the MRC committee are serious about pay-for-performance, then the leverage to make that effective is crucial, and careless wording in a contract can erode or even nullify the ability to redress poor performance. Other items to watch are how "annual salary", "bonus", "evergreen" and "non-compete" are defined.

3. **Understand the true costs.** Hiring is an especially dangerous time in the development of the employment relationship for it may seem that a hiring bonus is a small price to get a key talent to join the team. That could be the case, but if the "hiring bonus" affects the long term, what is its true cost? As another example, suppose that a highly effective consultant has worked with the company through its formative years and is now prepared to join the CEE Suite full time, but wants tenure to be defined to include those years as a contractor. The intuitive response may be to agree, but what do those added years cost? Does your company have a pension plan?

Would he or she qualify for a longer vacation as a result? How will it be seen by other employees?

4. **Stress test for the worst case.** Experience suggests that every contract should be viewed under the worst imaginable situation for the company. Calculate the full costs, consider the effects on other employees and stakeholders, and be realistic about the probability of this coming to pass. It may be an item to place on the list of risks to be monitored.

Demographics inform us that we are about to face talent shortages and the regulators are telling us that greater transparency around pay and benefits is expected. The MRC committee will have broader responsibilities and operate under a sharper focus in the coming years.

The Governance and Nominations Committee

An article by David W. Anderson, PhD, "Governance Committees Come of Age", opened with the sentiment that directors may be tiring of the incessant pressures to comply, and the author went on to say:

> *"We must resist equating compliance with governance. Compliance, while necessary and sometimes helpful, is largely about following rules and regulations. The outcome can only be as good as the rules themselves. Compliance-driven governance, being common within a given jurisdiction, does not generally confer competitive advantage. It is legally necessary but does not relate directly to performance."*[1]

Necessary but not sufficient, is absolutely correct.

In a small company, and especially a start-up, the GNC's responsibilities can be shared among all directors, at least for the first year or so. This likely implies that the chair of the board ought to be the champion on governance issues in the early going, a reasonable expectation in any case. However, even for small companies the situation shifts as the time to nominate the next board appears on the horizon. When you read the section of Chapter Nine called *Right from the Start*, you will learn that the chair of the board and the CEO agreed on the competencies that were needed when the company was formed, and the directors were recruited accordingly. You will also learn that the board of this company formed a Governance and Nominating Committee by the end of its first six months because it wanted to ensure that the board was the major influence on director selection as the company approached its first annual general meeting. That is rather unusual in a small company, but a great model to emulate.

---

1   David W. Anderson, "Governance Committees Come of Age". Reprinted with permission from the February, 2007 edition of the ICD *Director* newsletter, published by the Institute of Corporate Directors (www.icd.ca).

There are at least two salient reasons for striking a GNC sooner than later, regardless of the size of the company. First, by creating a standing committee with a charter emphasizing governance and taking responsibility for nominations, the board focuses accountability on the GNC chair. Second, the demands of modern governance standards create a lot of work, and a dedicated committee helps to divide the load.

Balancing the Work

The increased work to conform with the disclosure standards in public companies, the heightened expectations of private company owners, the increased emphasis on DOC, the added risks, the push of change — it all adds up to a director's workload that has at least doubled within the last 10 years. The work will not diminish in the foreseeable future and, in my opinion it should not, assuming a continued endorsement of high standards of governance. Further, we have seen the shift to audit committees that are composed only of independent directors, and there are strong indications that this will soon encompass the other standing committees. Balancing the workload of the directors has become an important part of managing the work of the board.

The board of directors	Standing committees of the board		
	ADC	MRC	GNC
Board chair	Visits but does not sit on committees		
Red		MRC chair	Member
Green	Member	Member	
Blue	Member		Member
Brown		Member	GNC Chair
Black	ADC chair		
President & CEO	Ex-officio	Ex-officio	Ex-officio

In this simplified example, there are three standing committees, as presented earlier, with a board of seven directors, six of whom are independent. The suggestion is that the chair of the board does not sit on any of the committees and the ADC chair does not sit on either of the other committees, given the work of the audit committee. While the actual workload is bound to change according to the situation, this distribution of duties is a reasonable balance, given the board calendar common for many companies.

The Annual General Meeting (AGM)

All Canadian business corporation acts view the company's annual meeting as the main accountability forum in which shareholders can ask questions and express their views. They are informed by the annual report, which is expected to be published and distributed in advance with the board's proposed slate of directors. The contents of the annual report are prescribed to a significant degree. Typically, it opens with a letter to the shareholders, and this is almost certain to be followed by MD&A of finances and operations. Then come the consolidated financial statements for the year just completed (usually compared with those of the previous year), which are an account of the stewardship of management and the board. The report will include the auditor's report and a statement of management's responsibility for financial reporting. Although the annual report is delivered in advance, it is received formally by the owners at the AGM. Note that they are not asked to approve the financials, merely to receive them, although the AGM is the moment for the stockholders to question the company's financial situation and learn about the future directions of the business. Private companies and NFPs may take a more casual approach to the AGM, but it is the most important communication with the stakeholders, and the advice here is that the board's interest in full and clear disclosure is demonstrated by a meeting that answers all their questions.

Best practices for those in the chair commence with advance preparation, striving for what one friend describes as a "well-planned spontaneous event". Prepare a checklist or countdown of things to do during the run-up to the AGM. The corporate secretary ought to do much of this, but the chair cannot shunt this aside; the AGM is simply too important. If your company is private and new, take note that the CBCA requires you to hold the first annual meeting not more than six months after the end of the first fiscal year and each one thereafter. The Ontario Business Corporations Act (OBCA) allows 18 months' leeway for the first AGM after incorporation, but after that you must meet every year, with not more than 15 months between any two meetings. If your company trades its securities on the TSX you must file your audited statements within 90 days after year-end and hold the AGM within six months of the same date. Specifics such as timing vary somewhat from one province or territory to another, between exchanges and over time.

Write a script so as to avoid embarrassing omissions, such as forgetting to introduce one of the directors or mentioning that a key shareholder has travelled several hours to be present. Elicit shareholders to make and second motions, and provide a written form of the relative statement, again guarding against the inadvertent or momentary lapse, such as one situation where the chair forgot to present the consolidated financial statements until reminded just as he was about to conclude the meeting. A script ensures that shareholders are reminded to register with the scrutineers, that a quorum is declared, that the meeting process is explained and so forth. Having agreed that a script is an essential, the wise chair never allows it to become a straitjacket, turning the meeting into a pre-ordained sequence.

Wisdom, as well as the law, dictates that transparency rules the street, and so it should be at the AGM. Having ensured that the legal niceties have been observed (directors elected, auditors appointed, resolutions passed) the AGM is an occasion for transparency — and some careful publicity. It is an ideal forum to present the company's vision of the future and as much of the business plan as is prudent from a competitive standpoint, always avoiding the pitfalls of too many adverbs and adjectives, all superlatives and any hint of guidance. This is the moment for the CEO to stand before the owners and show them why they should have confidence in management, to give an accounting of what has been done and what is about to be done.

The first meeting of the newly-appointed board should follow the AGM immediately, with an agenda of organizational issues, including electing the chair of the board, appointing the officers of the company, attending to the committees and their chairs, and confirming the board calendar for the year.

Finishing Touches

Superb craftsmanship produces world class tables and chairs, the furniture of governance. Business has borrowed from all the traditional styles and structures, from organized religions, from the military and from bureaucracies of all sorts to design corporate governance circa 2008. It has become a strong and reliable structure, but there are many finishing touches or refinements to be added. While fine in-lay and meticulous joinery have been crafted over the centuries, corporate governance is still in need of the plane and the sander.

If it is not yet clear, let me say it again: corporate governance is as critical to private companies as it is to those that have issued shares and listed themselves on a stock exchange. It is of equal importance to the oversight of managing an association, leading a charity or operating a government commission. There are close parallels between disclosure to the public-at-large because someone might decide to buy or sell shares and disclosure to shareholders interested in their privately-held company or stakeholders monitoring the efficacy of a human services agency. The boardroom is the forum where the interests of executive management and those of the shareholders or members are debated, where strategies are formed and decisions are made. The chairs and tables in the front row of corporate governance must be well built.

Chapter Seven:

Conundrums Faced

Many years ago, the *Winnipeg Free Press* provided its readers with a fresh test of lateral thinking with each issue and, thus, I became acquainted with conundrums. Their riddles used a play on words to perplex and bemuse (which led to a pun virus and a lifelong affliction!). Little did I realize that conundrums, or at least puzzles of a less pleasurable variety, would become part of my daily fare when I became a corporate director. Perhaps "daily" is an exaggeration, but only just.

Sensational disclosures and disgraced newspaper barons to the contrary, those who are truly bad apples are a miniscule part of the population of people in the business world. As a generality, everyone wants to do what is correct and proper, and their intent forms one view, the simple and straightforward face of the coin. The obverse is seen through a cloud formed by the absolutely astounding amount of bumf (Refer to page 306 of the *Shorter Oxford English Dictionary* and discover that one meaning of this word is toilet paper!) perpetrated in reaction to the miscreant minority. With a regulator in every capital, assorted stock exchanges, a sprinkling of professional standards organizations and a few self-regulating ones, there are enough busy pens to maintain a torrent of new rules and regulations, new interpretations of old rules and regulations, warnings, cautions, national instruments — but you get the picture. Directors, especially those on the boards of public companies, have a surfeit of information and advice to absorb. To apply it with wisdom is to balance the coin, spinning it on edge, for most situations demand something from each face. Achieving this balance is one of the director's conundrums and, frankly, I do not have an easy answer.

This chapter examines a few other coins and it opens with the perplexing issue of public versus private.

Conundrum One: Public — or Private?

One of the more profound choices before the board of a company is whether it should be public or private. There are many arguments for either option, but the final choice is ultimately situational, and it takes a clear and thoughtful perspective to make it correctly. It is a most difficult choice, for the lure of the public market may be irresistible to the majority of the shareholders, so that the discussion is moot. Do all that you can to keep the discussion alive until you are certain that becoming a reporting issuer is the best course for the company — which is where a director's duties lie, as opposed to many who may urge the board and management into a course which meets their priorities but may not be best for the company.

One of the older texts on my shelves is *Going Public in Canada: The Facts and the Fads*, written by Peter McQuillan in 1971, with advice and insights that remain fresh today. He suggests that, while there is a lengthy list of reasons to go public, in practice, only a few may apply to the situation at hand and many others turn out to be platitudes favoured by financial writers.

The capital markets are huge, beyond the comprehension of all but economists of the first order, and then only dimly. According to the Securities Industry and Financial Markets Association, the US bond market in 2006 had a total value of $27.4 trillion, while the stock market was valued at $21.6 trillion. Your company will be a miniscule part of a vast ocean, and the currents and trade winds are ferocious.

As you know, an IPO is the first sale of the shares of a private company to the public, hence the term "going public". The company might also achieve a public listing through an RTO, which could be accomplished in concert with any other publicly-listed entity, including the Canadian device known as a Capital Pool Company (CPC). The characteristics of each may vary, but the result will be a publicly-traded company, and this section addresses the merits of that stance while leaving aside the intricacies of how each approach works in practice.

The first consideration for the board is to answer the question, "Why are we doing this?" The foregone conclusion is that this is about money, so the very next query should be whether this is the optimal way to get it. Perhaps another private shareholder could bring the same financing to the table or a fund might be interested in becoming part of your growth story. Would debt be a more advantageous strategy? It would be less dilutive, but obviously it has to be repaid at some point and it has to be serviced in the meantime, which could be a chunk of your cash flow. If you decide to seek debt, the company must choose between senior debt, convertible debt and so forth. Good governance demands that all alternatives be examined before deciding on the optimal strategy for a given situation.

An IPO is often used by emerging companies of all sizes seeking capital to expand, but choosing to become publicly traded is equally a means for owners to extract their capital. If the latter is one of the reasons, the company may include a secondary offering, which is a sale of securities by a shareholder of the company, as opposed to the company itself. For example, Google's IPO included both a "primary" offering (issuing Google shares from the Google treasury) and a "secondary" offering, which was the sale of Google stock held by founders Larry Page and Sergey Brin, plus a few original employees. As an aside, the Google IPO in August 2004 brought in $1.67 billion and gave it a market cap of $23 billion. The Google IPO created an enormous pool of cash to fuel growth and expansion, while also giving its founders a huge payday. Two objectives, and both were satisfied.

The Arguments for Being Public

When the shares of a company are offered to the public market they immediately gain value because they are more fungible, they have value when sold for cash, they have intrinsic value when traded for other shares, they are an asset to secure a loan and so forth. The funds from a public offering of treasury shares can satisfy multiple objectives. They can permit growth via both acquisitions and organic expansion, a broadened equity base may result in a lower cost of incremental debt and increased debt capacity when it is needed, and greater exposure to the financial community can result in new sources of capital (for example, institutional pools, subject to investment policies that restrict or prohibit the purchase of private company securities, become prospective investors). The access to a broadly based market for the company's stock may be viewed by lending institutions as a possible debt refunding source, hence reducing the perceived lending risk and, therefore, the company's cost of debt.

Certainly, marketable securities are more easily bought and sold, they are more liquid and so are generally perceived to have greater value than privately-owned shares. Liquidity is the key factor in making securities more acceptable as an exchange medium for potential acquisitions or mergers, or as collateral to secure loans. That same feature is afforded to the owners of a public company when they sell part of their holdings through a secondary offering, which enables them to reduce their risk. The benefits of liquidity extend to residual holdings since they are also marketable and are more easily valued.

Public companies can contemplate acquisitions using their publicly-traded shares as a currency beyond cash and other tangible assets. Using the shares of a private company in transactions can be prohibitive, as their true worth is unknown and may be discounted by the valuation process, since the vendor and the buyer are virtually certain to hold different assumptions about the variables included in the method used to arrive at the value of the purchase. This is frequently resolved by an "earn out", meaning a sale price based in part on future performance, but this solution of a current problem creates a future constraint because the company must set aside cash reserves for contingent payments. A publicly-traded share has a value established by the marketplace and ready transferability, making it as acceptable as cash to a prospective vendor, and the share exchange is not taxed. Share ownership in a public company can be an incentive for management of the acquired company to remain with the merged operation, and the subsequent availability of share purchase options for management can be an incentive for high performance. Finally, the exposure of a public company in the business and financial community can help to generate unsolicited acquisition or merger opportunities that might not come to the attention of a private entity.

The shareholder's agreement is a dominant governor of the affairs of a private company, and a customary stricture has to do with what happens when a shareholder departs. When his or her shares are sold to other shareholders in a private company, the conditions may be pre-determined, eg, an agreed valuation, timing or other terms. If a shareholder dies, the shares pass to his or her estate and unknown conditions can come into play, at least as far as the family is concerned, such as the satisfaction of the shareholder's debts. A public company eliminates the shareholder's agreement as an issue and settling the estate can usually be accomplished with ease through the sale of a portion of the holdings, or with monies borrowed against the security of such holdings.

There is a constant battle for talent, especially keen in small companies, and a publicly-held corporation may be able to attract new employees who add depth and breadth to its competencies, to the extent of gaining the sought-after edge in the marketplace. Though stock option plans no longer offer the attractive tax treatment of prior years, a public company remains in a better position relative to a private one, if it wishes to implement such a plan to motivate employees. Highly qualified employees can be attracted via stock options or restricted stock units (RSU) when the company may not be able to match the salary demands with cash (see the addendum to this section). As well, if a company wishes to inculcate a "culture of ownership", such as the well-advertised WestJet, the task is made easier when the company is public. A public corporation can offer its securities to employees, and the broader ownership base can make attraction and retention easier. In addition, as the shares are now publicly traded, the administrative burden of the phantom stock plans used by a private company is removed.

The benefits of being public include certain tax-related factors, such as the tax-exempt status of dividends received from other taxable Canadian corporations, the possibility that public scrutiny might increase corporate vitality, perhaps a positive effect on public relations and the more dubious benefits of free and unsolicited media coverage, and the contributions of the investment banking community, which would not be interested in a private operation.

Finally, a successful IPO distributes the company's shares across a wide geography, and this effectively takes the company's name and knowledge of its products to new customers in regions where they may not otherwise have had any exposure.

The board of directors has not been mentioned as a reason for being public, but perhaps the ability, in fact the need, to attract outside board members could be a partial reason to be public. I am frankly unconvinced of that, because those who are directors are as likely to argue for remaining private as they are for going the IPO route, putting aside those who are also founding shareholders anxious to extract some of their capital gains. First, let us assume that the decision to go public has been made, for any or all of the reasons just listed, and turn to how that happens.

Getting There

Unlike the old saw, getting there is not necessarily half the fun. The decision to become a reporting issuer is only the first step along an occasionally tortuous road to selling the company's securities and bringing in the cash to execute the plan that was the rationale in the first place. According to the CNQ (Canadian Trading and Quotation Systems Inc.), "Canada's new stock exchange", a reporting issuer is defined as:

> *"A company that has issued shares to the public and is subject to continuous disclosure requirements by one or more of the provincial securities commissions."*

The term is defined in each of the provincial securities acts, and there may be slight differences from one act to another. Generally, a reporting issuer is an entity that has raised capital from the public and that must file annual audited financial statements with a securities commission. Notice that this does not say that the company is trading on a stock exchange. Being a reporting issuer and being one with shares trading on an exchange are not always the same thing, and meeting the requirements for trading ought to be a factor in the board's deliberations as it decides to go public. First, a quick segue along the possible routes to public status shows that these are an IPO or an RTO, of which there are at least a couple of varieties.

The path to an IPO starts with a prospectus. The securities laws in the US and Canada require a full, true and plain disclosure of all material facts in an offering prospectus, the legal document used to present the merits of a share offering. The prospectus is usually the main source of information for an investor prior to the IPO. The prospectus must be filed with, and approved by, the appropriate regulator, such as the US Securities and Exchange Commission (SEC), the Financial Services Authority in the UK or one or more of the provincial regulators in Canada. The prospectus document provides investors with detailed information about the company's business, financial statements, biographies of officers and directors, their compensation, any litigation underway, real properties and any other information sufficiently material to affect the decision to invest. As the board of a private company is considering the facts of public life, the prospectus is often its first true encounter with the demands of compliance — which will become all too familiar if they continue down this path!

Companies can become public issuers through an RTO, wherein a private company is merged into a public one and the resulting public organization takes the name of the formerly private company, hence the "reverse" part of the term. Aside from those operating on the fringes of the tax avoidance world, a public shell suitable for use in an RTO comes into being in two ways. A company that had an IPO, operated for a time and then sold its assets or became an undeclared bankrupt is a common form of shell. (Recall my tale of an undiscovered liability following an RTO into a supposedly "clean" shell?) Another version is a purpose-built entity, a public vehicle created as a shell, and in some Canadian provinces this can be accomplished through a CPC. In either case, the RTO is simply an alternative to an IPO, another means of "going public".

Suppose that your company completed an RTO with a shell company listed on the TSX Venture Exchange (TSX-V) and that company is not currently trading because it is dormant. As a general rule, the public company involved in an RTO is just such a shell. A shell corporation is defined in *Barron's Finance & Investment Handbook* as "a company that is incorporated, but has no significant assets or operations." Thus, if the combined assets or revenues of the shell plus your company do not meet the requirements of the relevant exchange, the new entity is a reporting issuer but unable to trade. Each exchange sets forth the requirements to be met before shares are listed and allowed to trade. For example, the TSX-V has two broad sectors (technology and industrial, or research and development) with two tiers for each sector, and up to three different categories. It is not unusual for an RTO to be complete from a legal process standpoint, but trading is unable to commence until funding is completed and a net tangible asset or working capital requirement is met.

The board has some interesting considerations as it chooses its path, some of which are:

1. Given the decision to go public, what are the advantages of an IPO versus an RTO?

2. What is the balance between raising as much money as possible today versus unacceptable dilution?

3. What is the appropriate price for the new shares? How will that price be derived or calculated?

    Your board should consider setting a reasonable offering price, slightly on the conservative side, to ensure that the new offering will receive strong initial support and will then be able to "perform" well in the medium term. This will be balanced with trying to capture the public market's support and enthusiasm at the highest acceptable price. Ask yourself, "What will the board communicate in the MD&A by this time next year?

4. Will some or all of the founding shareholders want to avail themselves of a secondary offering, and how will this affect pricing?

Your company will get professional assistance on many of these questions from the investment dealer chosen to manage and underwrite the initial public offering of shares. Take your time over this choice, for the underwriter has responsibilities beyond simply selling the securities. In Canada, all underwriters or brokers are members of the Investment Dealers Association of Canada (IDA), the national self-regulatory organization of the securities industry. The IDA regulates the activities of investment dealers in terms of both their capital adequacy and how they conduct their business. To qualify as a member firm, a brokerage must meet stringent capital requirements, demonstrate an ability and willingness to conduct its business in a manner consistent with the by-laws, rules and regulations of the IDA, and be subject to ongoing supervision. It would be time well spent to become familiar with the IDA and how it operates as one piece of education prior to selecting an underwriter — they are far from being equal or even similar in many respects.

5.   Have a frank discussion involving the directors, the CEO and the CFO. Ask yourselves, "Do we have, collectively, the financial sophistication and experience to choose a broker or an investment banker?" The biggest investment bank is not necessarily the best, a "name brand" is not a guarantee, either. Your best choice could be an adjunct of a chartered bank, or a tier-three boutique. If this is the rookie season for everyone, get some seasoned advice.

The principal objectives of the issuer are to obtain capital from investors at the best possible terms, while benefiting from the conversion to a public entity with marketable securities as share capital. The principal objectives of the underwriter are to obtain the best possible price per share for the company, in the context of a successful IPO, and to assist the company in its transition to public-company status. The brokerage should advise the company on the amount and the form of securities to be issued. After designing, preparing and purchasing the security issue, the investment dealer undertakes to place the shares with a wide variety of investors, retail and institutional as appropriate, to obtain proper distribution and help establish a healthy "after market" of share trading. The underwriter will continue as a market advisor and — in the best circumstances — will offer tangible support through writing an analyst's report on the company, although these are supposed to be separate events.

At the time of selecting an underwriter, a guaranteed price at which the shares will be sold generally cannot be quoted. There is usually about a 10-week lag between when the issuer decides on a managing underwriter and when the issue actually is priced in the market. The issue will be priced in light of market conditions at the time, thus only an approximate price range can be discussed in the initial stages. It is an important job of the underwriter, however, to give a close estimate of the expected price, usually based on some multiple of historical or expected future earnings per share, and not to "highball" a price in order to secure the business of the issuer.

The "promised" price of an issue should not be the only deciding factor in choosing an underwriter, since the market establishes the final price.

Creative financial ideas, the province of the broker and the investment banker, can affect the company's cost of money, the company's image in the financial community and even its long-term financial health. Personalized services are not tangible and cannot be measured on a best-price basis, nor generally can they be tested, at least not in advance. The company might make its choice based on the firm's reputation for past performance, including during times of market or company distress, which is probably the best indicator, and the company might also consider a quick survey of the other investment dealers. The three or four months prior to an IPO or RTO are stressful, and company executives (and perhaps directors) will be working closely with the team from the investment dealer so the personalities of the individuals who will work on the issue should be a factor as well.

The Private Side of the Coin

Whether regulatory compliance is at odds with the best principles of good governance may be a question, but there is no doubt of its side effects on reporting issuers. Compliance is a fact of life for public companies and fulfilling it should be a consideration when determining the wisdom of public versus private. It can be a sobering experience, for although exemptions may be sought when a disclosure could be harmful, the transition to public status means that previously proprietary financial and trade information, plus at least an overview of all IP, will soon be in the hands of competitors and customers alike. The board may wish to consider whether the disclosure of high profits and returns might attract new competitors, and if that added risk is worth the reward.

Then there is the compliance regime in Canada. Directors approaching the decision to go public in the domain of the maple leaf face a burden not felt by their American counterparts, that is, operating in a land where there are no fewer than 13 regulators. The roots of this peculiarly Canadian problem lie with the statute that formed the country, and multiple jurisdictions have been a nuisance ever since. Adaptation is a necessity of life and recent research by the Canadian Banker's Association found insights into this amazing circumstance:

- companies limit the number of jurisdictions in which they raise capital, restricting them to two to four provinces or territories;
- expenses increase with the number of jurisdictions, regardless of the size of the issue;
- the regulation-related expenses of a listing in all 13 jurisdictions is double that of a single jurisdiction;
- raising $1 million in all 13 jurisdictions costs more than 15% of the capital raised; and
- Canada currently spends about 50% more on financial sector regulation than the UK and more than double the amount spent by Australia.

In other words, beyond the disclosure aspects of compliance there is its cost. There are recurring out-of-pocket costs simply to be a public company, and they are especially burdensome for small companies because they loom so large proportionally. An original listing fee is payable, related to the number of shares to be listed, and there is an annual sustaining fee to keep the listing in good standing. After the initial listing, fees are levied for listing additional shares, stock splits, stock consolidations and name changes. Along the way are the costs of quarterly and annual reports, registrar and transfer agency fees, auditing fees, legal fees, board expenses, directors' fees, shareholders' meetings, investor relations, increased insurance costs and on and on. The delta between public and private often amounts to a multiple of the total for a private company, and your board should expect recurring costs of between $1 million to as much as $3 million for a public company with a modest $50 million in annual revenues. It is easy to see how that affects the bottom line, and it is equally obvious that there is a scope and scale threshold to public company status. A director at your boardroom table should query any decision likely to consume 2% of net earnings, especially one that brings risks with it.

The board should think long and hard about how public status for the company will affect the shareholders as individuals, whether they are themselves the owners or their proxies. A private company, while remaining well within the law and accepted practices, can easily alter its financial arrangements with a principal owner so as to optimize that person's financial position. Full disclosure combined with regulations on non-arm's length transactions restricts those opportunities. Dividend policies cannot be adjusted in accordance with the cash flow needs or tax status of an individual, nor can loans and shareholder advances be made, even for defensible business purposes, and expense allowances and non-taxable benefits may have to be reduced sharply. Annual bonuses become a function of performance rather than the personal financial needs of the individual owner. "It's my company and I will decide" no longer holds.

The principal shareholders are now "insiders" and must report publicly if they sell or purchase any shares in the company. If the owner sells shares to pay for a renovation, the market may misinterpret the sale as bad news, assuming that the owner is acting on inside knowledge. Simultaneously, the personal worth of that same shareholder may fluctuate with the market, a notoriously volatile and emotional entity, and this could constrain certain personal actions.

Then there is the "hassle factor". It will rear its head the moment the company is public. For those who have yet to experience it, being a reporting issuer can truly spoil your day. When principal owners or even directors who have had a significant role in building the company face this sudden shift it can be unnerving and often irritating. Start with the simple, perhaps obvious, fact that the moment that your company accepts money, an obligation is created. That obligation takes different forms and there are different expectations depending on the amount, the terms and whether it is a loan to, or an investment in, the company. The owners and directors must now share their power and authority with the person who wrote the cheque, and that is the source of the hassle — which can become a major issue following entry into the public markets. For example, an owner may have grown accustomed to a close working relationship with a partner in a local auditing practice, but suppose that the firm does not wish to audit public companies or perhaps it does not qualify for such work? Further, the auditors of public companies are tending less to report to management and more to report on management. Accounting practices may impose new constraints which, when combined with minority interests and outside directorships, can become irritants to the principals. Finally, an owner who has always played a major role in a trade association will find that public communications are suddenly considered to be "core documents" subject to disclosure rules.

Wearing their hats as managers, the owners will discover that they are now accountable to a much larger number of shareholders as well as the outside directors. Suddenly, management must devote considerable time to inquiries from shareholders, financial analysts, outside directors, journalists and the like, and there are the same 24 hours in the day. For public companies, quarterly audits and MD&A become facts of life, consuming more time and effort. Business becomes more formal and is subject to the many regulations protecting the public shareholders, while top management becomes more visible to recruiters and to the investment community. Personal transactions are scrutinized for insider trading, and the street wonders if friends or associates have used privileged information for their personal advantage. The compensation package of every member of the senior management team must be disclosed. The world of the private company disappears, replaced by the fish bowl of the public market. The group of owner-managers, owner-directors and outside directors considering the options should think long and carefully as to how it will affect them.

Summing Up

The public-versus-private decision is a conundrum because it encompasses such a range of variables, many of them unknown or difficult to predict. Your board may see the strategic value of access, but the realities of the public capital market include so many imponderables that your board should question the choice for that reason alone. After all, if there were a similar number of unknowns imbedded in any other crucial decision, your board might well decide that the risk is too high. It is tough to predict what the stock will do on its initial day of trading or in the near future for that matter so the soundness of your choice may not be determined for a very long time. Consider the track record of those in the financial services industry, spending millions to manage risk. They have entire departments, replete with the best analysts they can buy, who study market, credit, liquidity, and operational risk. They have the resources to model every conceivable possibility. But when the sub-prime juggernaut rolled through in mid-2007, Citigroup had a write down of over $10 billion, leading a parade that included, among many others, Merrill Lynch ($7.9 billion in losses), Bear Stearns ($700 million) and a couple of the major Canadian banks, each with several hundreds of millions in losses from bad decisions. By the way, these were the tallies at the time this was written — and many predict that they will rise.

One friend, who has used the IPO route three times and always to advantage, uses the analogy of a long automobile trip when he says, "If you have to get there as quickly as possible, you don't want to stop for gas, so fill the tank and drive hard". I agree — if the car is in great shape, the road is dry and the map is clear. This analogy has its limits, and we would be well advised to see access to the capital markets in an even-handed and clear way, great strengths balanced by significant constraints and costs. Markets carry risk, and when a company is going through a transitory growth period and is subject to uncertainty regarding its future value, the decision becomes profound. In my opinion, the threshold to becoming a public issuer is roughly $100 million in revenues, given the incremental costs in dollars and distraction. Of course, your company may take the plunge in advance of that amount of revenue when there are compelling reasons to believe that the momentum of growth is such that the company will break through the barrier within a year or so. As always, the twin conditions of the company and its market will be major considerations, and your company's appetite for risk will be the final major determinant.

When a company is public, it generally cannot choose who invests in it, but there are certainly some investors who are more desirable than others. Dr James Gillies, Professor Emeritus at the Schulich School at York University, when speaking at the Tenth Annual ICD Awards Banquet on May 31, 2007, offered an important insight when he said:

> "Are an owner and an investor the same? Not if they are speculators. Real owners — not investors — have an abiding interest in their customers, suppliers and employees."

I want to close this section by repeating my earlier statement that I am neither for nor against becoming a reporting issuer. I have emphasized the risk of the public markets because so many board determinations of public versus private ignore aspects that are unknown or only suspected. The prospect of "gas in the tank" mesmerizes the directors and public equity may be the correct choice. It is not the only choice, and when DOC has truly been completed your board may find another. Good luck is sometimes better than good management, so — good luck!

Stock-based Incentives:
Addendum to Public versus Private

Many books have been written on incentive-based compensation generally and stock-based incentives in particular. A full bibliography would be unwieldy and almost impossible to compile in any event, so I provide only the following notes. Beyond that: find an expert.

A stock option is the right to purchase a share of a company's common stock at a pre-established price, known as the grant or option price, during a specific time, known as the vesting period. Companies that issue stock options are granting the right to own a portion of the company. Employees who are granted stock options are presumed to have a vested interest in the performance of their company's stock, and their performance is expected to be reflected in the profitability of the company and thus the price of the stock. In addition, because stock options tend to be granted in regular schedules, with vesting periods at intervals in the future, stock options increase employee commitment to their company. Stock options are a cost of doing business and will thus affect your company's financial statements, perhaps the subject of a conversation with your auditor.

Restricted Stock Units (RSU) are grants valued in terms of company stock, although shares are not issued at the time of an RSU grant and, therefore, there are no immediate tax implications for the recipient. After the recipient of a unit satisfies the vesting requirement, the company distributes shares, or the cash equivalent of the number of shares used to value the unit. Depending on plan rules, the participant or donor may be allowed to choose whether to settle in stock or cash.

Once an employee is granted an RSU, he or she must decide whether to accept or decline the grant. If the employee accepts the grant, he may be required to pay the employer a purchase price for the grant. After accepting a grant and providing payment (if applicable), the employee must wait until the grant vests. Vesting periods may be time-based (a stated period from the grant date) or performance-based (often tied to achievement of specific corporate goals). When RSUs vest, the employee receives the shares of company stock or the cash equivalent (depending on the company plan's rules) without restriction. Your company may allow or require an employee to defer receipt of the shares or cash equivalent (also depending on the company plan's rules) until a later date. As a rule, an employee receiving an RSU is not taxed at the time of the grant.

There are many variations to employee stock option plans (ESOPs) and RSU programs. They may be useful devices for your company, but expertise and sophistication are required.

Conundrum Two:
A Secret is Something Only I Know — How to Talk to Analysts, the Media and Your Brother-in-law

The second conundrum involves secrets and how to keep confidences. Directors are insiders, with access to valuable information well in advance of the rest of the world, which includes many who would dearly love to have that knowledge. The curious hang on our words and parse them for meaning, hoping for a "hot tip". Allow an unguarded moment of conversation with that delightful fellow in the window seat on the flight home, and the flapping of your tongue could be much like that of the fabled butterfly's wing. So, mum is the word, we will never discuss business with anyone who does not possess a company card.

The other side of this particular coin might be described as "disclosure" and here is what Maureen J. Sabia and James L. Goodfellow in *Integrity in the Spotlight: Audit Committees in a High Risk World* (Canadian Institute of Chartered Accountants) say:

> *"The corporate reporting environment continues to change and evolve. No one today should view corporate reporting as being restricted to the financial statements. Corporate reporting now encompasses a broad array of additional disclosure matters. No longer focused on historic accounting results, it now includes information on what drives performance and how value is created as well as prospective elements, such as guidance on future revenue and earnings targets. Moreover, disclosure of a growing number of non-financial performance metrics is being demanded by analysts, together with an ever-increasing number of financial metrics."*

This lengthy admonition places directors of public issuers squarely in the middle. On one hand, watch what is said and then, on the other, disclose everything to the world or at least the entire investment community. And, yes, I am being simplistic, but only because many small companies have never had to consider such situations until they became public. Family-owned companies are dissected at the dinner table along with the roast, because analysts, shareholders and senior management are all likely to have been invited to the meal and they already know everything in any event. Small, closely held companies operate in the same manner. The world changes when either accepts capital from the public market. At that moment directors and other insiders are part of a process of "continuous disclosure", or at least they are except when the rules say they are not.

The wonderful charade known as a "blackout" is a special case. For readers who have yet to experience the joys of a public company please know that it is mandatory to enter a period at the end of each quarter when all communications become constrained and certain financial information is "blacked out" or proscribed along with trading by insiders. There is a certain amount of latitude in setting these periods, but the specifics of a particular situation are not the issue. The point is, that starting sometime just before the end of a quarter and continuing until the consolidated statements are filed, the company is under a blackout. This happens four times a year and for obvious reasons the blackout at the end of the fourth quarter is likely to last longer while the year-end audit is completed. It is quite unclear what can be said during this period. You and your board might believe that you can say nothing, but that is a very difficult act to perform, so some balance is needed, but where is it to be found? The safest course is to refer to information provided before the blackout period, eg, at the AGM, in a press release, in the annual report and so forth. As you can imagine, these are not always satisfactory responses, but the company may not say much more.

With the passage of Bill 198, directors became painfully aware that every syllable communicated by a company's representative can be viewed in some circumstances as a director responsibility. This is, of course, a generality and not strictly accurate — but prudence suggests that it be taken as a truism whether the company is public or private. Obviously, anything said around the boardroom table is privileged, as the Hewlett-Packard (HP) directors discovered a couple of years ago.

In that well-publicised situation, the board suspected an internal leak and decided to conduct an investigation of its own members, as well as certain members of the press, to find out who leaked confidential information to the media. The investigation used a technique known as "pre-texting," to obtain portions of directors' and journalists' social security numbers, which were then used to misrepresent the directors and obtain their phone records. HP's former board chair, Patricia Dunn, who ordered the investigation, and four others who conducted it were charged with felonies for using deception to obtain the personal phone records of board members, HP executives and nine reporters.

The fallout from the HP debacle made it clear that companies should take a hard look at how they deal with the board book, agendas, attendance, minutes, committee materials and other corporate governance documents. For directors, these are the tools of the job, and it is easy to treat them casually. By handing sensitive material over to be copied or by leaving it on the corner of a desk, controls begin to erode and the risks of leakage blossom. Though disclosure can be accidental, reducing the risk is critical in protecting your company's intellectual property and reputation.

Most companies rely heavily on some form of electronic distribution, perhaps a musty old fax machine in shipping, but more likely the Internet. This would seem to be efficient while avoiding the problem of documents lying around for prying eyes, but the board book is usually large and directors prefer to read a paper copy, where notes can be added prior to the board meeting. One way around this dilemma is to use a mixed media style of dissemination to the board, sending printed board books in the traditional manner while using a website secured by encryption for especially sensitive information. Encryption known as Secure Socket Layer or SSL is the daily protection of millions of consumers and businesses as they perform transactions, such as online banking and purchasing. It is an easy method of controlling the valuation of an acquisition, for example, by revealing the information only online and restricting the ability to print it. Paper copies can be provided at the board meeting and collected at its end.

During the Second World War, the phrase, "Loose lips sink ships", graphically illustrated the disastrous outcome of treating information casually. Directors are required to ensure the disclosure demanded by compliance regulations, but they need to be equally assiduous in protecting information that might threaten the company by attacking its position in the market, its reputation, its bargaining position during an acquisition and so forth. Given their responsibilities with respect to risk, directors ought to ensure that everyone in and around the company is trained on what can and cannot be said under all reasonable scenarios — and some unreasonable ones. Think about the unguarded moments, when what may seem helpful or simply polite is actually akin to selective disclosure or revealing a competitive advantage. Imagine the damage when a competitor learns the secret of the company's ability to respond so quickly on bids or when someone from the media hears that the company is in negotiations to buy its chief rival.

One DOC issue is to ensure that everyone with access to sensitive information is required to sign a confidentiality agreement, and the more binding it is, the better. It is good risk management. At the time of writing, at least four companies are struggling to repair the damage caused by former employees using company secrets for their personal benefit. Sleeman Breweries is suing a former regional sales executive and his new employer for $3 million and the return of stolen confidential documents describing everything from business strategy to customer incentives. Toymaker Mattel is also suing a former sales director, and First Financial is suing a former vice president of operations, and there are remaining echoes of the recently settled Air Canada suit against WestJet for taking flight and pricing details from a confidential website.

As one commentator put it, "Let's not pretend business is a friendly game".

Never forget, not even for a moment, that a secret is secure when it is known to one person, and the risk of its discovery rises with the addition of each and every person added to the pool of those in the know.

Conundrum Three: Best Practice — or Regulated Practice?

Those of us in Western economies think of civilization as including more complex patterns of ownership and exchange than less organized societies. Generally, we live in one place and accumulate property, and we trade for goods and services in a market system. We have agreed to use money as a universal medium of exchange for these often complex transactions, and we have developed equally complex rules and regulations as to how we will manage them. We should not be surprised that sometimes those concepts come into conflict with one another and corporate governance is not an exception. The following anecdote is one such instance.

Atlantis Systems Corp.

In December 2006, the OSC notified Atlantis Systems Corp. (I was chairman of the board at the time) that it wished to question the company's continuous disclosure and other pertinent aspects of its public reporting. On the surface this seemed like a normal course review, with nothing unusual about it.

Atlantis' number had been drawn. In the manner of these procedures, questions were asked and answered, with each set of answers followed inevitably by more questions. It quickly became clear that the OSC was focusing on a particular aspect of revenue recognition involving a very large contract with multiple deliverables. The Contracted Flying Training Support contract consisted of two major parts, the first part was worth approximately $60 million and was to be completed within the first 30 months of the contract. The second part was for about $20 million and was a 20-year agreement to supply support and upgrades to the original work. The issue centred on whether there were two contracts or one and whether the revenues should thus get different revenue recognition treatments.

The company had consulted Deloitte and Touche, the external auditors, and everyone had concluded that the contracts were separate, one for the initial work, and one for the support programs. As the inter-play with the OSC ground slowly forward, the regulator gradually became satisfied on all issues except the argument over which decision of the Emerging Issues Committee (EIC) of the CICA was applicable. For those so inclined, it was an argument over applying EIC 142 (Revenue Arrangement with Multiple Deliverables) versus EIC 143 (Accounting for Separately Priced Extended Warranty and Product Maintenance Contracts).

The backdrop to all this was, ostensibly, the imperative of the regulator to protect the investor by ensuring that all listed companies have full and complete disclosure, a most agreeable goal. The origins of inquiries such as the one that arrived at Atlantis in December 2006, lie with the work of the CICA Accounting Standards Board and its EIC, which examines various sections of the *CICA Handbook* and issues interpretive abstracts on a monthly basis. In other words, although all this discourse and change is within GAAP, the fact is that the interpretation of the rules of engagement keep changing. Notice that I did not say that the rules are always changing, although occasionally they do, but that their *interpretation* evolves, and it does so constantly. Atlantis was quite aware of the difficulties imposed by shifting sands and sought help from its auditor. A very carefully considered decision was taken. Later, it was found to be different from that of the OSC.

The 2005 results were restated to reduce revenue by $697,000 and costs by $483,000, a net change to the 2005 bottom line of $214,000 as both revenue and costs were moved into 2006. To the extent that these changes represent shareholder value, they were moved from one year to another. There was no net change over 2005 and 2006 taken together.

The period from early December 2006 through late March 2007 saw the CEO and the CFO completely distracted by this process, with extraordinary amounts of time and effort by various members of the accounting and finance group, plus the board of directors. Accounting and legal fees went through the roof, together amounting to almost $200,000, an interesting sum to compare with the amounts being moved from year to year. Of course, since the share prices did not react positively to the restatements, the cost in professional fees was a net loss in shareholder value.

Conundrums Faced

The reader may be left to ponder how this tale illustrates what seems to be a conflict between best practice and regulated practice. Certainly, it cannot be both, for surely the best practice would always accrue value to the company and its shareholders and, in this case, the only change was to issue cheques for professional fees. Investors were not protected more completely, there was no wrongdoing and disclosure was not improved.

Let us go to another example.

The Toronto Stock Exchange

On November 16, 2005, the TSX Group Inc. (TSX Group) restated its consolidated financial statements for fiscal years 2003 and 2004. The Revised 2004 Management Discussion and Analysis states that, "TSX Group has retroactively changed its revenue recognition policy for initial and additional listing fees to comply with Canadian Institute of Chartered Accountants' Emerging Issues Committee Abstract EIC-141".

The EIC, around since 1988, was created to provide "a forum for the timely review of emerging accounting issues that are likely to receive divergent or unsatisfactory treatment in practice in the absence of some guidance". That is laudable, but occasionally the folks who write the rules create situations which are more than passing strange. Such was the situation with the TSX Group and the fees to list on the exchange. The revenues in question, which are non-refundable, must now be recognized over a 10-year period; before EIC 141 became effective in January 2004, such fees were recognized at the time they were received. When the encyclical arrived the TSX Group consulted its auditors, one of the Big Four, and reviewed its accounting policies. It was agreed to continue declaring listing fees in the year in which they were paid. Then, as stated in the revised MD&A for 2004, "the interpretation of EIC-141 — evolved and precedents have been established". The TSX Group and its auditors were sent back to the drawing board and two years were restated.

Leaving aside any speculation whether the 10-year amortization is appropriate, the net effect is that the TSX Group consolidated statements now carry a whopping amount of deferred revenue, well over $300 million and rising quickly. So here is my question: how would you design a performance management system for executives in this situation? Good design creates strong links between achieving an objective and the reward for that performance. Usually, this takes the form of a bonus in addition to the base salary, and it would certainly be paid in the year earned rather than spread over 10 of them.

Reading through published materials, it seems that turnover is low at the TSX Group, even though financial executives are a hot commodity. One might assume that when a bonus is earned it is paid, so my guess is that the dilemma has been resolved by a reckoning to provide the basis for performance bonuses, whether it agrees with EIC-141 or not. One might ask, "What am I supposed to do when bonus calculations cannot be based on what we disclose, because that is not the way we run the business". I have no idea if there is a ruse to resolve the discrepancy between performance rewards in a given year and revenue recognition over 10 years, but it has probably been found. So there is compliance on one hand, good management on the other.

Conundrum Four: The Misplaced Comma

Those who toiled through grammar and punctuation classes, wondering whether there was a point, would have been surprised to read a *Globe and Mail* article on August 21, 2006. Millions of dollars apparently hung in the balance on the existence and location of a comma.

The story began four years earlier, when the Rogers Cable company signed a contract to string its video cable on telephone poles owned by Aliant Inc. (now Bell Aliant) and power line poles owned by the New Brunswick Power Corp., at an annual rate of $9.60 a pole.

When an agreement between Aliant and New Brunswick Power Corp. changed in 2004, the annual rates jumped to $18.91 a pole, and since Aliant could not pass this increase on, it told Rogers in January 2005 that it would terminate the contract in February 2006. Aliant's interpretation of the contract said it could be broken at any time with one year's notice, whereas Rogers believed that the contract was in effect for five years, until May 31, 2007.

In 2006, the Canadian Radio-television and Telecommunication Commission (CRTC) ruled in favour of Aliant, saying the placement of a comma in one part of the contract allowed its cancellation at any time as long as Aliant gave one year's notice. Rogers fought that decision on the basis that the French version of the contract clearly stated that it was to last for five years and that the English text was ambiguous due to the placement of the comma.

On August 20, 2007, the CRTC reversed its previous decision, explaining that it was "appropriate to prefer the French-language version as it has only one possible interpretation". The regulator, however, cannot force Aliant to stick by the lower rates in the contract because the Supreme Court of Canada ruled in 2003 that the CRTC does not have control over electric power lines.

There — you understand all that, of course?

Summary

The spate of corporate scandals that sparked SOX is, for the moment, behind us. We have time to reflect on their origins, and I want to pose a small question about situations that were described as fraudulent accounting. Misleading accounting certainly abounded, but then it still does. Imagine that you are a bank manager and you hold the mortgage on the home of one of your customers. When everything proceeds as expected, your bank receives a payment on the mortgage every month, probably by deducting it from the customer's account. The bank views that mortgage as an asset, but it cannot know with absolute certainty that the loan plus interest will be repaid until the last payment has been made. In fact, if there is a provision for accelerated payment, the bank cannot know the absolute amount of money to be received as repayment of principal or interest on the mortgage. In the interim, the mortgage is carried as an asset, perhaps with some allowance for risk. The bank has made a prediction and then placed that estimate in its books of account, and we all agree that this is acceptable, correct?

You probably know that IFRS are just over the horizon, and your board may have begun considering what it will do about their arrival in 2011. Aside from your corporate considerations, do you realize that — if the current practice prevails — the insurance policy on your house or car will become a financial instrument? In other words, under IFRS it will have a fair value in the hands of the insurance company, which must recognise revenue by matching it with risk, ie, over the life of the policy. This may be good or bad. No comment, but it will have effects that flow downhill, just like everything else. It is another example of a regulation or standard likely to have rather dramatic effects beyond the original rationale for its existence. The IFRS are likely to provoke the "Law of Unintended Consequences", which, as you know, operates in the manner of a bus on a city street in winter when it zips past with a load of passengers while spraying pedestrians with lumps of mushy snow: great intentions, with side effects. SOX and its progeny have certainly done that, and so have the increasingly difficult interpretations of various GAAP, regardless of their origins, in the way in which they obscure the day-to-day operations of a company.

Good governance, sound management and much of common sense are remarkably similar, but compliance with one-size-fits-all regulations is often at odds with all three and the intricacies, especially the interpretations, of GAAP rarely add clarity. Finding an accommodating path is a conundrum for directors.

Questions to Ask

One of the questions put to each of the Wise concerned their reasons for joining a board in the first place; an issue that never occurs to those who want a directorship so badly that their acceptance follows the invitation in a heartbeat. That is most unwise, and the following anecdote will make the point.

In the summer of 2005, I was asked to join the board of a sliver of a company and become the chair of its ADC. It had been essentially bankrupt before the president and CEO had convinced the majority shareholder that he had access to intellectual property that could be brought into the company and that he could secure financing to turn the company around and make something of it. This same shareholder had taken the company public through a reverse takeover during the dotcom years, but his reach had exceeded his grasp, and it had languished ever since.

Chairs and Tables

It looked like more work than it was worth, but the president was enthusiastic and answered my initial questions quite well. The company was about to raise equity, and an independent chair for audit would be valuable, so I contacted the other three independent directors. One of these was a former deputy minister in a provincial government and a successful entrepreneur in IT. He appeared to be solidly supportive of the CEO, as were the other two directors. Further, the company was in a technical field where I was comfortable and could make a contribution. The date for the proxy mailing was at hand and I agreed to let my name stand, but I signalled my intent to complete a thorough due diligence and warned that I would resign if there were problems.

A family illness intervened and I was distracted for about three months, so that the fiscal year-end was approaching when I finally began serious due diligence. I reasoned that I might accomplish some of my investigations while I prepared for the year-end audit. I made arrangements to meet the external auditor and scheduled a meeting with the comptroller after sending along a list of documents that I wanted to examine.

I will cut the story short at this juncture, for a novel in the style of John Grisham could be written about the next few months. For reasons that are now obvious, I have not identified any of the players in this little saga. It started when I looked at the audited statements from the previous year. Among the liabilities was a loan from the founder, who was still a significant shareholder at 18%, and the fact of the debt was not necessarily a concern. Then I asked to see the debt instrument, but it could not be produced. The provenance of the loan quickly became murky and an indicator of possible risks. When it became evident that the external auditor had accepted the situation without a document to substantiate the loan, I demanded a sworn affidavit from the founder. When the answers to questions put to the auditors were evasive, I changed firms. Next, I found that the CEO was being paid as an independent contractor, in spite of the fact that he was an officer of the company, that he was obviously working full time for the company and that he was on the company's benefits plan. Statutory deductions had not been made. Things went downhill rapidly as we began the audit. Ultimately, the president and CEO was suspended and later released for cause. Among other things, he had falsified his PIF with the TSX-V and had admitted to fraud.

It is a long and sad tale, but it did teach me lessons. The experience did provide insights into human nature, and it certainly taught that even a reasonably careful due diligence process might not discover a bad apple if it is far enough down in the barrel. First, the audited financial statements were initially accepted at face value, a reasonable thing to do and, but for a chance remark by another director, the founder's egregious loan might never have been discovered. The comment was not in the context of the loan, but it rang the alarm that sparked a much deeper investigation. Had we not had that short conversation, I would not have looked, the loan would have gained validity through another year's audit and the accommodating external auditor might still be in place. Second, as the audit progressed, it raised serious questions about the probity of the president and CEO. I had not checked his background beyond the apparent support from the other directors, and the fact that he was the chair of a large healthcare organization. This was a government appointment requiring a police check of his background and obviously he had passed muster. The true circumstances were hidden, because while the president and CEO had admitted his fraud to the organization that he had conspired against, and then paid a partial restitution, he had never faced a charge before the courts. Ergo, there was nothing for the police check to find.

The conundrum just described is the amount of time and effort to invest in due diligence when asked to join a board. The easy answer is, as much as it takes, but how much is that, exactly? How far must you go to satisfy yourself that you should say yes? This experience has been related to a few other directors, and it is not unique except in its specifics. The lesson for all directors, especially at the point of joining a new board, is that you cannot ask too many questions and you cannot rely on what seems obvious. It is completely appropriate and you are fully justified in putting the company on notice that you will not consider yourself finished with due diligence — and thus committed to the new company — until after an audit has been completed. You might also ask to be part of the audit process for that year whether you are on the ADC or not. It will contribute to your orientation and round out the due diligence that is good management of the risks to you as a director.

Chapter Eight:

Special Relationships

The central role of the board of directors carries with it a group of important, relationships, some of them crucial, and this is as true for small companies as larger ones. As the keystone in the arch that spans corporate governance and management operations, the board and its chair must present many faces to many views, which have to be collectively coherent. There is the obvious relationship with the shareholders and, if the company is public, with the investment community at large. Also there is an interface with the regulatory bodies, corporate counsel, the external auditor, the stock exchange, the government and so forth.

There is a particular significance to the relationship with both the CEO and CFO; perhaps the most important is the partnership between the chair of the board and the CEO of the company. This chapter begins with a case study of how this latter relationship played a crucial role in helping one company recover financially and then move on to grow and prosper.

The Chair and the CEO: The Atlantis Systems Case

The redoubtable Snoopy always began his epics with "It was a dark and stormy night" — but he was writing a novel and, while this is a good tale, it is fact rather than fiction. It is the story of Atlantis Systems Corp, how it was reinvigorated and the role of corporate governance during that passage and today. Atlantis is a small company, only now (mid 2007) approaching $40 million revenue, so readers may need a bit of background to set the context.

Atlantis was founded in 1978 by engineers with a passion for aerospace and a belief that simulation was the key to training people in complex and often dangerous situations. It grew modestly in its early years, and then in the mid nineties it had a break-out success when it developed the first flight training device to be approved for training purposes by the US Federal Aviation Authority. This substitute for a "full flight" simulator had 80% of the capabilities, but cost about one sixth of the large, mechanically complex simulators that were the standard to that point. Growth brought in venture capital and, as the company outgrew its founders, new management. In 2001, Atlantis became a public company (Atlantis trades on the TSX under the symbol AIQ) through an RTO, and the future was very bright — until the events of September 11, 2001.

Commercial aviation was thrust rudely into a steep dive, from which it is only now recovering, and Atlantis was, just as suddenly, in deep trouble. It turned to military aerospace, and the creativity and technical strength of its engineering team won a major contract to design and build maintenance trainers for the Boeing F-18 fighter plane. This continued a tradition of engineering excellence that had produced many technical success stories: maintenance trainers for the Boeing F-15, the flight training device that had been sold around the world, a pilot selection system and others recognized for their engineering excellence, high quality and the fact that they just did not break. By early 2004, the excellence of its products and its high standards of quality had been recognized with ISO certification (International Organization for Standardization), acceptance by world-class companies and militaries.

There was, unfortunately, another side to the story. Musical chairs in the executive suite and the lack of a clear vision had created a culture of uncertainty and, with deep financial woes, a chronic habit of finger pointing. The tools and trappings of professional management were missing — no job descriptions, no performance management, no emphasis on learning and development, no marketing and no business planning. While justly known for high quality, Atlantis was equally well known for late delivery. Finally, the term "corporate governance" was seldom if ever heard at head office.

That was the situation confronting Andrew Day, the new president and CEO, on April 1, 2004 as he arrived to continue the financial reorganization and rebuilding of the company. He had led a successful financing that kept the wolf from the door, but unless the company could deliver on a major contract due in November it would all be for naught. The priority was saving the company, but the employees had been disappointed many times and their lack of trust was a major obstacle to both productivity and the acceptance of change.

The previous board of directors had graciously stepped aside and an entirely new board was presented at the AGM on August 26, 2004. The new board immediately confronted a slate of tough, but basic, issues. These were not unexpected, but knowing of their existence did nothing to lessen their import for the critical first months. In addition to the multitude of operational issues facing the CEO, the directors had another layer of challenges. The new chair had been involved with the deal from the outset, and he and the CEO had recruited directors with an eye to the future. One very practical implication was that the new directors were largely unacquainted and some were complete strangers.

But in spite of multiple and diverse issues, many intractable in the short term, the new board and management team deliberately chose to set their sights on achieving full compliance within 18 months. (In August 2004, this meant the TSX 14 points with "harmonization" in progress.) It was a tall order, requiring careful thought if there was to be any chance for success. Atlantis was of modest size and resources, and those resources had to be rationed carefully.

Wisdom and governance alike dictate the separation of the chair and CEO jobs, but that very separation creates a relationship between two powerful roles with differing goals. True, they overlap, but only partially, and the board-CEO relationship predicts much about the creation of enduring value as well as effective governance. Like most relationships, it is all about chemistry, communication, collaboration and focus. The chair and the CEO of Atlantis wanted to get that mix right. They were accustomed to an open, transparent working style based on mutual respect, trust and confidence in each other, and they wanted to embed this style into the company and the board, as well as between the two. They made some deliberate choices of catalysts to get this started.

The president and CEO immediately instituted monthly town hall meetings for employees, and the chair attended informally even before the new board was elected. The practice continues today, and after the new board was in place, directors were welcomed and frequently still attend, especially the chair. Informal feedback suggests that employees regarded director involvement of this sort as a strong indicator of serious, long-term interest, an important factor in alleviating their historic uneasiness at this company.

Another tactic was Monday morning teleconferences for the board, so that the CEO could give a condensed, informal overview of operational issues and events. These sessions, a substitute for the orientation that might have been available in other situations, helped develop the director-manager interface and added a frequent input to the management team at a time when this was sorely needed. Eighteen months later these teleconferences became a bi-weekly event that still continues today for its value in maintaining director knowledge of key strategic and operational issues as they emerge.

Directors were invited to meet members of the senior team and develop their knowledge and understanding of them and the company. Neither the board chair nor the CEO were present for these meetings, which had some of the same goals as the Monday briefings, and all directors carried through on a slate of them. In some cases, this led to directors becoming mentors for fast track employees. The practice continues and, while the CEO is always aware of the meetings, directors are encouraged to contact senior management directly at any time.

The chair of the board led "lunch and learn" sessions on corporate governance to instill an understanding of what it means to work for a public company. Short presentations were followed by question and answer sessions as employees learned not only what the new governance rules implied, but how serious the new board was about their implementation.

The chair and the CEO collaborated on extensive workshops to tease out operational issues and to start the process of defining new corporate values. By early 2005, business cards with five key values were in use, with posters in high traffic locations.

An important side effect of these tactics was their role as visible demonstrations of the working partnership between the chair and the CEO. The fact that the chair and other directors attended regularly at head office was tangible evidence of interest and a willingness to help that underscored the efforts of the CEO to impart a message of hope to a workforce that badly needed it. When the chair and the CEO appeared together at sessions involving dozens of people at a time, their working relationship was a window into a new style, and it instilled confidence and began the work of building a different and more transparent culture in the company.

Within a few months of taking office the board began considering draft versions of the documents that are important underpinnings for compliance, eg, charters for the board and committees, position descriptions, disclosure policies and codes of conduct. The board had six out of seven independent directors from the outset, all chosen for particular competencies individually and as a team, and all are of the "roll up your sleeves" variety, ready to work at securing the foundations for governance. Today, several are members of the Institute of Corporate Governance, one holds an Institute of Corporate Directors Designation (ICD.D), and another is enrolled in the director's education program.

All of this is helpful, perhaps essential, but the main characters in the tale were, and are, acutely aware that their personal working relationship is a key ingredient. Convinced that moving good governance beyond ticking a few boxes is a "joint and several" responsibility, they work at it. These pages noted earlier that the chair and the CEO had mutual respect, trust and confidence in each other at the outset, but they also knew that the strains of growth and risk can erode even the best relationship. So, they met frequently at the company offices, they shared breakfast, they stopped for a beer after work, and occasionally, they found time for dinner together. They exchanged text and voice messages, and they "pinned" each other from their BlackBerry. Importantly, each placed a high priority on the other person.

Lessons Learned

Before drawing any conclusions from the case, it is appropriate to relate the results of the first three years. First, Atlantis is proud of the fact that it is fully in compliance and compares very well with the governance and best practice benchmarks set by companies many times its size and with many times its resources. Then, there is the Fast Fifty Award that the company won in 2005 and again in 2006. There is the score of 100% on the ISO certification reviews conducted by third-party auditors. There is the fact that Atlantis is now an "on time, on budget" supplier. The company was recognized by the Ontario Chamber of Commerce as the best small company in Ontario in 2006. Finally, from revenues of about $16 million in 2004, Atlantis more than doubled revenues within two years.

What insights can be taken from the story? Three stand out. They were, and are, important to Atlantis and, I suggest, to all small companies.

1. **Mutual respect and trust are the key ingredients** in the mix that forms the chair-CEO relationship. Develop them in whatever manner works for you in your particular situation, but develop them you must. Failure to create that bond will threaten the company and your shareholders' investments.

2. **Work at it.** The chair and the CEO spent a great deal of time injecting fundamental values into the corporate culture mix. They knew what they wanted, but trust and openness had to be earned, and they chose to conduct much of that work in a visible way that itself was part of the transition to a new style.

3. **Maintain the focus.** The diagram in "Head In, Hands Out" describes how the allocation of chair and board time changes as a company grows and matures — but it also shows that it is never 100% in either domain. The chair may be challenged to switch roles frequently, but the focus on oversight must be kept constantly in mind.

This short summary describes a highly collaborative relationship between a CEO and a chair, something both strived for because they believed that was to the significant advantage of the company. Readers should not conclude, however, that this diminished the role — or the accountability — of the CEO. A corporation cannot be run effectively with different voices of authority. Harry Truman knew that the "buck" stopped at his desk, and so does every other CEO, a basic principle to be heeded by every board.

While this case was written about the chair and CEO as they struggled to save a company, a longer and more complete story would have brought other members of the CEE Suite onto the stage. The section on standing committees of the board noted the dotted line relationships between their chairs and functional leaders in the company. After the CEO, the next interface is with the CFO.

The Chief Financial Officer

Readers will notice in the charter templates and in other references at the end of this book, that the view expressed herein is that the board should be involved in the selection of all members of the CEE Suite, not solely the CEO. That is certainly true in the case of the CFO, a stance supported by the requirements of CEO/CFO certification and the importance of that process not only to the company and investors, but to the level of risk borne by the directors.

Chairs and Tables

The ADC is the best vehicle to carry the board's interests when the CFO is being selected. This group includes those closest to the demands of the job, people who understand accounting and finance both as a function within the company and as the key to public disclosure and relations with shareholders. The chair of that committee plus the committee members should be deeply involved in developing the job description for the CFO and the profile for the right person to fill that job at a given time. And this is exactly where the relationship between the players takes on its special nature. In many companies the CFO is the right hand of the CEO, who will want and must have the final decision on the candidate, because the chemistry between them is too important to risk any other approach. Accomplishing the several goals of the process can be ensured by having all of the final candidates for the job match the profile agreed by one and all, so that regardless of which one the CEO chooses, that profile is in place. When everyone is pointed in the same direction this rolls forward in sequence: job, profile, a candidate pool, screening to finalists and choice by the CEO.

Assuming that all this has gone smoothly and the CFO is in place, what should the directors expect of the person running finance and accounting? We all know that the CFO should report to the board on all key performance indicators with a financial tone plus alert the directors to risks; that is the one-line job description. Those with board experience also know about the sometimes impenetrable masses of paper that pass for "reporting to the board". It need not be so. To illustrate, this is how one truly effective CFO tackled her relationship with the board. Anne Mackenzie is not her true identity, but the real life CFO in this anecdote will recognize herself, so, "Anne" please accept a well-deserved tribute.

The value of this CFO lies not in her knowledge or experience, although both are formidable, but in the way she applies them, with creativity and a view that the board is a customer. The comprehensive exams for her Chartered Accountant (CA) designation were dispatched with ease only a year after she finished a four-year honours degree in business administration and she forsook public auditing after a rapid rise to manager level and a terrific offer from a client. From there to controller, another move to a first job as CFO and then, happily, to the role where we met when she became the VP Finance and CFO of a company where I was on the audit committee.

Anne made her value known immediately. Within the first month in her new role, she had interviewed all seven directors, even though three of them had previously interviewed her during hiring. She asked each director the same question, "What information do you need to carry out your duties as a director?" This tactic of walking around the table to our side was greeted warmly, and our answers formed the basis for a draft overview of the information that she planned to provide. This was followed by a few quick iterations on our preferences for graphics, level of detail and means of access. Anne then sent the directors access keys to a new web portal where we discovered that all our questions had been answered, plus some enlightening additions. As CFO she knew the key metrics used by management to run the business, some of which had been missing from the director's list because they simply did not know them. We knew there had always been a gap between what the board and management considered important, but had never quite bridged it. The CFO added key internal variables to the usual operating results against budget, plus trends and insightful ratios. All this was arrayed with sales and revenue results, covenants, cash flow and high-level indicators of the company's situation for the near and longer term. The package was fronted by a "dashboard" synopsis that led into charts, graphs and tables, plus interpretive commentary.

Importantly, the portal was linked directly with the accounting and finance system, which meant that the information was self-extracting. Once designed and implemented, the work was done; it was automated from that day forward, and it was always current. The directors quickly came to trust and rely on the portal. There was a marked improvement in their understanding of the business, and their questions became much more focused and certainly more penetrating. We now knew and understood the operational issues and the context they formed around the more strategic issues. The board could easily understand why something was, or was not, happening and how it fit with where the company was going. Anne McKenzie had boosted the quality of the board's strategic oversight.

This CFO had a talent for developing and maintaining a terrific and highly effective interface with the board and the rest of the CEE Suite. You and your board may not be able to find her equal, but the lessons that we learned from Anne can — and should — be applied universally. Directors are likely to have busy schedules, and even the most financially adept can find better things to occupy them than trying to extract insights from minutia. Do yourself a favour and find a CFO who understands (or can be taught to understand) the "care and feeding" of the board of directors.

The External Auditor

Since this book concerns itself with smaller companies and many of them are private, including some that are owned by the members of a family, I must explain why the "external auditor" gets a section. It is because, in my opinion, all companies should employ the discipline of the annual audit, a process that should be in objective and expert hands. My rationale is not complicated. I simply believe that a close-up and personal examination of the business model and how the company makes money, carried out at least once a year, is worth the time, effort and dollars that it costs. We could debate the value versus the cost, but that is a discussion for another time. I believe the costs of an annual audit are justified since, for example, keeping peace in the family or trust between shareholders are priceless outcomes. However, the intent of the next few paragraphs is to examine the relationship between the directors of the company and the external auditor, not debate the latter's existence.

The chain of delegation from board to ADC to external auditor implies reliance on the special knowledge and professionalism of the external auditor. Even the most sophisticated directors cannot match the currency of the auditor's knowledge, nor their breadth and depth of experience in resolving accounting issues. So, no surprise, the relationship relies on those qualities, and it engenders comfort.

With that said, directors would be wise to reach their comfort through a few well-chosen exercises, and again I lean towards similar, if not identical, practices for all companies, rather than specialize for those on the stock exchange. More than merely good practice it is essential for directors to understand how the auditors do their job. As noted in a previous chapter, the assumption is that all the directors are "financially literate", but they also need, and deserve, full knowledge and understanding of how an audit is done. This is a form of continuing education in which the external auditors keep the entire board up to date on the implications of changes in accounting and disclosure practices, while ensuring that the audit committee is at ease with the details that forced those implications into being. No one wants situations such as those described in the chapter called *Conundrums Faced*. Further, the external auditor should describe the annual audit plan to the entire board, again leaving the details to the audit committee. When the directors know the process, steps, timelines and checks to be completed, they have truly exercised DOC and are in a position to receive the ADC's recommendations after the external auditor is finished.

Public companies now face well-defined responsibilities for ICFR procedures. This is one of the more positive aspects of the changes to the compliance regimen in the past five years, changes which push companies to implement controls which good management should seek in any event. ICFR, as described by the regulators, may be part of public company compliance but they have equal value to the shareholders of any organization. The means of making and fulfilling commitments should have an honoured spot on the due diligence checklist of every director when joining a board, and there is tremendous added value when the external auditor comments on their efficacy. It is an insight into day-to-day operations vital to a director's DOC, and adding the auditor's opinions is worth the costs.

The external auditors should be hired by the ADC, and their selection should be approved by the shareholders regardless of company size and means of capitalization. In fact, in a family-owned business the directors will likely be the owners, and they will certainly be part of management, if not all of it, so this dictum is easily implemented. It requires little thought to see how it might work in other private companies.

All of this suggests that the working interface with the external auditors will be more effective, and certainly more pleasant, if there are positive interpersonal relationships among the major players, something to remember when hiring the firm. The partner who will service your account is as important as the name on the door of the auditing firm.

As a parting comment about audit firms, all the majors and many smaller ones offer complimentary services as part of their business development or marketing efforts. Look for seminars on governance issues, changes to

GAAP, emerging issues and a host of other topics. Check their websites, eg, the Deloitte Centre for Corporate Governance and the excellent "Directors' Series".

Corporate Counsel

We all enjoy jokes at the expense of lawyers — when this was written Google could find 2,130,000 results when prompted for "lawyer jokes" — but the laughter stops in the face of a serious issue. The law defines society's rules of conduct, of "how we play with others", and those rules were long ago codified by governments in an attempt to ensure consistency and fairness, sometimes called justice. It would be an understatement of major proportions to say that the law has become more complex over the years since Canada and the US began building their legal systems on a foundation of English common law. It is simply not feasible for an untrained person to find a way through the maze.

Let us start with what we should expect when we retain a lawyer, which is, broadly, the practical application of legal theory and knowledge to solve the real problems before us, or at least to mitigate their effects. In Canada and the United States, all those with the right to refer to themselves as a "lawyer" have had a substantial education and have then been "called to the bar". Law is taught at law schools, usually a part of a university, and entrance normally demands an undergraduate degree. Your lawyer should hold either an "LL.B" or a "JD", depending on where they went to law school, in Canada or the US respectively. (It is abbreviated LL.B. (or LLB): "LL." Is an abbreviation of the genitive plural *legume* (of *lex, legis f.*, law), thus "LL.B." stands for *Legum Baccalaureus* in Latin.) Following university graduation the licensing process usually requires the graduate to take further classroom law courses, taught by the provincial or territorial law society, pass the related written examinations, commonly referred to as bar exams, and complete a process usually known as articling. Articling exposes the student to the real world, outside of the academic environment, supervised by a principal of a law firm or a jurist qualified for such oversight. Finally, the new lawyer is licensed and "called to the bar" in a formal ceremony, swearing an oath and signing his or her name in the rolls of solicitors.

The "solicitor and barrister" can now practice law in the province in which he or she is licensed. A barrister and solicitor should not be called an attorney, at least not in Canada, Great Britain and Australia. In the US, an attorney at law is a person licensed to practice law by the highest court of a state or other jurisdiction. Depending on the jurisdiction there are distinctions between lawyers who plead in court and those who do not, and similarly the power to act as a notary public may be delegated or not, eg, in the province of British Columbia, licensed lawyers are automatically a Notary Public, but in all others this requires further licensing from another authority, such as the provincial Attorney General. While criminal law is consistent across Canada, Quebec retained French civil law (The Civil Code of the Province of Quebec) at confederation, and civil law advocates (or *avocats* in French) often call themselves "attorney" and sometimes "barrister and solicitor". Your company will discover the rest when you rent or buy property, hire employees, seek a licence or any of a myriad civil acts around your business in Quebec.

While this short tour through nomenclature may help with buyer beware, it is far from the sole consideration when retaining counsel. The recent acceleration in legal fees will be close to the top of the heap, perhaps followed by special expertise, eg, IP, contracts, labour, etc. Your company may want to consider hiring a lawyer as an employee, and this may be the correct decision, but likely for reasons other than legal fees, which will not disappear because you have in-house counsel, since a third-party opinion will be sought frequently. To their distress, small organizations do not get a fee reduction because of their size or financial circumstances.

In common with the external auditors, corporate counsel is an important part of the team and, once again, the chemistry is important. The issues that your company will probably refer to its lawyer are usually complex, often time sensitive and always stressful. Team members rely on trust and an open working style to work quickly and productively. Choose your legal personalities accordingly.

The Stock Exchanges

In 1602, a group of Dutch aristocrats and influential merchants convinced the States-General or Parliament of Holland to grant a 21-year monopoly on the highly lucrative trade with the merchants of India, China and Indonesia. Thus was born the Dutch East India Company, whose owners decided to spread the risk of launching the new venture through an innovative ploy. They raised the needed florins by selling shares or stock in their company, which they then listed for trade on another innovation; the Amsterdam Stock Exchange. Thus the Dutch East India Company became the first multinational and the first to issue stocks and bonds, more than 80 years before a stock exchange began in London.

Over 400 years later, the North American economy rests on its ability to pool capital and deploy it to create wealth, jobs and growth. Stock exchanges do that job and they are plentiful; in fact, there is a debate over the optimum number. Stock exchanges are themselves profit-making companies with their shares listed on the exchange that they own, following the model established by the Dutch East India Company. Each exchange has its own set of rules and regulations about when and how your company can list its shares, when those shares can be traded and so forth. The exchanges themselves are regulated by semi-judicial, non-profit organizations (see the following section, *The Regulators*).

Globally, there are over 100 stock exchanges, and they operate under wildly different rules. In the US, the National Association of Securities Dealers Automated Quotations exchange, or NASDAQ, has the most listings with well over 3,000, although the "Big Board" as the venerable New York Stock Exchange is known, is the world's largest by dollar volume. If the market capitalizations of all the companies listed on the New York Stock Exchange

(NYSE) were summed, it would be approximately $25 trillion. In Canada, the dominant player is the TSX, accounting for over 75% of the dollar value of all shares traded in the country. Other Canadian exchanges include the TSX-V, the Montreal Exchange (ME) or Bourse de Montréal, the Winnipeg Commodity Exchange (WCE) and the CNQ.

During the first few centuries after European settlement in Canada, colonial businesses and governments borrowed primarily from the London capital market to undertake major investment projects. Public shares of large corporations such as the Hudson's Bay Company, the Grand Trunk Railway and the Bank of British North America were largely held in Great Britain. In the mid-19th century, financial brokers began to emerge to handle the growing supply of financial instruments, such as government and railway bonds and bank and mining stocks.

In 1863, a board of brokers was formed In Montreal for the purpose of trading bonds and stocks, and it became Canada's first stock exchange in 1874 when the Montréal Stock Exchange (MSE) received a charter from the Quebec Government. In Upper Canada, Toronto businessmen met as early as 1852 with the intention of forming an association of brokers, but formal records are scarce, so we are left to follow their example and speculate. In October 1861, two dozen Toronto businessmen met in what is now the Masonic Temple at the corner of Yonge and Davenport. They passed a resolution to create the Toronto Stock Exchange. Fewer than two dozen companies, most related to banks and real estate, were listed. Trading was limited to daily half-hour sessions, and usually no more than two or three transactions occurred per day. In 1878, the Toronto Stock Exchange (TSE) was officially incorporated through an act of the Ontario legislature.

After a quarter century of desultory ups and downs, the TSE ceased operations for three months in 1914 when the British market for raising capital vanished with the First World War. The Canadian Government financed the war effort by issuing bonds worth billions of dollars, which were sold to Canadians and into the New York bond market. The war stimulated industrialization and generated such a demand for capital that the number of shares traded on the TSE grew to over 10 million a year by the close of the Roaring Twenties.

During the Great Depression, the value of stocks plummeted and the TSE merged with the Toronto Stock and Mining Exchange, its principal competitor. By 1936, the TSE had become North America's third-largest exchange. Since then, the trading volume and value have continued to grow, with a few sharp declines, such as the one that happened during the stock market panic of October 1987.

The TSE has played a leading role in adopting modern technologies and ideas. In the 1970s, the TSE was the first exchange in the world to develop a computerized system to trade some of its stocks. In 1997, the TSE closed its trading floor in favour of electronic trading. In 1999, in order to compete with foreign exchanges, Canada's major exchanges reached an agreement to realign their responsibilities. The TSE has become the sole market for the preferred or senior equities, the stocks that have priority in the event of company bankruptcy. The ME has become the sole market for derivatives.

Since April 2000, the TSE has operated as a for-profit corporation — the TSE issued its own stocks and declared its first quarterly dividend in January 2003. In May 2001, the TSE acquired ownership of the Canadian Venture Exchange (CDNX) and the TSE was renamed the TSX.

Today, the TSX Group is the home of many of the small- and medium-sized companies that provide the fuel for the Canadian economy. As noted elsewhere, the small- to mid-size companies regularly contribute more than three-quarters of all new jobs and more than 40% of Canadian GDP. Those that are publicly-traded are likely listed on the TSX or the TSX-V. As explained in another chapter, the CPC is a vehicle unique to Canada, offering an alternative to an IPO as a means of entering the public capital market. The TSX is also home to some of the largest companies in Canada, with about 200 issuers inter-listed on US exchanges.

This chapter is about special relationships, and it may seem unlikely that there can, or should, be much that is "special" about the relationship of a board and a stock exchange. My counsel is to take special care so that the relationship remains appropriately distant, and there are some simple steps to take. If your company is private and thinking about a public offering, learn those items that will appear at entry, such as listing requirements, blackout periods and the like. Ensure that all insiders have filed a PIF, a useful device in any case, and implement some routine to check that it is always current. If this is to be your initiation into the life of a public company, spend some time getting acquainted with some of the automatic information feeds that will help you track your company's fledgling shares. Finally, and importantly, learn the intricacies of SEDAR (System for Electronic Document Analysis and Retrieval) and SEDI (System for Electronic Disclosure by Insiders). Your company will be tracked by the former and you as an individual by the latter. As an insider you face hefty fines if you fail to comply, so learn the ropes or find someone who will do it for you. The corporate secretary is a great choice, since he or she has the advantage of regular access and therefore might help the directors avoid penalities for forgetting to disclose a trade in their own company.

The Regulators

In North America, the capital markets are regulated by semi-judicial bodies that have the primary responsibility for enforcing the securities laws and regulating the securities industry and its stock markets. The US has a national regulator, an arm of the federal government called the Securities and Exchange Commission (SEC), whereas Canada has no less than 13 regulators, one for each province or territory.

One way to view this striking difference in practice is to consider what might transpire from inception to listing on an exchange in either country. Incorporation is parallel, with both providing a choice of federal laws or provincial or state, depending on the country. There are differences, of course, but there is broad similarity through this stage. Entering the capital markets of either country might also be described as roughly the same from a marketing standpoint, that is, both require a prospectus, there are similar approaches to marketing the securities, and so forth. To illustrate the divergence, imagine two companies, both intending to operate across the boundaries of more than one province or state, as the case might be. Each intends to attract investors from at least all of the geographies in which they will be active and potentially any others who think the stocks might fit their portfolios. The American company must meet the rules of the SEC regardless of the state in which it is incorporated, where it intends to operate or where its investors reside. The Canadian company must obey the regulations of each and every province or territory in which it has a substantial operation, or in which its investors reside. The handy 10-to-1 ratio, a frequent rule of thumb when drawing an insight about one of the two countries when some fact is known about the other — is reversed in this 13-to-1 landscape.

Readers will draw their own conclusions as to the efficacy of the two approaches.

Canada

When Canada became independent on July 1, 1867, the British North America Act separated the powers of the provinces and the federal government, but with some "interesting" overlaps. Social and cultural issues were important and the regulation of trade, especially along the St. Lawrence River, was a major consideration for the original provinces in the dominion. As a result, they retained many rights and privileges, leading to the current situation of a regulator in every province and territory. (Remember the old tea commercial, "Only in Canada you say?") The 13 securities regulators have the statutory power to regulate the exchanges and define the terms and conditions under which they operate.

Securities regulators from these jurisdictions have come together to form the CSA, with the responsibility of creating harmony in Canadian securities regulation. The CSA describes itself as a "forum for the securities regulators of Canada's provinces and territories to co-ordinate and harmonize regulation of the Canadian capital markets". The CSA mission statement is:

> *To give Canada a securities regulatory system that protects investors from unfair, improper or fraudulent practices and fosters fair, efficient and vibrant capital markets, through developing the Canadian Securities Regulatory System (CSRS), a national system of harmonized securities regulation, policy and practice.*

The CSA's website is replete with words and phrases such as: "collaborating on rules"; "consensus seeking"; "avoid duplication"; and "streamlines the regulatory process". At the end of the day, it does not enforce, as it does not truly have the power to do so. In fact, it admits on its website that its major effect may be educational, "through its efforts to help educate Canadians about the securities industry, the stock markets and how to protect investors from investment scams".

So far, so good — but, as one immortal remarked — "you ain't seen nuttin' yet". The CSA has a super committee called the Policy Co-ordination Committee, formed in 2003 consisting of the chairs from British Columbia, Alberta, Manitoba, Ontario, Quebec and Nova Scotia. Its stated purpose is the "timely resolution of policy development issues". It also has a phalanx of permanent committees and project committees. Permanent committees include enforcement, market oversight, registrant regulation, investment funds and investor education. Project committees are formed around specific policy issues as they arise, eg, short- and long-form prospectuses, continuous disclosure, proportionate regulation and investor confidence.

Of course, each CSA member has people working on policy development and this regulatory thought enters the mainstream through their membership in the CSA permanent and project committees. Everyone beavers away to add transparency and clarity.

These earnest efforts on behalf of harmonization find expression in national or multi-lateral "instruments", a species of encyclical meant to deliver truth to the masses. For example, while each Canadian regulator is responsible for the marketplace of its own province or territory, the word "marketplace" is defined by National Instrument 21-101, which describes marketplace operations as including stock and futures exchanges, alternative trading systems, and quotation and trade reporting systems. The instruments are numbered using a code which can be unlocked to reveal the subject matter. Let us use CSA Notice 52-313, which brought us CEO/CFO certification, as an example. The first digit (5) is the subject matter category into which the instrument has been classified, in this case "Ongoing Requirements for Issuers and Insiders", ie, continuous disclosure. The second digit (2) is a sub-category of the subject matter. The third digit (3) is the type of instrument; a three is a CSA notice. The fourth and fifth digits (1 and 3) are consecutive from 01 to 99 within a particular sub-category, so this is the thirteenth CSA notice in this sub-category. You might want to consult the CSA website and discover how companion policies and forms are numbered — there will be a test a little later.

Lest you conclude that this is sufficient for the purpose, there are four more entities, the Self Regulatory Organizations (SRO), each with its own goals and objectives. The good news is that these particular SROs do not affect companies other than those few within the financial services sector and then only a select few:

- **The Investment Dealers Association of Canada (IDA)** is the national self-regulatory organization and trade association for the Canadian securities industry

- **Market Regulation Services Inc (MRS)** is a joint initiative of the TSX and the IDA, created to safeguard investor protection through consistent administration, interpretation and enforcement of a common set of trading rules in all markets in Canada

- **The Mutual Fund Dealers Association (MFDA)** is the national self-regulatory organization of the mutual fund industry. If you are a director of a company selling or managing mutual funds you will doubtless be more than aware of NI 81–107 and Independent Review Committees.

- **The Canadian Investor Protection Fund (CIPF)** protects clients' cash and securities held in an IDA member, or the TSX, TSX-V or ME member firm if that firm becomes financially insolvent

The major provincial regulators are the OSC, which regulates the TSX, MRS Inc., the IDA and the MFDA. The TSX-V is overseen by the Alberta and British Columbia securities commissions. This means that when your company's ambitions and financial circumstances reach a certain height, not only can it move from one exchange to another but it can "exchange" regulators (sorry, unable to resist). The Bourse de Montreal falls under L'Autorité des marchés financiers (AMF) l'organisme de réglementation et d'encadrement du secteur financier du Québec.

The CSA maintains two highly useful and informative electronic databases. The SEDAR was developed for the CSA to provide accessible public records of all companies publicly traded on the Canadian markets. SEDI is an online, browser-based service for the filing and viewing of insider trading reports as required by various provincial securities rules and regulations. Anyone with an Internet connection can go to SEDAR to view a company's recent news releases and financial statements, or go to SEDI to view insider trading reports.

The United States

Wall Street is a metaphor for the global financial market and how it came to dominance is equally the tale of how stock market regulation came into being in North America. Following the scent from earlier in this chapter, there was once the Dutch West India Company, operating from behind Peter Stuyvesant's Wall, which came to name the street across New Amsterdam. The Dutch had invented capitalism as we know it, and it was so firmly rooted in the colony that when the Royal Navy hove into the harbour and rolled out its guns, the merchants capitulated rather than lose their businesses and their fortunes. The British changed the nameplate with alacrity, and New York became a birthday present for the Duke of York, the heir to the throne of King Charles II. The British thus came into possession of an enormously valuable prize along with the wily merchants who had created it.

There were fundamental and profound differences between New Amsterdam and all the other American colonies. New England had its Puritans, Pennsylvania its Quakers, and Maryland its Catholics, all determined to build communities founded on faith, hope and charity, especially faith. It is indicative that when the Dutch finally got around to building a church, 17 years had elapsed after the colony had been hacked out of the forest at the southern tip of Long Island. They came to the New World to make money, and so they did.

It was many years before New York emerged as a financial epicentre, before it rose from number four among the cities on the Eastern Seaboard to become the home of the NYSE. This is not the place for that story but those with a flair for history might wish to read *The Great Game* by John Steel Gordon for an enjoyable and in-depth portrayal of how it all happened. Suffice it to say that the British were apt students for lessons in speculative technique, and Dutch teachers were plentiful. Gordon quotes Thomas Jefferson for one chapter titled "A Cloacina of all the Depravities of Human Nature". Evidently the affairs of the day were sufficiently odious to deserve attention from the goddess who reigned over the sewers of Rome.

It took about a century and a half before President Franklin Delano Roosevelt appointed Joseph P. Kennedy, Sr., to serve as the first chairman of the SEC. A lot happened along the way, and two wars and the engineering feat of its day were the place markers.

The War of 1812, when the US came to blows with Great Britain for the second and final time, caused the US national debt to climb from $45 million in 1811 to $127 million by 1815. The flood of federal bonds that financed that war was sold by brokers, particularly those in Philadelphia. This latter facet caused no end of envy among the New York brokers and was the motivating factor for the formation of the Board of Brokers, soon to become the NYSE.

Next was the engineering feat that created the Erie Canal. The valley of the Mohawk River divides the Catskills from the Adirondacks, the only way through the Appalachians north of Alabama, and is a direct route from the widely used Hudson River in the east to Lake Ontario and Lake Erie in the west. The first shovel of dirt was lifted on July 4, 1817, and the canal was inaugurated on October 26, 1825. It cost a staggering $7 million at a time when the annual spending of the federal government was less than $22 million. It was far beyond private capital, and the stock market thrived on its financing.

Finally, there was the catastrophic Civil War, when both the North and the South faced desperate financial circumstances. One legacy of that war was the forerunner of the Internal Revenue Service and another was the first "greenback" or federal government currency issued to pay for the war. With both greenbacks and gold coins in circulation a brisk speculation sprang up to trade on the spread in their respective values. However, that trading was miniscule compared with the flood of bonds issued to finance the government's debt, and when they were advertised widely in a patriotic appeal they became immensely popular. By the end of the war the percentage of Americans owning securities moved from about 1% to at least 5% in the north. The Wall Street securities market emerged as the second largest in the world.

There were other bumps in the road to regulation, not the least being the tumult around Vanderbilt and his railway interests, but by 1934 regulation finally arrived in the US capital markets. Established by the US Congress via the Securities Exchange Act of 1934, the SEC is an independent, non-partisan, quasi-judicial regulatory agency. It came into existence in no small part as a reaction to the Great Depression, in turn caused by the Great Crash of 1929. It was created to regulate the stock market and prevent corporate abuses relating to the offering and sale of securities and to corporate reporting. It is responsible for administering the six major laws that govern the securities industry in the US:

- the Securities Act of 1933 (also known as the "Truth in Securities Act");
- the Securities Exchange Act of 1934;
- the Trust Indenture Act of 1939;
- the Investment Company Act of 1940;
- the Investment Advisers Act of 1940; and
- the Sarbanes-Oxley Act of 2002.

The SEC website states:

The mission of the US Securities and Exchange Commission is to protect investors, maintain fair, orderly, and efficient markets, and facilitate capital formation.

The SEC can bring civil enforcement actions against individuals or companies found to have committed accounting fraud, provided false information, or engaged in insider trading or other violations of the securities law. It works with criminal law enforcement agencies to prosecute individuals and companies for offences which include a criminal violation.

To achieve its mandate, the SEC enforces the statutory requirement that public companies submit quarterly and annual reports, as well as other periodic reports. As part of the annual reporting requirement, the company's top management must provide a narrative account in addition to the numbers called the "management discussion and analysis" which provides an overview of the previous year of operations and how the company fared in that time period. Management will usually also touch on the upcoming year, outlining future goals and approaches to new projects. In an attempt to level the playing field for all investors, the SEC maintains an online database called EDGAR (the Electronic Data Gathering, Analysis, and Retrieval system) from which investors can access this and other information filed with the agency.

Quarterly and annual reports from public companies are crucial for investors to make sound decisions when investing in the capital markets. Unlike banking, investment in the capital markets is not guaranteed by the federal government. The potential for big gains needs to be weighed against equally likely losses. Mandatory disclosure of financial and other information about the issuer and the security itself gives private individuals as well as large institutions the same basic facts about the public companies they invest in, thereby increasing public scrutiny while reducing insider trading and fraud.

The SEC makes reports available to the public via the online EDGAR system. The SEC also offers publications on investment-related topics for public education. The same online system takes tips and complaints from investors to help the SEC track down violators of the securities laws.

In the years after the American Revolution the states were jealous of their rights. They restricted limited liability to those companies able to obtain a special, legislatively granted charter. All others, with charters granted under general laws of incorporation, were as exposed as partners in a partnership. It was a recipe for corruption. The Blue Sky Laws, enacted and enforced to regulate the offering and sale of securities at the state level, were a feeble attempt, so much so that the Investment Bankers Association told its members in 1915 how to avoid the Blue Sky Laws by making securities offerings across state lines through the mail. Today, the Blue Sky Laws of most states are patterned after the Uniform Securities Act of 1956.

A Plea for Sanity

It is said that when Rome found that it needed watchmen to watch the watchmen, the empire sank into decline. That thought ran through my mind when I read an especially pertinent version of "Lexington", one of *The Economist's* regular columns. This one had a provocative subtext, reading, "Of horse's teeth and liberty" (October 27-November 2, 2007). How could I resist a title like that?

The article opened with a couple of truly silly examples of regulatory overload, one about the unlicensed filing of horse's teeth in Texas, a technique which I learned was called "floating", and the other about barring miscreants who dare to do African hair braiding without the 1,500 hours of training demanded of "cosmetologists" in Minnesota. I took comfort from the fact that an organization called the "Competitive Enterprise Institute" (CEI) had intervened and both the floaters and the braiders had been rescued from their respective regulatory snares.

There are some fascinating Office of Management and Budgets data that you can find with a lot of persistence on the White House website but this version of "Lexington" did its readers a favor by doing the leg work. Would you believe that, between 1996 and 2006, the annual cost of the main federal regulations were between $40 billion and $46 billion, whereas the revenues (fines, fees, etc) from these rules yield between $99 billion and $484 billion annually.

These are huge sums, and there is more to discover. Jerry Ellig of George Mason University points out that the estimates are based on the estimates that various agencies make when they propose rules, with little or no testing after the fact. The CEI puts the true cost of all federal regulations at a mind-boggling $1.1 trillion a year by including price supports, barriers to entry and the battle to comply with the tax code. That is $3.86 for every man, woman and child in the entire US, based on the July 2007 estimate of a population of 301,139,947. But that is the entire population, it intensifies when you bring it down to people going out to earn a living. *The Economist* article calculated that it costs $7,600 for each employee, every year, simply to comply with federal regulations.

So, if my calculator is telling the truth, as we speak, an employee earning a package of base salary plus benefits equal to $76,000, will cost an additional 10% just to comply with the US Federal Government's regulations? Please allow an impertinent question. How many instances can you recall of fraud, embezzlement or other egregious activity being unearthed by anyone other than a whistle blower? Would that total lead to a reasonable return on that investment of $7,600? I assume that Canada spends less than the US on its regulations, but their efficacy at catching the bad guys is sub par.

A frightening thought is that regulations seem to proliferate, seemingly beyond the possibilities of amelioration. Politicians are reluctant to say what they think or even what their constituents think, especially if the regulation has anything to do with human life (just check those health care rules), a "special" group or anything green, most of which are not, but that is another issue. The economist Mancur Olson (Mancur Lloyd Olson, Jr., was a leading American economist and social scientist who, at the time of his death in February 1998, worked at the University of Maryland) predicted that interest groups will multiply until they push their host economy into decline, a typical parasitic result. Well perhaps we need not go to that extreme, but we do need to be cognizant of our predilection for regulation.

The *Globe and Mail*, on October 1, 2007, carried an article from Nancy Hughes Anthony, the president and CEO of the Canadian Banker's Association, which opened with:

> *"In the continuing debate about Canada's system of 13 securities regulators versus a common security regulator, the facts are missing in action — especially when it comes to the costs to small and medium businesses trying to raise capital today."*

The article was an excellent summary of the deleterious effects of multiple regulators on the Canadian capital market. As I write this, the *Financial Post* has just published a headline, "TSX, MX Talking Merger". That, too, would make sense in the Canadian economy and may influence the regulators. Without any hope of being heard, I enter here a plea for the sanity of a single, national regulator. We have too many regulations of an unusually opaque nature in any single jurisdiction; do we really need to multiply that?

I·R·I
INDEPENDENT REVIEW INC.

bringing governance and competitiveness together

Independent Review Inc. (IRI) is dedicated to the idea that any company can benefit from sound governance while fulfilling its compliance and disclosure obligations and still making money. It also believes that every company is different and demands a different solution. A customized soution will usually require the specialist knowledge, expertise and depth of experience that IRI can provide.

IRI specializes in reducing the exposure of public company directors to simple errors and omissions, small mistakes that should be avoided. For example, boards must now have a written charter plus a code of ethics, they must have policies on board operations, on disclosure and they need a whistle-blower policy. Every standing committee must have a charter. Director orientation is highly recommended, as is regular board assessment. There are a lot of issues to cover while simultaneously attending to corporate strategy, management oversight and creating wealth for shareholders. IRI can assist you in developing all of them, from a totally independent viewpoint.

IRI serves the governance needs of private companies, not-for-profit organizations, government agency boards and commissions. It works from a firm conviction that good governance is largely distinct and separate from the issue of compliance as this term is applied to reporting issuers. The IRI team includes senior executives, former regulators and experts in law and accounting, a well-rounded inventory to deploy on behalf of clients.

IRI provides a "Sounding Board" service for boards of directors seeking a sober, second opinion on any governance issue. It provides advice to small- and medium-size companies that are, or are planning to go, public; and it provides corporate secretarial support to all companies.

In addition to this spectrum of governance offerings, IRI has developed a particular expertise in the issues facing the mutual fund industry, where it has assisted numerous investment fund families to set-up and run Independent Review Committees under NI 81-107.

> **To avail yourself of our specialist sound governance services please call Don Hathaway or W William Woods on 416.849.1928**

www.independentreviewinc.com

Chapter Nine:

Head In; Hands Out

The directors of small companies are inevitably closer to day-to-day operations than those who sit on the boards of billion dollar enterprises, so the temptation to put their "hands in" to management's domain may be stronger. It may also be essential to the company's prospects. When a newly formed company first gets underway or when an existing one faces especially trying times, its smaller size will mean fewer executives at the table to confront the issues, and in many cases, those executives will have less experience to bring to bear. In such cases, the directors can be the seasoning that rescues the recipe.

For example, imagine a small company that has just passed through a change in control. The new owners are either on the board or close to the directors representing them. They deliberately targeted this opportunity because its problems could be corrected with a resulting gain all around. There was leverage in adversity, and the new team bought in because of it, and that included management and directors alike. Following the takeover there will be a period spent addressing the most serious issues, those that were major problems under previous management and caused the largest losses. In the diagram overleaf, this is the turn-around period, sometimes called "saving the company". This is likely to be followed in turn by time spent in transition to a new way of "how things are done around here" as policies, processes and people adjust to the new regime and eventually reach stability.

The graphic is a gross over-simplification, but it does illustrate a fact of life for directors of small companies passing through any dramatic change, be it a takeover, a financial crisis, or any significant threat. The amount of time spent solely on truly governance issues may be slim to none in the early going, as shown at the left of the diagram, but as the crisis passes and the company becomes stable the directors will be able to devote more and more time to their oversight duties rather than management issues. In the chart, management and directors are a single-purpose team during the takeover. Long hours are the norm, and weekends mean little. There is a constant exchange of information while the whole team is preoccupied with the biggest single issue before the company, and there is almost no distinction between director and manager. Then, this phase passes and the team members gradually assume their separate roles, and the directors shift the allocation of the time they are devoting to this company. As the turn around progresses, the directors become confident that the efforts will succeed and the company will continue into the future. They can now consider that future as their focus moves almost naturally towards their oversight duties.

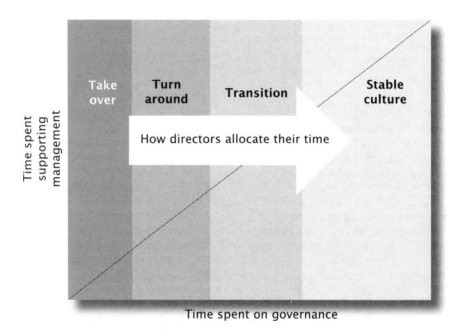

Time spent on governance

It is never this simple, nor is it as unidirectional, but the shifting allocation of time is not only common in small organizations, it may be fundamental to their effectiveness. A turn around is one situation when the amount of shift is pronounced, and another is that wonderfully exotic animal, the start-up. The phrase that is the title to this section should be taken as a goal, perhaps even a great and overriding one, but it should also be recognized as an ideal, something that may never be fully achieved. In fact, in smaller public companies and most private ones it may be neither achievable nor an ideal. When the directors of a private company include or represent the major shareholders, the goals of the company and its owners are likely to be closely aligned, so that their lack of "independence" may not be relevant. There are, of course, many variations, such as a shareholder that is a private equity fund that has goals that are different from other owners or a dominant shareholder who has a personal agenda that may not be in the best interests of the company or the remaining owners. While "head in, hands out" might be applied straight from the bottle for a large public entity, it is too simplistic for undiluted application to the many situations found in the world of smaller companies.

Starting from Scratch

Joining the board of a spanking new company has its own special allure, a siren's song that has caught my ear more than once and, yes, my boat ventured too near the cliffs during a couple of those temptations (referred to during cocktail conversations as learning experiences!). Shipwrecks aside, you might wish to listen to the words of the song because the new tune might be a hit, but keep your navigational aids engaged. Whether you are approached to join a newly minted board because you are independent, or if you are a company founder going onto that self-same board as a matter of course, you are certain to hear one of the many versions of the melodies of growth. The sirens love these songs so you are certain to hear at least a solo — and a chorus could have your ship on the rocks.

This is a billion dollar market is one of those wonderful myths found in close companionship with "we'll all get rich". Such assertions usually rest on the sort of calculation that starts with the population of the entire country, to which is added an assumption that some proportion of that population will buy the new product or service, and the projected market is that number multiplied by the price needed to make the answer come out to a billion. The arithmetic is always flawless, the logic not so much. Before temptation takes over, demand, or do the research for, information that is reliable and substantiated, ie, at least the source data are credible. Establish reasonable estimates of the overall market size, its growth and trends, and spend the time to develop a full understanding. Follow that with close questioning of the assumptions behind the share the new company expects to gain. Request a profile of all competitors and an overview of barriers to entry and pertinent regulatory or other roadblocks. You are now ready for the most important step, crucial if you are serious about joining this company.

Once you are confident of the underlying information, calculate the market share accessible to the company under at least two scenarios, the worst case and the slightly better. Forget about the best case; if it happens the dream comes true, but it is likely to be a long night. You will be doing everyone a favour and saving management from embarrassment when the new company presents itself to outside investors.

Notice that I did not say, "Have someone calculate", the injunction was for you to work through the numbers. Read the Diadem Boat anecdote in Chapter Eleven in the section *Conspiracy of Ignorance* for an example of directors who ignored this step. If you cannot, or if you do not have the time, perhaps this is not for you.

Chairs and Tables

We have a window of 18 months is a belief that owes its existence to the quaint idea that whatever differentiates the new company cannot be copied within, you guessed it, about the same amount of time that it took it to reach this stage. Apparently the thought process was unique, there was never a possibility that another group of clever people were thinking along parallel lines, nor could someone use the original work to gain insights that allow a better version in less time. Be wary of the assumptions about obstacles to competitors intending to enter the market or about the time it will take to imitate a new product. The prudent assumption is that the "window of opportunity" is almost closed. To do otherwise is to add an unnecessary risk.

The technology is ready — and the cheque is in the mail. This myth might refer to the IP that is the *raison d'être* for the budding enterprise or it may simply be an enabling package, such as the loading dock receiving system or the system to manage customer contacts. It does not matter, really. The statement implies new technology or significant alterations to the current state, so assume that this is an "iffy" situation. If its state of readiness is on the critical path, assume that "ready" should not appear in any sentence discussing it. If there has been a "field trial" visit the site and walk through the trial, paying special attention to the results on the day you visit. If a beta version has been released to a few customers, meet them and ask questions. This is not the place to describe the faults in the logic that lead organizations to create new versions of the myth, but please accept my misgivings about pronouncements on the readiness of technology. You might add outright scepticism if the creators of the technology are a research team more or less removed from the realities of commercialization (read: any laboratory, anywhere). As a director, insist on a "Plan B" that takes into account the risk from any and all delays in the availability of the technology, whatever that means in your situation.

The management team is complete is an assertion that should raise more suspicion than it does simply by virtue of the fact that most teams in most companies are *de facto* incomplete at any given point in time — and this is a start-up. This wish arrives in full bloom when the three or so founders of the business have concocted a structure for the new company and have an available name for each box drawn on the chart. I was present at one meeting where the founding president, an engineer, having omitted sales and marketing from his structure explained all with, "There will be so much demand for our widgets that all we need are order takers." The same guy also proposed that a good bookkeeper was all that was needed in accounting, though he expected the company to start preparing for an IPO almost at once. Yes, I am exaggerating, but only a little. Directors joining the board of a start-up should interview the senior team members very carefully, as if considering them for employment. Wisdom suggests that the same team might then be scrutinised in the light of the company's growth plans and the changes those will bring. The truth will out, with luck before any damage.

The business plan will be achieved is a true statement — sometimes. I would love to witness the successful fulfillment of the first business plan of a new company. Directors in the early days of a company will hear its founding president assert that the business plan will absolutely happen; there is no room for doubt, etcetera. To date, I am on hold. You should do two things. One, as a director or even as an advisor you should ask the tough questions that raise the possibility that the business plan might not be achieved. After all, can anyone claim that their assumptions are 100% accurate? You have read rather a lot of newspaper accounts of forecasts and estimates missed by established companies, presumably rooted in experience and full knowledge. Imagine being a seer in a start-up! Your second task is to start developing the governance context by commencing the oversight process even as the board is forming, setting the tone of the board and CEO relationship. In the future, the CEO must seek board approval of the business plan; the initial one may be the only time when it is not subject to the rigour of board scrutiny. Your questions as you do your due diligence may also do the CEO a favour.

The CEO is willing to shift roles. This is a myth propagated by the CEO in question as often as anyone. It seems to arise from self-imposed modesty, a sop to those who question the capacity of the CEO to lead a larger company, or from the CEO's belief in his or her ability to manipulate the situation. Aside from the existence of this chameleon quality, would you expect the combination of self-confidence, ego and exuberance that started the company to countenance a shift to another role? What role do you think that might be? Do you think the CEO will agree to a *lesser* role? Some growing companies have promoted the CEO to become the chair of the board, and while it is a solution it is equally likely that the company will then have a chair without much experience in corporate governance and a strong tendency to invidious personal comparisons.

Summary

Such wondrous myths survive and are perpetuated because boundless optimism is a prerequisite of the entrepreneurs who start new companies. And if unbridled enthusiasm is the mother of optimism, its other child is unthinking assumption. Add a lack of experience, and the combination becomes lethal. In spite of this, the rate of new company formation is strong, with many more starting than failing, so the net number of small, entrepreneurial companies keeps increasing.

Should you be approached to join the board of a new company, please consider it carefully, neither accepting nor turning away. Let us assume that your background is a reasonable fit with the competencies that the new venture is likely to need on its board. You must ask yourself some of the same questions that a board ponders when it considers a new venture, and the first ought to be, "What is my tolerance for risk?" Further, think about your tolerance for ambiguity, for start-up companies are never certain about very much and you could find yourself in the midst of a very uncertain situation for quite a while. Assume that you will need to spend more time than expected, and that will remove another disappointment. Clarify at least these factors first, and then put some serious effort into due diligence, asking all the questions and investigating every angle.

Remember to consider the board-management interface, an important variable over time. As the management team matures the directors will be able to shift away from a consultant or advisor role — if they wish. In some small companies at least, the original directors prefer these roles and a dependency can easily arise. What style does this particular collection of people, this board of directors, prefer? How much experience have they had as owners and operators, ie, what is their understanding for, and tolerance of, the vagaries of a small business — and how closely do they wish to be involved in day-to-day operations?

This is the juncture to reflect on where you gained the experience that is being sought for this board. Have you ever worked in a company of this size? It is equally as difficult for a big company executive to understand small companies as the reverse. This may require a penetrating stare into Pogo's mirror. Please do not blink.

Corporate governance is as important to a start-up as to any other business, and there is an opportunity to make it a way of life for the new company. What things must be done to enable modern standards of governance? Will the company be able to be fully compliant within a year or will it take longer? Please note that I am not differentiating between public and private, because your opportunity is to do it "right from the start" as the following section describes. If you can reach a more or less positive conclusion you should join that board and enjoy the thrill of building a business from the ground up.

Right from the Start

I would like to think that this story will become a case study at a business school, but I am using it here as an example of how one company was determined to include benchmark practices in corporate governance "right from the start".

The true origins of NetFX Concepts Inc. are rooted in the mid-90s, when the people who eventually started the company were still developing their interests in, and knowledge of, telecommunications and IT. They had yet to meet each other. The story is still unfolding as this is written, but this is not a progress report so much as the process by which the founders of NetFX implanted governance practices as a fundamental in that company's culture, while it was still developing as a corporation.

From a purely legal perspective, the company was incorporated in 2006, but its true origins lie in the coalition of the five people who became its founders. Various pairings had existed among them in previous years, but the originators of NetFX truly came together while attempting to rescue another company in early 2006. They arrived too late for that party, but they discovered their mutual interest in the business communications sector and quickly recognized common values and operating styles. By early May, they had formulated the basic plan for the company that was to become Net FX.

At incorporation, all five founders were directors, a legal necessity they planned to change after the financing and acquisition phase at the inception of NetFX. An important turning point occurred in June as they began considering possible directors for the new enterprise after financing was complete. The founders are all experienced senior business executives, either entering or passing through middle age, and they could easily have decided to constitute the board personally while the company remained private. They chose to create an independent board.

Knowing that their investors would expect liquidity within a year or shortly thereafter, they decided to "build a board for the future". Each of the founders had an impressive Rolodex, so there were more than enough candidates, but the list became slimmer when the group concluded that they wanted to operate NetFX in the manner of a publicly-listed company "right from the start". Business instincts drove the choices, helped by a matrix of the competencies judged to be of most benefit to the company in its first years. In the aftermath of that meeting, the founders concluded that one early choice was no longer qualified, and they found another candidate. It was a telling decision, and that meeting became the hallmark for other corporate governance issues. The founding directors implanted governance basics plus the expectation that the company would operate at the highest standards of public company oversight and disclosure, even while it was private.

Governance at NetFX

Here are the rafters and joists in the corporate governance structure built at NetFX:

1. **Board composition:** was largely independent from the outset, with six of the initial nine directors meeting the definition of independence as set forth in the rules for the ADC of a Canadian public company. This was not, strictly speaking, a necessary characteristic, but the founders recognized the value of the tone at the top, and how these early steps would form a board culture consonant with the demands of rapid growth and the triumvirate of evaluate, acquire and integrate.

2. **The chair of the board:** was independent. The roles of chair and CEO were separate as a matter of course, with the founding directors deciding to take this tack from the outset. Crucial to this was the trust relationship that developed between the chair and the CEO who had known each for only a short time and had never actually worked together. Vastly different personalities, they shared traits such as a belief in hard work, dedication, strong organizational

skills and a tendency for bluntness. They used these as common ground and quickly built mutual respect and trust — the basics of the operating relationship between a chair and a CEO.

3. **The board agenda:** includes an in camera session at the end of every board meeting as a normal and expected practice. The chair and the CEO made an early decision to use an executive committee to deal with the fluid blend of operational and strategic issues characteristic of an early-stage company. The executive committee included the chairs of audit and compensation, the CEO, the CFO and the COO, with the leadership baton passing between the chair of the board and the CEO, depending on the issue. The executive committee participates in a weekly teleconference, thus removing virtually all operational issues from the board table.

4. **A board mandate:** was written and adopted in draft form by the company founders and passed on to the independent board for review and approval when that body came into being, only six months following incorporation. The content of that mandate is consistent with the requirements of North American benchmark standards for corporate governance.

    a. **Director responsibilities** include strategic oversight, risk management, succession planning, communications, ICFR, and the overall approach to and process of corporate governance.

    b. **The board code of ethics** is an appendix to the mandate and is used as the benchmark to determine the board's satisfaction with the integrity of the CEO and other executive officers. It is also the basis for a similar and largely identical code for the company.

    c. **Direct feedback to the board** is assured through a defined method by which shareholders, if they wish, can contact any of the independent directors without going through the CEO or CFO.

    d. **Position descriptions** for the chair of the board, the chair of each committee, for directors generally and for all members of the senior management team, were written for board approval. The position descriptions for directors include the standard expectations for attendance at, and preparation for, meetings. Directors are also expected — a slightly different concept — to make some additional contribution to the success of the company.

5. **Orientation and continuing education:** was embedded in the board charter and in the position descriptions for directors and chairs. When its first major financing was completed, the

company founders and senior team held two days of briefings and discussions to provide orientation to the independent directors joining the board. The chair of the board took a leading role in encouraging continuing education.

6. **A code of conduct and business ethics for the company:** was written in draft form by the founding directors and turned over to the independent board when it was formed. It was reviewed, modified and approved within the first months of the board's inception.

7. **Nomination:** of the original slate of directors was by the five founding shareholders, using a competencies matrix aligned with the company's first business plan. A fully independent GNC was formed during the first year, and it selected the slate of directors put forward for the company's first AGM.

8. **Standing committees:** were formed soon after the board came into existence, two immediately (ADC and MRC) and then GNC within a few months. All standing committees have written charters approved by the entire board.

9. **Board assessments:** were a feature of NetFX governance from the outset, but its board elected to use a third-party assessment process.

NetFX is the result of combining separate companies, each with an important ingredient to contribute to the overall mix that became the package of business communications services offered to the small- to medium-sized business market. The founders were acutely aware of the pitfalls facing any single merger, and their decision to attempt several within a short time was not taken lightly. On the other hand, they had been party to, or observers of, the complex situations that can arise during the integration of a merger or an acquisition and knew that this is the phase which creates problems. They believed that they could avoid these problems through transparency, respect and hard work. Integration of the day-to-day operations of the component companies began well before the various deals were formally closed, slowly at first, and accelerating as the groups in question came to understand the values and methods of the new company as it emerged.

Let us step back a moment. This is not intended as a "how to do a merger" seminar. The point in presenting this brief overview of an incredible amount of hard work is to provide insight into how the board was formed and how it interacted with the senior team as the entity called NetFX emerged.

Two factors stood out. First, and foremost, was the simple fact of working closely together during an intense and somewhat stressful period, when issues abounded and the days were long. The other factor was the habit of setting very high expectations for the performance of the emerging senior team and the directors in waiting. For example, this group started with a few members and grew to about a dozen. During just over four months, they talked to each other at nine o'clock every weekday morning. Every morning, with everyone on time and with full attendance unless otherwise assigned. These were people intent on getting the job done and using each other to make that happen. This created trust, rapport and familiarity with each other's working styles. Team building was job one for the senior management team, and the directors were "in the room".

I am not suggesting this as a universal approach, but it worked wonderfully for the cast of the production of NetFX. Most would agree that trust is earned, not given, and that mature and determined people can accomplish a lot. That is what happened, and when the first meeting of the board was held, everybody was on the same page, because they had been reading the book for quite a while.

Chapter Ten:

The Director and the Law

Most of us know remarkably little about that brow-knotting collection of the arcane known simply as "the law". We get by with the basics of the Highway Code, knowing the filing date for our tax returns and the mores of playing nicely with others. Our first lesson may have been instructions about traffic lights or an edict such as "Don't touch that, it doesn't belong to you". The rudiments were absorbed slowly and more or less casually, often as part parental instruction, part object lesson. As a result, many of us scarcely know the difference between social custom and behaviour truly prescribed by some statute written somewhere by some authority with the power to do it. All that changes the day you accept a directorship and with it the additional responsibilities emanating from the act which created the company and the complex legal environment in which it operates. Here is what highly respected Carol Hansell had to say when she gave the luncheon address at "Dialogue with the OSC" in 2005:

> "Directors need not be wrong to be sued — they are very conscious of that. Even directors who are confident of the decisions they are making would be foolish not to be aware that when significant dollars are at stake, lawsuits are always possible. Does this influence the decisions that directors make? It is hard to imagine that it would not, in some circumstances".

Assuming that you are a typical business person is tantamount to assuming that your knowledge and understanding of things legal is relatively modest. However, with a directorship in hand you owe it to yourself, your fellow directors and the company to modify that. This is not to say that you need to enrol at the nearest law school or even take an introductory course for it would not impart what you need. Fortunately for all of us, there is a shortcut. True, it is 232 pages of shortcut, and you cannot afford to miss any of them, but Carol Hansell's book *Corporate Governance: What Directors Need to Know* (Thompson-Carswell, 2003) provides the crucial legal basics essential to being a competent director. Read it, then read it again, and resolve to keep it handy as a reference.

Beyond that advice, these pages offer an update and some other references to help point directors to sources of further understanding of their legal responsibilities and how to discharge them.

The Board and Civil Liability

As the clock on Toronto's Old City Hall tolled midnight on December 31, 2005, about a kilometre away in Queen's Park an amendment of the Ontario Securities Act by the Ontario Legislature passed into law, effective with the chimes. Much discussed and long anticipated, the "Keeping the Promise for a Strong Economy Act", commonly referred to as Bill 198, brought civil liability into the corporate world, at least in Ontario, when it established a new civil regime for companies either listed in or operating in that province. More specifically, Bill 198 established civil liability for secondary market disclosure, meaning the trading of securities after the IPO of shares. The Bill received Royal Assent on December 9, 2002, and certain portions came into effect in April 2003. The remainder, including the statutory regime, arrived with the New Year in 2006.

The Act is broadly applicable. It applies to all companies listed on the TSX or the TSX-V regardless of the location of their offices. Further, the term "registered issuer" is defined so as to mean that the legislation applies to issuers of publicly-traded securities on foreign exchanges if they have a substantial connection with Ontario, such as a local subsidiary or a significant share of the market for their goods, services or securities. The net thus captures much of Canadian business, including the Ontario operations of companies from outside the country.

The crux of the new rules is the requirement that more information be made available in a more timely fashion. Bill 198 requires that corporate disclosure extend well beyond the previous bounds of an offering prospectus or an annual statement. Complete, timely and accurate disclosure must encompass all of what are now defined as "core documents". These include any or all of quarterly statements, MD&A, AIF, press releases and even presentations to analysts and brokers. In fact, any communication could be considered as "core" if it contains information that might influence the purchase or sale of the company's shares. Given this, any misstatement by a senior executive, or an optimistic forecast in a company newsletter without the proper cautionary language could result in a lawsuit that would drain both financial and employee resources and have a detrimental effect on your company's reputation in the marketplace. In summary, disclosure must be accurate and on time, without any hint of misrepresentation, and if an error is made it must be corrected at once.

The teeth in Bill 198 are the risks to a broad class of presumably knowledgeable people, especially directors and officers, but including experts, insiders and other influential people, plus the public issuers *per se*. Companies face liabilities of 5% of their market capitalization, up to $1 million. Directors, officers and those speaking on behalf of a company could be fined up to $25,000 or one half of their compensation from the company and its affiliates for the previous year — but there is a catch. The liabilities are limited only when the sinner is unaware of the sin, meaning that the limits apply only when the defendant *unknowingly* authorized or permitted a misrepresentation. If it can be shown that the defendant knowingly authorized or permitted the representation, then he or she is liable for the total of the plaintiff's proven damages.

With Bill 198 a fact of life, it became much easier for an aggrieved party to launch a costly class action suit. In criminal law the defendant is innocent until proven guilty, and the court system ensures that there is a reasonable body of evidence before action is taken. In civil law, the burden of proof comes to light only after the parties are in court, when a costly and stressful process is underway. The Act allows shareholders the right of action to sue public corporations, directors and officers, influential persons, and experts for public disclosures containing materially inaccurate, incomplete, misleading, or untimely information.

In addition, the CSA, which represents the provincial and territorial regulators, has issued a series of regulations and notices to expand communication requirements relating to Disclosure Controls and Procedures (DCP) and ICFR. Multilateral Instrument MI 52-109 and proposed amendments set out reporting criteria required for 2006, 2007 and beyond. Combined with Bill 198, these new rules will have significant implications for audit committees, directors and senior management of public reporting issuers. The appendices provide a list of some of the pertinent regulations, rules and policies.

During one briefing on the topic, a lawyer postulated that Bill 198 could as easily have been called, "Making it Easy to Bring Securities Law Class Action Suits". He presented a litigator's to-do list containing only nine steps from "find a stock price with dramatic changes" through "look for as many defendants as possible" to end at "consider a settlement strategy". He offered a fascinating — and terrifying — statistic on why it may be prudent to settle rather than fight. The basic approach to such actions is of the "boil the ocean" school of thought, meaning that the plaintiff's legal team will produce an absolutely mind-boggling amount of information, so much that the defendant cannot afford to review it. If 100 gigabits of e-documents are filed, there will be about 5,120,000 documents or roughly 6,400 banker's boxes of printed materials to review. At 42 documents per hour, at a cost of $150 per hour (what does your lawyer cost?), the price tag to prepare for court comes to $1,828,571! He closed that presentation with, "Litigation is a business — and you are inventory". The directors in the audience got the point.

DOC and the Law

The Caremark Case decision by the Delaware Chancery Court may have practical relevance to director liability in Canada. The outcome of the case suggests that part of a director's duty of care includes giving attention to corporate compliance programs designed to prevent the breach of applicable legal requirements, that is, they must monitor the monitors. In his judgment, Chancellor William Allen said:

"I am of the view that a director's obligation includes a duty to attempt in good faith to ensure that a corporate information and reporting system, which the board concludes is adequate, exists, and that failure to do so under some circumstances may, in theory at least, render a director liable for losses caused by non-compliance with applicable legal standards."

Note the words, "a duty to attempt in good faith to ensure". Imagine how many ways that could be interpreted! The decision underscores the increasing importance that courts, regulators and professional bodies are placing on directors overseeing corporate monitoring systems and the role that these oversight activities play in limiting directors' liability.

In Canada, the Competition Bureau has distributed its Information Bulletin on Corporate Compliance Programs. And as part of its Guidance for Directors: Governance Processes for Control, the Canadian Institute of Chartered Accountants has described how a board can discharge its responsibilities, which include "approving and monitoring the organization's ethical values".

A report by the TSX's committee on corporate governance stated that "in supervising the conduct of the business, the board, through the CEO, sets the standards of conduct for the enterprise." That report went on to say that "those standards include the general moral and ethical tone for the conduct of the business, the corporation's compliance with applicable laws, standards for financial practices and reporting, qualitative standards for products of the business and so on".

This is "tone at the top" writ large. Directors are being warned that their DOC extends beyond having codes of conduct and policies ensuring their active implementation. When I first sat on a company board, I was advised by an old hand to demand that every meeting receive a statement to the effect that all statutory deductions have been made. That was good advice, but we have gone well beyond payroll deductions as a source of concern. Directors must ensure that the standards are set, that processes are in place to implement those standards and that the board receives information on their ongoing effectiveness. To do otherwise is to offend DOC.

What about SOX?

The Sarbanes-Oxley Act (SOX) of 2002, also known as the Public Company Accounting Reform and Investor Protection Act of 2002, is a US federal law passed in a hasty and somewhat controversial reaction to the corporate and accounting scandals that plagued corporate America at the turn of the century. It got its name from its two chief proponents, Senator Paul Sarbanes and Representative Michael G. Oxley. SOX was passed quickly and with little dissent, with a vote of 423-3 in the House of Representatives and a unanimous 99 to 0 in the Senate. The legislation is wide ranging, to say the least, for it established new or enhanced standards for all US public company boards, for the management of public companies, and for public accounting firms.

The Director and the Law

The act contains 11 titles, or sections, ranging from additional corporate board responsibilities to criminal penalties. It caused the SEC to implement rulings on how companies and boards are meant to comply with the SOX regulations. Supporters believe the legislation was necessary and useful, while critics believe it does more economic damage than it prevents.

The first and most important part of SOX establishes a new private sector, non-profit corporate agency, the Public Company Accounting Oversight Board (PCAOB), mischievously known as "Peek-a-boo". It is, in effect, an auditor for the auditors and is charged with overseeing, regulating, inspecting, and disciplining accounting firms in their roles as auditors of public companies. Its stated purpose is to "protect the interests of investors and further the public interest in the preparation of informative, fair, and independent audit reports". Although it is a private entity, the PCAOB has many government-like regulatory functions, making it in some ways similar to the private SROs that regulate stock markets and other aspects of the financial markets. SOX also covers issues such as auditor independence, corporate governance and enhanced financial disclosure.

Once in place, institutions like PCAOB are virtually impossible to dislodge, quickly becoming "part of the establishment". Not only are there fewer risks for its officials than for being a director of a public company, but the pay and benefits are not stingy. PCAOB members serve full-time, five-year terms and its chairman is currently paid $556,000 per year, while the salaries of other board members are $452,000 annually. The PCAOB has a staff of over 300 and operates from its headquarters in Washington, DC, with an annual budget of approximately $100 million. The budget is subject to annual scrutiny and approval by the SEC and is then funded by fees paid by US issuers. We might think of this as a disincentive for change.

As a final note on SOX, I enjoyed the views of Alan Greenspan in *The Age of Turbulence: Adventures in a New World* (Penguin Books, 2007): He said, reasonably enough, that while US corporate governance has had its share of shortcomings, it has to be admitted that the US economy has done rather well in spite of them. Therefore, the corporate directors must have got it right at least some of the time. The man has a point.

The Oppression Remedy

Section 241(2) (c) of the CBCA, also known as the "oppression remedy", is unique to Canadian law. In its broadest sense — and this is an unusually panoramic and flexible concept — the remedy addresses conduct that may be viewed as oppressive, meaning *unfairly prejudicial*, to the interests of any corporate stakeholder. It can spawn an action against the corporation itself or its officers and directors. The oppression remedy allows a court to consider the manner in which the company, its directors or its officers have used their powers. If the exercise of that power is found to be have been "oppressive or unfairly prejudicial" to the interests of any stakeholder, the court may make any order it deems appropriate to redress the grievance. In his remarks to the Institute of Corporate Directors on June 1, 2006, Justice Robert Blair described the remedy as a "judicial brake" on abusive powers, but he also said:

"Your corporations — and you, personally, as their corporate directors — are the prime targets of this statutory howitzer".

Given that the oppression remedy can be "brought to bear" by anyone who can qualify as a complainant, Justice Blair's reference to a howitzer is all too apt. The complainant is usually a shareholder, but creditors have been included, as in the case that follows. The director's defence starts with the twin factors that have to hold for them to be liable in the first place. First, the directors must have either taken a specific action relative to the complaint, or they must be shown to have been specifically negligent or inactive when they could have alleviated the conditions causing the complaint. Second, if the directors are to be required to compensate the complainant it has to be shown that there was some benefit to the director through his or her action or inaction. This means that with a private company, owned by a few family members or a couple of partners, the control over the company and the benefits from it are so inextricably linked to the owners and directors that all three parties may be held liable under the oppression remedy.

Peoples v. Wise (David S. Morritt, in the Osler Update: Creditor Claims Against Corporations and Directors: Canada's Supreme Court Highlights Importance of the Oppression Remedy, November 2004)

When Peoples Department Stores went into bankruptcy it started a chain reaction leading to a landmark decision in corporate governance. It all started when the trustee in the bankruptcy of Peoples sued the two Wise brothers, who were former directors of Peoples, for breach of fiduciary duty. In 1998, Mr. Justice Greenberg of the Quebec Superior Court granted judgment in favour of the trustee, finding that all directors owe a fiduciary duty to creditors when a corporation is "in the vicinity of insolvency", a broad definition that could include the time when a company is actually under protection from its creditors or when it is in such financial trouble that it is "in the vicinity". Five years later, in February 2003, the Quebec Court of Appeal reversed that decision. It held that the directors owed duties only to the corporation, representing the interests of shareholders, and that they had not breached any of those duties.

This was appealed by the trustee, and on October 29, 2004, the Supreme Court of Canada declared on *Peoples Department Stores Inc. v. Wise*. Not only did the Supreme Court dismiss the trustee's appeal it delivered long-sought clarification of the duties of directors toward creditors. Simultaneously, it bestowed potentially broader rights to creditors than had been recognized previously within or outside Canada, giving explicit recognition to the rights of creditors as stakeholders of a corporation and requiring directors to owe them a DOC. It also gave directors very wide latitude for honest, good faith and informed business judgments. Ultimately, the Wise brothers prevailed on appeal because both the Quebec Court of Appeal and the Supreme Court of Canada held, on the facts of this case, that they had acted honestly, in good faith, without negligence, and that their actions did not cause the corporation's bankruptcy.

A Director's Considerations

The oppression remedy has very broad purposes, and when those are coupled with statutory language and the vagaries of its interpretation, the best advice is to "be prepared" and ward off the arrival of a suit. Here are a few indicators, more rumble strips at the edges of the business straight and narrow, suggesting the possibility of a suit for oppression relief:

1. **A transaction which is not supported by a valid corporate purpose** may well indicate that an officer is motivated by goals other than those of the company. The individual may not necessarily be seeking personal gain, the impetus could just as easily be a prejudice or personal preference rather than pecuniary advantage. As a director, your signal may be the answer to the question, "Which business plan objective would suggest this action?" If the answer to that question does not make sense, you have another kind of question to ask, and a different issue to resolve.

2. **Failing to ensure an arm's length transaction** is a strong signal that someone is acting in a manner that may attract a suit. For example, one company let the contract for clearing the snow from the parking lot of its manufacturing plant to the same person for years. The cost of the service, when compared with others in the town, caused a new controller to wonder why this particular contractor had been selected in the first place. He expected that an initial low bid had been escalated over the years, but it turned out that the contractor was the president's nephew.

3. **The context of the relationship between the potential complainant, the company and other stakeholders** can be deadly if it includes facets that lend themselves to wide interpretation. These are especially risky when changes or a new view are likely to engender hurt feelings. In one example, the tender spot was an unwritten understanding between the president and a business colleague. They were both involved in the start of a new venture, with a tacit understanding that, while one was the CEO and the other a vice president, they would really be "partners" in the deal and share equally in the rewards. Eighteen months later, the board was faced with Siamese twins: terrible performance by the vice president and an unsuspected context that cost the company a year's salary to resolve.

4. **Contracts which are ignored** will become a mushroom cloud. When a contract written with good intentions under one set of conditions is ignored, it can become a huge issue when, for example, payment

terms become far more onerous simply due to an unthinking change in policy.

5. **Evidence of bad faith** should be a prime suspect. There is no requirement for evidence of bad faith when a complaint is lodged and the oppression remedy is sought — but as a director, if bad faith is discovered in any form, settle the case as amicably as possible for this one is as deadly as nightshade.

6. **Discrimination among shareholders** is less than admirable and when its purpose is to benefit the majority to the detriment of the minority, it is solid grounds for an oppression remedy action. Note that this most definitely includes those situations when there is a grand design to eliminate that pesky minority shareholder. This situation is depressingly common in privately-held companies where two or three shareholders are dominant, perhaps they are the executive team, and they wish to rid themselves of a founder who invested at the start, but has not been active since then.

This list is far from complete, simply a few examples to help tune your antennae.

Please keep the "business judgment rule" in mind, for it offers protection from the court when you can show that business decisions have been made honestly, prudently, in good faith and on reasonable grounds. The court is not about to put itself in your shoes, meaning that it will not try to second guess what it might have done in the circumstances. You were the director, you had the delegated authority and it was your duty to act. On the other hand, this is not an *a la carte* menu. Your choices will be tested to determine if they were reasonable, consistent with the reasonable expectations of the complainant, and did not inflict prejudice.

As a director, you must be able to show conclusively that the business judgment rule was exercised and the decisions taken fall within a broad spectrum of reasonableness. In this regard, you might wish to become familiar with the Repap case, or have your counsel explain it and its implications. Since the transparency of your thoughts and actions may be of crucial importance later, this is another instance of ensuring that the documentation and communications around the situation are complete, candid, detailed and analytical. Obviously, this must be done before the fact instead of becoming the subject of later regret! Finally, read the board minutes thoroughly and challenge their level of detail, for they must show that the directors were engaged and considered all aspects of the situation before taking their decisions. A log of questions and comments could become a vital account of how the directors thought and decided.

I hope this is a familiar refrain by now, and that you identify it as the DOC.

The Director and the Law

The Bre-X Case

In spite of the most careful scrutiny by the most attentive directors, defending against outright fraud is well nigh impossible. It is a sad fact that some people are dishonest, and the rest of humanity pays the price. A recent article in the *Globe and Mail* tells the tale of the Southwestern Resources Corp. and its Boka project, now revealed as a scam effected by altering the documentation of drilling results. The promise of three million ounces of gold in the hinterland of China has evaporated, and an $800 million market cap in mid-2004 has melted as shares dropped from $6 to well below $2. Sad as this story is, it pales in comparison to the granddaddy of all resource sector scams: Bre-X.

On July 31, 2007, John Felderhof was acquitted of all charges in the infamous Bre-X Minerals Ltd scam, Canada's most notorious mining scandal. When Bre-X claimed that it had discovered huge amounts of gold in the Busang region of Indonesia the company's shares soared from penny stocks to peak at $187.55 a share. Paper fortunes were made overnight. The wind changed in early 1997 when tests carried out by another company showed there was virtually no gold in the Bre-X deposit. The original assay results had been "salted", meaning that the samples had been sprinkled with gold from other sources. The fable unravelled quickly, and the stock sank like a rock. Investors lost millions in actual cash and as much as $6 billion in evaporated market capitalization.

The former vice chairman of Bre-X, and also its chief geologist, John Felderhof was the only person to face legal charges in the decade-old case and with the verdict of Judge Peter Hryn, the saga drew to its sorry end. Its inclusion here is not to speculate on the abundant rumours and mysterious events surrounding the demise of Bre-X, but to draw attention to the grounds for the acquittal.

The judge ruled that Felderhof "reasonably believed Busang was a legitimate gold find" and the so-called "red flags" that might have led him to question the reliability of the gold estimates were not as obvious as the OSC had alleged. The judge also said that the tampering of thousands of Bre-X core samples had been so sophisticated it would have been difficult to uncover.

Felderhof has always maintained that he did not know that the tampering had happened. We might note that, after a false start in medicine, John Felderhof graduated in geology in 1962. At Jason Mining in Australia he quickly earned a reputation as a skilled geologist. Further, the initial interest in the Busang Region was through Felderhof's knowledge of the area. Bre-X was promoted in Calgary by David Walsh while Felderhof remained in Indonesia to oversee the team of geologists. Finally, he was the vice chairman and the chief geologist. The claim that he did not know about the tampering is reminiscent of Enron's Kenneth Lay, another person who did not know what was happening in his company.

Nevertheless, Judge Hryn found for the defendant and the verdict hung on those words "reasonably believed". While the case may yet be appealed, it is unlikely.

An infamous scandal has played itself out, dismissing its accusers because there was a reasonable belief. Without commenting on right or wrong, justice served or denied, there is a clear message in these two cases, and in other examples in other sectors: crooks will be crooked. In spite of the most scrupulous care, the most attentive pursuit of possibilities and suspicions, once in a while, the guys with the black hats fill their saddlebags and ride out of town.

Get Understanding

Steve Forbes, the editor-in-chief of his eponymous magazine, writes the "Fact and Comment" pages and just below his by-line is the quotation, "With all thy getting, get understanding". That excellent advice could apply to many, many topics, but we are talking about directors and the law. For those on boards, get a broad, comprehensive but general knowledge of the legal environment in which your company operates, and find competent corporate counsel to take care of everything beyond that basic understanding. You must never for a moment yield to the penny-wise-and-pound-foolish temptation of dodging legal fees, and when you accept complexity and law as inseparable siblings that urge will dissipate as if it never existed. The risks to the company and to you personally are simply too great to proceed in any other way.

With that caution in **bold** letters there is much that can be done to get understanding of the laws and regulations applicable to the business that you oversee. Here is some practical advice, presented as if you have just joined your first board and, incidentally, it does not matter if it oversees a public or a private company, or, for that matter, a charity or a government agency or commission.

> **Start with the foundation**, meaning the articles of incorporation and by-laws if the board is for a company. They should be included in the information package sent to you when you agreed to join the board. While the CBCA and its provincial counterparts are quite similar there are differences and you must know them, and there may be specific constraints embodied in the founding articles and by-laws.
>
> This is a good time to include the wide variety of not-for-profit organizations, some of which are charities. Some trusts, foundations, unincorporated associations and, in some jurisdictions, specific types of companies may be established for charitable purposes or change into a charity after formation. An NFP is usually defined as an organization formed to support an issue of private or public interest while operating without monetary profit. They are active in a rainbow of arenas, including the environment, the arts, social issues, charities, early childhood education, health care, politics, religion, research, sports and so on. The formation and management of an NFP

is regulated by law in most jurisdictions, and it is beyond the scope of this book to delve into the topic with sufficient depth to guide you. Please know that many are required to comply with a corporate governance regime, which probably includes publishing audited financial statements and in many ways acting similar to businesses in spite of their significant differences. Directors of many NFPs owe a fiduciary duty and a DOC very similar to those for a company. Please pay very close attention to the exact details and the interpretation of every clause of the Canada Revenue Agency view of the status of the NFP.

Regardless of the type of organization, you should become familiar with basic by-laws such as the quorum for a meeting, the protocol for meeting notification, whether a director can be added to the board in the middle of the year and so forth. Given a solid legal foundation for the organization, it is part of DOC to ensure that board meetings and processes are on solid ground as well.

Industry regulations come next. Every sector has laws, regulations and standards peculiar to it, brought on by its history, its technology, its economy or other forces germane to the industry and its incumbents. For example, if your company is in the telecommunications sector please feel welcome to the world of the CRTC. The CRTC has been a fact of life since the first Royal Commission on Broadcasting in 1928 and is easily one of the most complex and arcane regulators — but if you are in that sector you cannot afford to be ignorant of its dictums and its *modus operandi*. The advice is equally applicable to many other sectors. Think of the complexities of the pharmaceutical industry, the overtones of aeronautics, the environmental hazards of mining, the effect of labour laws on railways and manufacturing and the paranoia of militaries. The list goes on — know the ins and outs of your world.

Public companies have an added layer. Every province has an act respecting securities, many called the "Province Securities Commission", but with variations such as the Securities Commission of Newfoundland and Labrador, the Prince Edward Island Securities Office, the Saskatchewan Financial Services Commission, and the AMF in Quebec. Beyond these primary regulators some provinces have a commodity futures act, and there are specifics relating to public companies in Canada and provincial business corporations' acts. These are, by definition, the rules of the road prescribed by whichever exchange carries your company's listing, and whether that stock market is in your country or another, whether it is a junior or senior exchange, and so forth.

International trade, the exchange of goods and services across international boundaries or territories, means international laws, treaties, tariffs, licences, restrictions — it is a long list. Even if your company does not have a foreign subsidiary and does not engage directly in importing and exporting, your customers and suppliers probably do. If you have a foreign subsidiary you will encounter "mind and matter" issues, that is, where does real control lie? For example, this admonition (Roger Hanson and Ronan Guilfoye of dms Management Ltd. as reported in Opalesque newsletter) about the governance of hedge funds which, by the way, are usually small companies. Note the words, "location, composition and degree of activity" as the appearance of these and similar words or phrases are indicators of a mind and matter issue.

> *"Ensuring that the full board of directors is located outside of the United States and that they hold regular board meetings, indicating that mind and management are not located in the United States - - - - We welcome more attention to the location, composition and degree of activity of the Board of Directors of offshore funds, as part of investor focus on the broader issue of corporate governance."*

Canada's merchandise trade with its North American Free Trade Agreement (NAFTA) partners has increased about 125% since 1993 and is now about $600 billion. Our NAFTA partners account for over 80% of Canada's total merchandise exports and about 60% of services exported. You may not need a course in economics or foreign policy, but a grounding in NAFTA is basic. If your company becomes serious about spreading its wings abroad, contact the Department of Foreign Affairs and International Trade and Export Development Canada. There is a lot to learn.

Understand the future of regulations specific to your industry and to business generally. As an industry-specific example, in November 2006 the International Civil Aviation Authority passed a new world standard for licensing airline pilots, called the Multi-Crew Pilot's License. Implementing these standards in any given country is the responsibility of that country and the world must wait while that happens, but in the meantime boards of companies in affected industries should educate themselves on how they may or may not affect their particular companies. That tenet holds for every economic sector. If there are certainties beyond the grim reaper and the taxman they are the frequency of changes in the regulations governing our world. DOC advises that directors keep a weather eye on the horizon and, when a cloud appears, commence a little personal education as to what the new regulations might mean for his or her company.

Aside from the ubiquity of environmental laws, a prime example of a generally applicable regulation is the emergence of IFRS. These are standards and interpretations agreed and adopted by the International Accounting Standards Board (IASB) and now rolling into place in many countries. Canada's move to IFRS (to arrive by June 2011) will affect all publicly-traded companies and other publicly-accountable enterprises, and implications are certain for companies with international operations, public or private. Due to the extent of the IFRS changes and the fact that the first actions and decisions will be required as early as 2008, directors need to understand that this transition will go well beyond auditing and permeate the organization.

Within Canada, something to watch is the emergence of the XBRL. On January 19, 2007, the CSA launched an XBRL voluntary filing program. Beginning in May 2007, reporting issuers participating in the voluntary program were able to file financial statements in the XBRL format on SEDAR. In the US, the SEC has a similar program using XBRL to file on EDGAR. History teaches that when processes like these become more and more common their use becomes a *de facto* mandate, or they pass the tipping point and become law.

Making it Happen

The five layers of law just described probably sound like a lot, and the busy director may put off until tomorrow what seems avoidable today. You may argue — if you must — that having the general knowledge just described is not a "reasonable" expectation and should not be expected. That is counter to the concept of DOC, at least as expounded within these covers. It is always possible to react after the fact, but why not avoid legal issues in the first place and reduce the risk to your company at the same time? While the directors may not be close enough to notice new industry-specific regulations even as they develop (although one wonders why they would not) it is certain that someone in the company will be tracking them. Your auditors certainly know about IFRS and your corporate counsel is familiar with disclosure issues and trends. Most of the major audit and legal firms have director education programs (they are really marketing tactics, but they are professionally done, complimentary, and quite educational). You may be surprised to find that one of your colleagues on the board is a closet expert. The point is that there are readily available sources of education for the board and it should never be caught napping.

Watch Your Back

Part of getting understanding is realizing that while all directors face the same slate of risks when viewed from a strictly legal or regulatory standpoint, the directors of small companies are beset with a few that derive simply from scope, scale and financial stability. While class action suits are a danger, they usually target large companies simply because the potential payoff is bigger, whereas smaller companies have a higher likelihood of financial problems that could lead to bankruptcy, or an inability to address an environmental issue, or to be wary of employee confidentiality issues, all with the attendant risks for the directors. I meant all those things that I said about the rewards of being on the board of a small cap, but you should watch your back.

Assume that the DOC will be your best defence and never stop adding sandbags to the levee. This implies that, first and foremost, you never accept a board appointment unless you are able and prepared to commit the time for DOC.

Understand that you and Caesar's wife have much in common. An overly zealous (and somewhat less than fully informed) media has feasted on the few truly egregious instances of governance abuse to the point that the ordinary citizen views all directors with suspicion. You must not only perform well, your performance of DOC has to be patently obvious to all. Here are some ideas to consider:

- **Ensure that your name is in the minutes.** Your presence is not enough, you need to participate and be able to show that you did. Move or approve a couple of motions or resolutions at every meeting, or initiate an issue or ask a question that will be recorded. Make sure the approved version of the minutes includes your efforts.

- **Ask that statutory deductions be certified** at every board meeting. If this is not a standard item on the agenda, ask that it be added and ensure that either the CFO or the CEO presents the information for the minutes. While this should be unnecessary at a larger company, small ones often make quick decisions to conserve cash flow — and the directors are liable. If cash flow is known to be an issue, satisfy yourself that payroll is current, including vacation pay and the ability to pay for unused vacation time in the event of a serious situation. This should be unnecessary in a public company with CEO/CFO certification in place.

- **Ask for regulatory compliance to be recorded.** It is a good practice to ask, perhaps twice annually, if the company is in compliance with health and safety regulations, employment equity, environmental protection and the like. These vary between provinces and states, so knowing the broad strokes is part of "getting understanding" so that you can ask the right questions.

- **Record your disagreement.** There will be times when you cannot agree with a decision of the board, and the wisest course is to ask that your dissent be recorded in the minutes.

My generation of engineers was taught to maintain a journal that recorded everything they did. Every page was dated and if it included an especially important drawing or calculation, the engineer's stamp was added and it was signed so that it became a legal document with the status of a blueprint. I suggest that directors draw a lesson from that practice, for DOC is effective because it is proactive and a good journal can be a cornerstone. I hasten to add that my friends in the legal profession disagree, apparently because the rest of us could not possibly maintain notes that are sufficiently clear and complete to do other than provide ammunition to attack their writer. Such notes can be demanded by a subpoena, and then every word will be interpreted, so the risk is genuine. On the other hand, you can be subjected to discovery and your memory will be in contrast with that of other people and such documents as are available. While conceding the potential risk, I will continue the practice. I record the main points of every business event of any significance, with a summary of what I concluded at the time and why I thought this to be so. My journal includes phrases such as, "as is my practice" or "as usual" so that it is obvious to any future reader that I am following a conscious and consistent regimen.

D&O insurance is essential. Never go onto a board until D&O insurance is in place and the fees have been paid. Having said this, it is equally important to have your lawyer provide an exact description of what the insurance covers — and what it does not — and the circumstances that trigger either case. You should also understand whether the policy pays any costs as they are incurred or if you must defend yourself and then make a claim. There have been very sad cases where a director or officer was virtually bankrupt paying legal bills while the litigation went forward, with a claim possible only after the court proceedings were over. You might review the plight of the central players in the proceedings following the Nortel debacle as an example of the disaster when D&O insurance has holes.

Small company boards are not small jobs. You should be prepared to spend as much or more time as a director of a small company as you would for a larger enterprise. First of all, large or small organizations face the same regulatory and disclosure hurdles and clearing them takes roughly the same amount of time and effort regardless of the company. Small companies, however, are unlikely to be able to place the same resources at the disposal of the board, so directors may be left to their own devices to fill the gap. That translates into time, your time, attending to DOC issues that would be covered by staff in a larger company. It is for this reason that all parties should have a sober second thought during the recruiting process of a director without small company experience.

The management-board interface is less defined. The directors of smaller companies are often called upon to help resolve an issue that would never reach the board in a large corporation. It is a slippery slope, lubricated by interest, flattery and the natural desire to help. It is all too easy to slide down it only to discover that independence has been threatened or perhaps compromised. Having issued the caution, there may not be an alternative. When you possess knowledge and experience not present in the CEE Suite of a small company, and they are needed in a direct way, unwillingness to get your hands dirty will not be in the best interests of your company and its shareholders. Maintaining your independence of thought may be more difficult — but that is simply another aspect of being a director of a smaller organization.

Indemnification should be automatic. Companies are allowed to pay for, or reimburse, directors and officers for the expenses or liabilities incurred in legal actions or proceedings — and you should insist on indemnification as a condition of joining a board. When you check the acts of incorporation you will find that they allow for indemnification, but they do not make it compulsory except in a few specific situations. You should scan the company by-laws for a clause that not only allows, but mandates that all permissible indemnifications be paid.

Summarizing a director's safety net is a tall order, since this section is a collection of the tips of many icebergs. It is impossible to cover everything in depth, perhaps it is impossible to cover even some of it, but this short selection will go a long way towards warding off a bolt from the blue. The most frequent answer from the Wise when asked about how they satisfied themselves about DOC was, "Work at it".

Director Education

DOC relies on knowledge; and there is no substitute for an ongoing, never-ending and focused process of learning and maintaining awareness, and you can choose your own agenda or seek a formal program. There are seminars and courses of various sorts, but there are also focused programs available to those who wish to obtain significant education in corporate governance. They are the Director Education Program from the ICD, offered by leading universities in several cities across Canada, the Chartered Directors Program sponsored by the Conference Board and operated by McMaster University, and the program from the College des administrateurs de societes, sponsored by the Caisse de depot and delivered at Laval University in Quebec City. All three are excellent and provide the opportunity for professionalism through study and examination. Each is also tangible evidence of the sea change in beliefs and opinions as to what constitutes the appropriate preparation to discharge the duties of a corporate director.

This is somewhat of a parallel with the changes in thinking about management that began in the middle of the last century and continue to the present day. In 1967, J. Kenneth Galbraith's best seller, *The New Industrial State*, predicted that professional management had become ubiquitous and could never be displaced, even by shareholders or governments. That was something of an over-estimate, for when Drucker wrote his epic book, *Management, Tasks, Responsibilities, Practices* (Harper & Row) in 1973, he pronounced, "While it has run its course, the management boom has nevertheless permanently changed the world's economic and social landscape". It was Drucker who viewed management as the "organ" responsible for leadership, direction and decisions in all institutions but particularly in businesses. As such, he saw it as a generic function with an essential core that remains unchanged although adapted to the circumstance.

The ensuing years have seen the realization that most of the techniques of management are generic, that tools and methods are heedless of boundaries.

While the issue of whether leadership can be taught is still a debate, the evidence is in to support the teaching of techniques. The question is, "Will corporate governance come to be seen as a generic function common to all social institutions but especially to business?" Will that mean that it can be taught, examined and certified, so that the consumer, boards and citizens alike, can have confidence in a corporate governance designation? The issue is far too large for these pages and must be put aside until another time.

Chapter Eleven:

Strategy in Small Packages

It is easy to agree that corporate strategy is fundamental to the success of any business — but it is easier said than done. The art and science of creating strategy remain mysterious, and based on results they seem more than a little difficult. For that matter, many directors and managers are uncertain as to what strategy is, in spite of pronouncements such as that of Michael Porter, "Strategy renders choices about what not to do as important as choices about what to do". This statement is especially applicable to the director's role in making the critical choices that continually confront a company. They have an ideal vantage point from which to advise and counsel the CEE Suite. They have at least some of the objectivity of a third party while operating within the circle of confidentiality. The board as a whole likely has a collective diversity of experience and knowledge much broader than the functional focus of the CEE Suite members. They know the company and its markets, they are driven by the desire to increase value and they are removed from the operational issues whose resolution is so easily taken for strategy. Finally, they have a strong vested interest in the company's success.

Large companies frequently have someone who carries the lion's share of responsibility for corporate strategy, at least in the sense that he or she is the catalyst in the process, the one who ensures that markets are researched and competitors analysed, and who may be accountable for writing and communicating the final plan. Many companies are fond of "strategy retreats" with a program lasting a couple of days, usually at a resort or conference centre. These sessions may include outside experts, the board, the CEE Suite and others. There are many pundits on the efficacy of various approaches to strategy but, while certain lessons can be drawn from how the big dogs do it, there is little of true value for the small cap company. Business texts are sparse generally, and they seem unable to offer more than admonitions about "strategic oversight" when it comes to the role of the board, regardless of company size. Perhaps this is why one of the Wise commented, "The average director understands strategy in the same way as my five-year-old granddaughter".

Chairs and Tables

This chapter attempts a small contribution, recognizing first that aside from the more obvious differences from its larger colleagues, the typical small company has some unique challenges in formulating strategy. As is frequently the case in the world of the small- and medium-sized business (SMB), these factors affect executives and directors alike.

Resources are always constrained in smaller companies. The time to think and consider is a precious commodity, there are fewer people to do things like market research, and money to hire experts is scarce to non-existent. Admittedly, the smaller company operates with less scope and scale, and this is something of an offset, but many small companies make serious mistakes simply because they cannot allocate sufficient resources to thinking and planning. This is both a threat and an opportunity for the board.

Risks have more leverage in an SMB. The relative impact of a given setback has a more pronounced effect within the context of a small company. When one division of a major company spills red ink it is a serious issue, but when there is only one division the receiver is just around the corner. Curiously, the directors of many small companies adopt a fatalistic view, accepting the unacceptable because they do not believe there is a choice, and there is a lot of wreckage around because risk was not managed creatively.

Strategies have a shorter half-life in small companies, indeed some would claim that in the smallest of the small, long-range planning is what to do after lunch. A common phrase is, "We have a window of opportunity, and it will last until..." Those who think this way are willing to pin their future, and their company, on a guess about when other competitors will appear, for example, or when a replacement technology comes to market, or similar simplifications. Further, even when the strategy is well founded, evolution in the small company will shift more quickly, meaning that board and management must quite literally rethink their strategy frequently, perhaps almost in a continuous process. In a fast-changing industry, the small company would be wise to adopt a rolling 18-month approach, continually casting its plans forward and refreshing its world view.

A Short Test

You have no doubt assimilated the conventional wisdom that the strategist need answer only two short questions: "Where are we going?" and "How are we going to get there?" Well, it may be just a little more complicated than that, but those twin inquiries are the basis for a test that might be useful when you are trying to determine if management really has a strategy, as opposed to a combination of tactics propelled by a wish list. It takes the form of a simple graphic.

The suggestion from this quarter is that the inquiring director might sketch a chart like the one below (white boards are ubiquitous). Explain it, and ask management to portray their proposed strategy on the diagram. Point out that each line crossing from left to right is a specific strategy for the company's intentions in a given market sector. The choice of that sector and the targets in the top right corner (Future) are the answer to question one, while the shape of the curve and the data appropriate to the vertical axis will go a long way to answering question two. It is a simple test, but the answers will be illuminating to one and all.

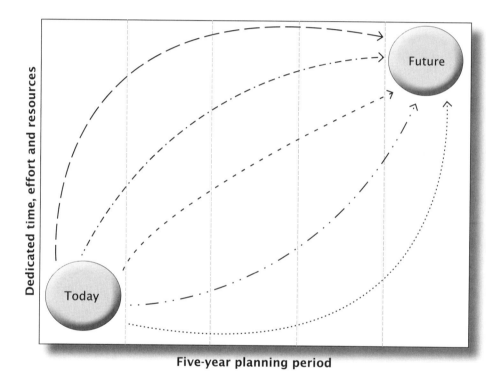

Five-year planning period

Once the picture has been drawn you might ask questions such as these:

- Which curve, ie, strategy, is the best match for the company's tolerance for risk? At this point you may find it necessary to have a conversation about "tolerance for risk" beyond retorts like, "We are all entrepreneurs".

- Are the resources arrayed on the vertical axis available now – or must they be found? What is their cost and how long will it take? What do the answers imply for the viability of each strategy, especially strategies one and two?

- Will this allocation of resource inputs produce a sustainable competitive advantage — in each case — and which is best?

- Assuming that we are reasonably certain of next year, how does that confidence fall off in each succeeding year? Are we agreed that the fifth year is a wish more than a defined goal? Or, if your small company is in natural resources, the five-year horizon is probably too short, so the question may address a time 10 or 20 years in the future.

- What is the sensitivity to (fill the blank) on each strategy?

Those are enough examples — mould them to your company and multiply their number — DOC will have been done and oversight achieved. There is a more extensive list in the following section.

Small companies cannot afford the time and dollars to delve into every nuance of every possibility — but equally, they can ill afford to scrimp on a deeply intensive workout of their chosen strategy, once that decision has been made. As a director you would wish to satisfy yourself that such thinking has taken place. Experience has shown that a couple of hours attempting to fill the blanks implied by the graphic will be beneficial to the company overall and very informative to the director.

Strategy as Seen by a Director

The DOC has been fulfilled when each director is engaged in all aspects of strategic oversight, and that is so much more than attending an annual retreat and eventually approving the business plan. Fair statement, but what are the specific issues beneath its assumptions? Consider the implications of any of the eventualities under the four headings below. Whether it is one or more of the possibilities from that list or some other, ultimately the board must make a choice to balance risk and reward, that is, what is best for the company in its present circumstances and with an eye to the future? The next four headings are a lens through which the plans for that future can be viewed.

1. What is the vision and overall strategy?

a. Has management and/or the board articulated a clear statement of what the company does? For example, when defining what the company does, would an officer refer to its industrial sector or the company's intellectual property? Consider the difference between "We are in the automotive parts aftermarket" and "We design and install proprietary inventory control systems". Both statements are from the same company and reveal confusion as to what the company does for a living and a lack of coherence in its message.

b. What are the core businesses? Which strategic business units or divisions provide the lion's share of the EBITDA every year? If the company is crafting a new strategy, will they remain as the core or will the emphasis shift? Will the synergies between the various strategic business units (SBU) become stronger or weaker with the new strategy?

c. What is the long-term vision for the company? Will it have the same scope and scale in 10 years or something quite different? Does management have a vision of very rapid growth — or geographic expansion — or diversification?

d. Do the core businesses or IP (or something else) define what makes this company different and thus sustainable? Which elements of differentiation could be strengthened? Does a major competitor rely on differences that could be diminished?

e. What is the explicit strategy for the creation of shareholder value? Should short-term profits be sacrificed to get revenue growth? Has the time come to go public, or, if public already, should the board consider going private?

f. What is management's assessment of the external and internal factors, trends, opportunities and threats that shape its view? Has "conventional wisdom" been tested for validity?

g. Are there unmanageable constraints, such as trade restrictions, an environmental regulation or a patent dispute in the path of the company's plans?

h. How risky is the explicit strategy — and is the risk within acceptable limits? Has management presented a coherent and thorough risk-versus-reward assessment? Does it provide the information for the board to make a well-informed decision?

2. What are the key performance drivers?

a. What are the drivers to create value for investors? A Formula One race depends on carefully calculated pit stops for fuel — so what is the equivalent in company performance?

b. In what ways must the company excel to fulfill its vision and strategy? For example, must the company achieve a cost-of-sales level substantially lower than the industry average to deliver the projected earnings — and how reasonable is it to do that?

c. How will management and the board know that the company is going in the chosen direction? What performance indicators signal progress — versus stasis or worse? Are those indicators sensitive enough to detect a trend within a month, a quarter, a year?

3. Does the company have the capability to deliver the desired results?

a.   Have the resources to execute the strategy been quantified — and are they available, ie, can they be re-assigned from their current deployment?

b.   Have both financial and non-financial resources been considered? Have time constraints been considered for both, but especially when the resource includes finding and recruiting new people, or acquiring a security clearance, or getting an export licence, or completing an environmental assessment?

c.   Are these resources available within the company? If they must be found elsewhere, what will they cost financially or strategically?

d.   Does the company currently have the systems and processes to execute the strategy with full knowledge and understanding, ie, even if the KPI are well known can they be monitored by the current systems?

e.   Will those systems support reliable disclosure to the capital markets while the strategy unfolds?

4. What confidence is there in the plan and the expected results?

a.   What is the recent track record — how well has the company performed and what underlies that performance? Can the board be confident that management will deliver, based on performance?

b.   Do the actual versus the planned results impart confidence? Presuming that the planned goals are met, can the board be confident that this success was earned or circumstantial?

c.   Is this plan believable in the eyes of the outside world? If the vision and plan are dramatically different, what will be needed to explain them to the street?

d.   Are the results sustainable? What percentage of the most recent revenues was recurring, and what must be sold next year?

This four-step examination has been characterized as a lens to view the future, in this instance, a tool for directors questioning strategy and the process that developed it. Readers may be interested to learn that it is an adaptation of ideas presented by Deloitte and Touche at a seminar in late 2005, but then the advice was directed at assessing the MD&A disclosure framework. It is the consistency of director's oversight that allows the same four sets of questions to facilitate a quarterly task and an ongoing responsibility equally well.

Major Choices

Across many years as a consultant to business, I found that most organizations could brainstorm or otherwise devise impressive lists of options which appeared, at first blush, to have sufficient merit to deserve serious consideration. But, as noted, small companies cannot afford to model every possibility, stress test it, do sensitivity analysis, add market research and so forth. Small companies must do a thorough job but when there are many competing possibilities, which one gets the resources?

The chart below is a summary of a simple method to resolve the issue of many seemingly sound opportunities, but only limited resources to support the choice process. As before, I recommend that directors bring such tools to the boardroom, especially during the formative stages of the company when their experience adds depth to the management team.

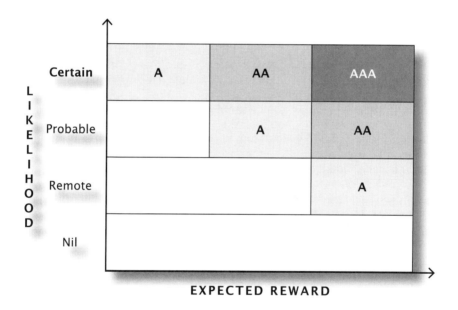

EXPECTED REWARD

You might start the process as soon as the list of possibilities is complete. The group will likely discard a few seen to be fanciful and then be ready to tackle the list in earnest. The next step is to judge two dimensions for each alternative, that is, what is the likelihood that a given opportunity for the company will materialize and, second, what is the expected payoff? This is not an exact science nor is it a detailed analysis; it is simply the best thinking available in the room, assigning broad categories of "likelihood" versus "reward". These "guesstimates" are mapped onto the chart.

Chairs and Tables

Obviously, if the team identifies one or more triple-A opportunities, everyone will be delighted, but this happy outcome is unlikely. Should it seem to occur, ask "Why has no one else seen this before now?" Experience teaches that identifying — realistically — a couple of double-A possibilities is a great day for the company. It also means that all the rest can be shelved, at least under the current circumstances, and scarce resources can be applied to a full blown workout of the best chances.

Finally, do not scrimp on analysis after making the apparently ultimate selection. If your company cannot afford to make a fully-informed choice it cannot afford to pursue the opportunity.

A Conspiracy of Ignorance

I hope Kurt Eichenwald forgives the close parallel to his great title. This tale is about a group of well-intentioned people who spent a lot of money and caused a lot of heartache through simple ignorance.

The story concerns an east coast boat builder, identified here as Diadem Boats. In the late 70s, one of Canada's Eastern provinces, called "Maritamia" for this case, had embarked on a major economic development program. It attracted the attention of Diadem Boats, a major European firm specializing in police, fire and other harbour craft with a reputation for speed, reliability and sea worthiness. In spite of the fact that the company had never been in the pleasure and recreational boat market, it was convinced by the Government of Maritamia to come to Canada and build a new line for the North American market. Tax breaks, training incentives, marketing assistance and ease of entry induced Diadem to design two entries, one at 25 feet and one at 37, both luxurious, well-appointed power cruisers at the high end of the market.

While a few boats were sold, at the end of only two years the Canadian company was in financial difficulty and our consulting practice was asked to determine the problems and suggest solutions.

A single trip to New York to visit the offices of *Yachting* magazine either provided information immediately or directed us to where to get it. In as little as two weeks, we understood the basics of the luxury power boat market in North America, and two inescapable facts emerged. First, the Diadem plant in Maritamia needed 17% of the entire market for luxury cruisers simply to reach break even and, second, Chris Craft, which was unlikely to stop selling while Diadem caught up, led all competition with only 15% market share.

At the conference with management which followed we also learned that we had been the first to bother calculating that same break-even volume. Further, no one in either board or management had a reasonable estimate of how many high-end, 25- and 37-foot luxury boats were being sold in North America each year. When the board was apprised of our findings, the directors were astounded, some doubting the veracity of our statements. During the same meeting, we pointed out that their municipal tax holiday would end the following year, worsening the situation, only to discover that everyone seemed blissfully unaware of this tidbit. It was a difficult afternoon for everyone in that boardroom.

Diadem halted production, closed the plant within six months, sold the inventory at a loss and withdrew from the Canadian market. Ignorance had conspired to invest millions, relocate trades people, divert tax dollars from alternatives and waste an alliance that could have been successful under different circumstances.

To underscore the point, market information was readily available at little cost and in a short time, and it needed only rudimentary analysis to find the fatal flaw. The Maritamia plant was an unnecessary and avoidable flop perpetrated by people who did not do their homework. Government, management and directors alike may have been focused on creating jobs and, thus, gave no thought to their durability through the long-term viability of the new company. It was indicative that the directors of the company, appointed by local and provincial governments, were not chosen with manufacturing experience and oversight of the company in mind.

Lest you think goofs like this happen only in small companies, consider the situation facing Tom Enders when he arrived as the new CEO of Airbus in the summer of 2007. One of the first issues confronting him was the lack of options for engines for a new plane, the A350 XWB-1000. On his arrival, there had been only 20 orders for the A350 XWB-1000, all coming from Qatar Airways. The customer was supposed to have a choice between Rolls Royce and GE engines. The Rolls Royce engine was ready, but Qatar wanted the GE engine. This variant of the A350 is a "stretch" aircraft, and the generally available GE power plant is only sufficient for the two smaller versions of the A350. The stretch version requires more power, and given the customer's choice of GE, this would imply the GE90, being built for planes like the Boeing 777. Airbus seemed to think that the GE90 engine or a variant of it would be a quick and easy option for its new plane. Unfortunately, Airbus failed to talk to the supplier. The A350 XWB-1000 was designed to be in direct competition with the Boeing 777 and GE has a contract with Boeing to make engines exclusively for the Boeing 777. The GE90 was not available for the Qatar order. Undoubtedly, this matter never came to the board until after the fact. It is included here as a classic example of failing to close the loop even though the information was available for little time and effort.

Please do not follow these examples!

More Grey Zones

This chapter has provided a couple of tools for directors to use in questioning company strategy and plans. It closes with a simple listing of Grey Zones, places where risk may surface, or should be brought to the fore by the use of the director's tool kit. The basis for the list was found in Leighton and Thain's book, *Making Boards Work*, and their work inspired the updated and extended version that follows.

A.   **Critical discontinuities, such as:**

- Major changes of critical employees; such as replacement due to death, retirement or separation of anyone in the CEE Suite, particularly the CEO, or a powerful thought leader or a developer of the IP at the heart of market differentiation.

- Change, or a major threat of a change, in ownership or control, including taking the company public or private, or a major shift in government policy.

- Threats from competition, markets, technology, economic conditions, or major changes in the regulatory regime (for example, think about the implications when the CRTC allowed telephone number portability in March 2007).

- The appearance of major opportunities, such as possible acquisitions, expansion or divestments.

B.   **Periodic major reviews, including:**

- Redefinition or reconfirmation of purpose – vision, mission, goals and objectives, branding and so forth.

- Development and/or approval of strategy, with directors becoming more involved in the development as well as the approval processes.

- Approval of annual operating and capital budgets – where the thoughtful director will have an eye to the role of ICFR in monitoring and reporting progress against the budget.

- Approval of specific major capital appropriation requests and how these either fit against, or alter, the strategy of the company.

- Annual performance and compensation reviews of the CEE Suite.

C.   **Routine interaction with management is a crucial aspect of DOC, and one which many directors take too lightly. More is said elsewhere on the following bullets, as this is DOC in action:**

- monthly and quarterly reviews of operating results;
- periodic progress reports and updates of special projects or initiatives;
- informal discussions with individual managers;
- facility tours and special off-site meetings;
- requests for issues and opportunities to be put on board agendas; and

- review of board meeting minutes and follow-up by inquiries on topics discussed.

Directors might ask themselves, "Am I really satisfied with the timeliness and quality of the information that I receive as a matter of course?" In a small company, this might include a selection of operating information, as long as it is remains as information, not the basis for, "when I was running the widget company..."

D. **External interactions and research:**

- Reaction (but not over-reaction) to investment analyst's reports which question or criticize company performance and results.

- Monitoring of media reports concerning the company and its political, social, economic, and technological environments.

- Outside business and social contacts that often yield useful, sometimes critically important information.

A Strategic Summary

It is now conventional wisdom that the board of directors at least approves and may actually determine the strategy of the organization. But corporate strategy is an elusive topic, or at least that is what one might conclude after putting the question to many executives and directors, something that has been a habit of mine over a few years. The folks in the big management consulting practices put strategy consulting near the top of the listings, the assignments that everyone wants, with big fees, glamour, prestige and a step toward a partner's office. I discovered early that strategy engagements carried a hidden bomb that has to be defused if survival and fees are to be assured. The explosive device lay hidden in the simple fact that virtually everyone, clients and consultants alike, were substantially confused about strategy, generally and specifically, as well as both theory and practice. When the project deliverable was a strategic plan, well, you understand the problem.

It was during the get-acquainted, earliest stage of one such assignment that one of our clients provided an insight that I adopted instantly and have used ever since. The discussion was becoming mired around terminology, especially words like mission, vision and the like, including strategy. Our client began by reflecting that the word "strategy" originally meant something like "general's tactics" and, having placed that before us, he asked, "How will we know if our strategy is successful?" Many possibilities were offered, and after a moment the same client said, "What each of you has said can be reduced to a single word: winning. That was the general's objective, too."

Chairs and Tables

Strategy is successful only when it wins. It can be simple or convoluted, written in a few lines or several chapters, but its goal is always the same. Reaching the desired future defines success. That objective may be to sell more, or earn more, or develop the best technology, or even to survive an economic recession, but it is always about achieving a given end better than the company's rivals in the market. The diagram on page 187 shows five different paths travelling from the bottom left to the top right, each emblematic of a different set of choices, a different strategy. Each path implies an alternative deployment of resources — different strategic decisions — but they all converge on the chosen goal, the desired future for the organization. Just as battles can be won by different strategies, businesses have alternative ways to "win" their struggle for success.

If determining the best path is one of the board's chief responsibilities, actually making the choice is unclear. There is a tendency to be overly simplistic and take a stance that, while irrefutable as far as it goes, makes assumptions that may not be true or may change dramatically over the next few years. You may conclude, as Gabrielle "Coco" Chanel believed, "If you want to be irreplaceable, you have to be different." That sounds good, but how would it work in a market where an entire product category can be replaced by technological innovation? How would you apply the Coco dictate to the manufacturing of white label products? Would price be a sufficient difference, or would other characteristics be needed to leaven the mix — and how long would that advantage be sustainable — and at what long-term cost?

This chapter is a far cry from either a theoretical discussion or a "how to do it" manual. Its pages will have accomplished their purpose if directors and others come away with three simple thoughts. First, strategy is always about winning — however, that may be defined in your situation. Second, strategy decisions are complex and optimal choices are more likely to be seen most clearly in the rear-view mirror. Finally, attempting to predict the future is foolish, but your company can and should have a vision of the future and be prepared to make many incremental adjustments to accomplish what a mathematician would call an "asymptotic approximation".

May all your choices be in fortune's light!

Chapter Twelve:

A Word from the Wise

Where would you turn for good advice on corporate governance issues? I have included some references in the final appendix, well-known books and websites for example. While those are useful, nothing can take the place of thoughtful answers from those who have demonstrated their wisdom and skills through their accomplishments as directors and business leaders. In the introduction I mentioned those who agreed to share their wisdom with you, calling them "the Wise" for ease of reference. Each of the Wise had his or her first stint as a director on either a business board ("B" below) or a not-for-profit ("N" below), although they have all gone on to multiple directorships. Most have had direct experience with smaller organizations, while a few were included because of their stature and the undoubted breadth and depth of their wisdom.

The Wise

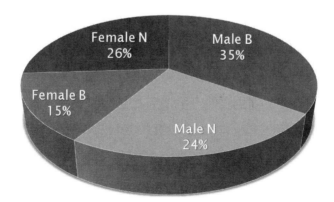

The final tally was some 46 people who consented to be interviewed. Their names form Appendix One, and this chapter is a digest of their thoughts and opinions.

Answers to the Questionnaire

The purpose of the interviews was to gain insights from respected practitioners, a cross section rather than an attempt at a statistical confidence level. Having said this, at 46 the sample was large enough to be meaningful, statistics aside, as the opinions of a relatively large group of thought leaders and experts who have significant influence on corporate governance in Canada. The interviews were relaxed conversations rather than interrogations, but some questions were consistent threads running through the sessions and here are the answers to those queries.

What was your first directorship and why did you accept?

Business boards or a start on an NFP board or the board of a government agency or commission were exactly even, with 23 each. As might be expected from such a large and diverse group their reasons were many and wonderful. Many of those now on several corporate boards started as a volunteer director, which may be why "making a contribution" was the most frequent reason for joining the first board with 13 votes or about 28% of the total. After that, the rationale for that first board did not have a real pattern, although "learning" had four votes and eight people joined their first board because they were investors.

What do you enjoy most about being a director?

The discussion from the first question carried over into the second and "making a contribution" was reinforced, although expressed differently, eg, "helping with growth" or "resolving problems". The overall favourite was intellectual exercise in some form, with answers that included "learning", "strategy", problem solving", "intellectual stimulation" and the like. It was interesting that none of the Wise mentioned director fees or options as either a positive or a negative, other than one casual comment to the effect that fees were irrelevant to that person. I did not raise the issue, and it simply did not come up for discussion.

What is the biggest headache for a director?

This question drew wildly assorted answers, often delivered with emphasis or even passion, and since each was expressed in a personal manner it was a challenge to sort the results. The most frequent answer was the easiest to record, since it was an immediate, single word: "compliance", the instant answer 13 times. Several mentioned the work of keeping abreast of regulations or similar answers, bringing compliance-related answers to a total of 17, a significant proportion.

Beyond compliance, there was a set of answers that, while expressed in a variety of ways, all lead to human performance, either management or other directors. The major management issues were "getting the right CEO" and "management mistakes", which got a total of 10 votes, and the problems associated with the transition from founders to professional management, which drew five mentions. Directors complaining about directors provided eight responses, but the issues differed among them. One of the Wise targeted a specific style of director, one who believes that his presence is all that is required, and his words are always worthy:

> "My headache is the grand old man, the very strong personality with a gravely voice and a grey suit, and a tendency to posture and pontificate, with many references to 'the way we did it' as the basis for all recommendations".

Three people mentioned their discomfort when a sudden demand on their time interfered with their personal lives with all three viewing their director responsibilities as priorities which had to be fulfilled.

What are the three crucial qualities or competencies in a director?

In an earlier chapter, I presented a personal opinion that there are three layers of competency, the first one a set of prerequisites, the second the "core" competencies and then a layer that is situational. I think this view was supported by the Wise, perhaps I am flattering myself, but some answers started with, "Well, integrity is table stakes" so there seemed to be support for prerequisites followed by other competencies in some sort of priority. Since the Wise were asked to rank their answers (first, second and third choices) and certain qualities would garner different rankings by different respondents, it was difficult to get a really clear preference.

Having offered this caveat, the clear winner as the most crucial quality or competency was integrity, getting 13 votes as the top priority, four as the second and three as the third, plus at least five of the "table stakes" variety. Further, several people combined integrity with other traits into a collective, such as "judgment", and I am certain that many simply assume that integrity is in place, though they did not mention it specifically. Instead, some of their underlying thoughts would come out when we talked about tone at the top or some other analog.

Second place was clearly time and commitment, with 11 firsts and seven thirds. All other choices were virtually impossible to detect, with many qualities receiving four or five votes apiece.

Personal reputation, independence and an understanding of governance each got five first place votes, plus a scattering of others. Team work was mentioned frequently, usually down the list, but often included. Consensus builders were valued, with a couple of the Wise stating that this competency is a necessity in a chair.

"Directors are responsible for gating, for channelling management in the right direction, and for that they must have commercial intelligence and a strategic sense."

Overall, the answers to this question suggest that the qualities sought in a director, beyond honesty and commitment, are as varied as those making the choices. In my view, the answers to this question are a solid endorsement for a well-considered competency matrix to drive the selection, rather than the opinion of individuals.

Where do you find those qualities — what sorts of people have them?

The Wise provided both conventional answers and personal thoughts on where to find directors. Executive recruiters were favoured by 11 respondents, and the recommendation was often accompanied by a comment such as, "You need to get outside of personal circles". Search firms also came in for criticism from a few of the Wise, who feel that recruiters are likely to perpetrate an existing board rather than find fresh thinking. There was a mash of other responses, but of note were the 11 responses suggesting a very broad scan of many backgrounds, seeking those whose lifetimes demonstrate their character and potential value as directors. A few of the Wise made a point of saying that, while a couple of former executives on a board could be invaluable, the old habit of recruiting solely former or current CEOs was likely to lead to problems such as "group think".

There were two interesting comments about those directors expected to provide the board with added depth in financial management. A couple of the Wise view this subset as different from the other independent directors, and while one suggested that merely a jaundiced eye was the necessary accoutrement, the other said that such directors should be "hugely cynical".

Given that the Wise have influential opinions, it is interesting to speculate on how we might broaden the fields where we recruit new directors in the future.

How would you describe the role of the chair of the board?

Of the 46 people who compose the Wise, all but six provided very individual one-liners for the role of the chair. Without exception, they cast the chair in a leadership role, managing the board and its work, so no surprise, but the characterization of how the chair is to fulfill that role was wonderfully fascinating in its variety. For some, the chair is a moderator or a facilitator while others emphasize the administrative aspects of the role. A small number would slant the chair's priorities towards management, others towards the directors, and some see it as a balancing act. Most agreed with the sentiment that directors do not want to be managed, but they do expect to be led.

A Word from the Wise

A few provided omnibus sentences, all very good, one of which was:

> "The role of the chair is to set the ethical and cultural tone for the enterprise, to manage the board, and to ensure there is an effective interface between management and the board".

An intriguing aspect was that seven of the Wise used an identical simile, all likening the chair to the conductor of a symphony orchestra. I wrote furiously in an attempt at capturing verbatim the words of one of the seven, and I hope she forgives my lack of stenographic talents and finds the following to be a reasonable facsimile of what was said

> "The chair is like the conductor of an orchestra. The conductor must have the ego to want the spotlight for a moment and the strength of character to give it up as soon as he taps the baton and attention shifts for the overture. Different musicians have different parts, a cadenza or a trumpet flourish, some forte and some pianissimo, each called forth to fulfill the score at an exact moment and in harmony with all the other players. When the music is over, the applause is for everyone who created it."

The other six were equally quick to suggest the simile, although perhaps less eloquently. Since the quotation was from an early interview I related it to them, and as I read it each exclaimed at how well it portrayed the role of a chair.

What are your comments about board evaluation?

There was very strong support for board evaluation, but not for the assessment of individual directors, at least with the tools presently available.

Only one person was actually against the idea of board evaluation, and there were another nine who were dubious or somewhat jaded on the issue, but 36 were supportive. Of these, 10 were strongly supportive, seeing board assessment as a best practice, and another 26 were simply in favour. However, a majority of those supporting board or committee evaluation added caveats about the methods and processes in current use. One person said, "Where have you seen this working well?" Several expressed discomfort around the inability of some evaluation processes to capture all the dimensions of board performance; questionnaires were singled out as especially lacking. Many agreed that, while the idea is a good one, the methods are "a work in progress".

There was general agreement that the process is at least as valuable as the results. One director stated that, "Assessment should cause a person to examine his working relationships" and went on to add that if this was done with an open mind and a serious purpose, any problems would be largely solved at the end of the process. Those with a similar view suggested that an open discussion at a quarterly in camera session was much more effective than more formal and, thus, constrained methods.

Evaluating the performance of an individual director was endorsed by only four people, while nine were opposed, but the bulk of the respondents are still uncertain of this practice. There were ten who believe that one-on-one sessions between the Chair and individual directors is the best plan, and the "problem director" becomes an issue for the Chair to resolve.

What things do you practice to satisfy DOC?

In short, work at it — and never stop. The Wise had favourite methods, such as a rostrum of friends who provide regular information and insights about an industrial sector, or an especially good trade magazine, or an electronic bulletin arriving daily with the most up-to-date news. A few claimed omnivorous reading as an essential tool for DOC. Some visit the company for quarterly discussions with members of the CEE Suite or they travel to a plant or a mine or an oilfield. The bottom line was consistent and substantial effort, well beyond the board book and preparation for a known agenda, by serious and dedicated directors. There were 24 who said, in effect, "I do a lot of work". It was a comforting experience.

What is your view of director certification?

The Wise are enthusiastic about director education and knowledge with each and every one of them providing strong endorsements. Some elaborated, others contented themselves with some version of "all learning is good, and since we are directors, then more education is terrific". The only caveats offered recognized the limits of education, such as "I don't think you can teach courage".

Those who had experienced one of the three corporate governance schools were loud in their praise for them — but they were more restrained when it comes to another set of initials. Earning a certificate is good; becoming certified raises questions. No one suggested that holding a designation should be a prerequisite to sitting on a board, in fact, a couple of the Wise shared discussions that they had with their boards where there was a certain amount of cynicism about a governance designation. Concerns were expressed that any program of study, no matter how well conceived and delivered, might replace experience and career success.

Overall, the Wise endorse director education in the strongest way, both for the content and the fact that programs such as the three mentioned here have sensitized so many people to the value of corporate governance.

A Word from the Wise

A Summary

Rather than attempt to summarize the collective views of the Wise, beyond the preceding paragraphs, I offer on behalf of all readers my gratitude for their time and interest and for the generous and open manner in which they shared their wisdom.

I joined a board for the first time in 1976 and have served on many in the interval. I believe that the overall commitment of the men and women serving on boards has increased and can be likened to a good investment, with continued and growing returns. Perhaps the best summary is this quote from one of the Wise:

"I am really proud of corporate Canada and its commitment to excellence."

Thank you, all of you.

Chapter Thirteen:

And In Conclusion

I would like to leave you with three summary thoughts: a final insight into what it takes to become a good director, a last comment about the work that a good director does (yes, more DOC), and a closing comment about governance and regulation.

First, please extend your thinking about what we expect of directors to include a willingness to learn more about the fundamentals of corporate governance *per se* than we have asked traditionally. I offer a parallel from a previous life, an insight from many years as a management consultant and, ultimately, a partner with two of the name-brand firms. They were good years, and we were proud of the contributions that we made to our clients, but the cloud over the sun was the urban myths about consultants, for none were complimentary. Perhaps you recall chestnuts like borrowing someone's watch to tell them the time and similar clichés. I spent a lot of time and effort in an attempt to bring higher levels of professionalism to the industry, first as the president of the Institute of Management Consultants of Ontario and later as the president of the national institute. The focus in those years was on developing a common body of knowledge and code of conduct and then understanding how to ensure that they were applied in the interest of the client.

The crux of the matter then, and probably now, was that if you had worked in industry or government apparently you were automatically qualified to advise organizations like your former employers or even those that were quite different. If laid off or semi-retired, you could move with alacrity into consulting mode. The practice was particularly noisome in government circles, which played the game of reducing headcount while adding "consultants", ie, former employees, to the roster. Most who enter consulting in this manner last only as long as their first couple of contracts, which are often provided as a means to ease them out the door and off the payroll. Then, reality dawns and the "consultant" learns that managing client expectations, delivering professional services and balancing work loads, all while earning a reasonable margin, is a formidable task. In the process some initiates glimpse the significant body of specialized knowledge and practice that differentiates a professional and a pretender, and they choose to accelerate their learning through formal courses or programs. The apprenticeship of those who learn while doing is detected only when they make a major mistake.

The comparison with the emergence of the "professional director" is interesting. Twenty-five years ago, professionalism as a director characteristic would have raised eyebrows, at best, and more likely would have been scorned. The idea that corporate governance might require a particular body of knowledge had yet to occur, and a view that such learning is an important underpinning in fulfilling the directorship role was not yet formed. If you were a current or former executive, especially a president and CEO, you were automatically equipped to take your place at the boardroom table. Rather than a new responsibility, it was often a reward for a career with the company. Even though most claimed that the role was chiefly oversight, and thus completely separate from management, none saw any difficulties in moving from one side of the table to the other. It was as if we believed that a professor teaching laminar flow could also fly an airplane or that a psychiatrist could do brain surgery. While we see the fatal flaws in those particular assumptions we seem blind to the equivalent error made when we sponsor a transition to the boardroom without asking for those competencies essential to fulfilling the responsibilities of directorship.

This brings us to the issues of director education and certification, a common topic in the conversations with the Wise. A few were in favour, a few against, but overall, the virtue in any certification process is seen to be the learning, not the piece of paper. As understood in North America, most of Europe and some other parts of the world, professional designations are earned from a professional society or institute. Some must be renewed periodically and a requirement to show evidence of continual learning or continuing education is common. Some professions use the relevant designation as a barrier to working in the field, enshrining these in law, such as CA, medical doctor (MD), professional engineer (P.Eng.) and others where certain knowledge or proficiencies would affect medical, economic, legal or other issues in a critical way. Designations in this category are highly regulated, and new ones are rarely added to the list. Industrial certification is common for skilled trades such as electricians, carpenters, plumbers and many traditional crafts. There are self-regulating organizations, such as the IDA, which have the mandate to license those in a given field. The licence, often earned through a combination of coursework and practical experience leading to formal examination, is a barrier to entry and thus a protection for the consumer.

At the time of writing, there are very few restrictions on who may become a director, leaving selection an open choice by the current chair, the nominating committee or, still in some cases, the president. The ICD has been, and continues to be, a strong and positive influence in its chosen role as a national body for the certification of corporate directors. It grants the "professional ICD.D. designation" upon successful completion of a substantial program of study, delivered by a university, and then rigorous written and oral examinations. The business community, the regulators and the exchanges are still some distance from a requirement for director certification, but the topic is on the table.

Experience is convincing. There are prerequisite competencies for a directorship, absolutes that must be in place as surely for a director as for other high accountability roles. These essentials must be held by all directors of all organizations if they are to have reasonably comparable foundations for the accomplishment of their responsibilities. Beyond these, the board as a "body politic" must secure a range of competencies from the collective of assembled directors. When we hire an individual we attempt to get as close to some ideal as possible, but that profile is within the confines of a single job. No matter how complex the role, it is meant for one person so it cannot contemplate the breadth demanded of the corporate entity called a board of directors. The solution — and the challenge — is to assemble the board's necessary scope and scale of competencies by accumulating them a few at a time from the assembled directors.

When each director is chosen with a clear and thorough understanding of what the organization needs, one might expect good corporate governance to follow, but we know from historical and current examples that this is not always the case. Perhaps that indicates that the whole board, the body politic, should be held to some standard, some form of certification in the manner of the licensed professionals. The CSA might claim that it does that with the CEO and the CFO, with everyone else falling into line, but the regulators are speaking of compliance not necessarily governance. We need a licence to drive an automobile, so that we do not injure ourselves and others. Why not a parallel for directorships? This is likely to be a controversial idea, but it is offered with the hope of sparking further debate.

This brings us to the second issue, the task of being a good corporate director once chosen. You have just joined your first board and your self-assessment has reassured you that you have the prerequisites, you are interested in the company and its industry and you have the time and the inclination to commit it to the new role. What comes next, aside from attending your first board meeting?

At the ICD Awards Banquet in May 2007, Victor Young advised us that, "A diligent director never rests". Excellent advice, but where should busy directors focus that time and effort, especially when newly anointed? You have, of course, been scrupulously thorough in your personal due diligence, so by now you know quite a lot about the company, its market, products and competitors, and you have met the senior team and the other directors. If any of these items is missing, now is the time to fill the blanks. Your first few meetings will bring familiarity with the culture of the board and the company and build your understanding of ongoing operations. That is an invaluable process, and while it progresses you might think about what your personal contribution is going to be, that is, what difference will you bring to the company and its many stakeholders?

Here is a suggestion. Go back to the interviews and meetings when you were being recruited and recall the questions asked. You were selected because you have a particular set of competencies that are an important component in the make up of the overall profile of the board, and those questions indicated the nominating committee's concerns, ie, the board's needs. Referring to an earlier comment, you are now a key part of the body politic of the board. The suggestion is that you think of your new role as a portfolio of accountabilities, a combination for which you are at least as well qualified as others and for which you are ready to be personally responsible. This is not a stretch, it is simply writing a version of the director's job description specific to you, one that reflects the needs of the board and your ability to meet a selection of them. The portfolio responsibilities will help focus your time and effort and, given a willingness to carry it on behalf of the board, your contribution can make a major difference. An example of a portfolio might be, for an exporter, monitoring the various international trade organizations, summarizing their deliberations and assessing the likely effects on your business. Or, you might track cases in which the business judgement rule is being applied and interpreted, summarize the results and digest the work for your board colleagues. Third, you could become the centre of expertise around the OSC interest in a "compensation MD&A". There are many possibilities for a focused contribution, and you might discuss the portfolio concept with your colleagues, since you are certainly not the only one who could contribute something beyond meeting attendance and pertinent questions.

Some suggest that the new rules and regulations around corporate governance are really old wine in new bottles and that a debate on the question would more likely be won through oratory than content. I agree with that. The underlying principles of corporate governance, like those of good management, remain unchanged, although selected practices and methods have evolved. This is especially true for the compliance issues facing public companies where, by and large, there have been improvements, such as separating the roles of the chair and the CEO, selecting directors with competencies geared to the company's strategic needs, and increased emphasis on financial controls and risk management. We have also seen the task become much more complicated, and here is an insight from one of the Wise, offered as a story.

The tale begins when my colleague, then a young lawyer, was frequently involved in preparing a prospectus, hammered out on an Underwood typewriter. He pointed out that there were always 12 pages in a prospectus at that time because printing was always by a local print shop and everything was in multiples of four pages. He confided that nine or 10 pages would have sufficed in many cases, but the rule-of-four prevailed. Time went by, the Selectric typewriter appeared on the scene, and the typical prospectus became 16 or 20 pages. By the late 80s, word processing expanded capabilities and the document so that it soon required a table of contents to navigate its 64 pages. With a document that size a summary was appropriate, but a single page became four as the prospectus swelled to 96. Some bright spark suggested another kind of summary, even shorter but "signed" by an executive or the chair, and so a couple of paragraphs began appearing just inside the front cover, which was soon the first page of 120 in the now hefty prospectus.

Let us pause and return to the start of all this, which was a 12-page document written to inform investors so that they could make a decision. That same goal motivated the summary and, later, the few paragraphs inside the front cover. What, you might ask, is the purpose of the rest? Aside from a small contribution to the paper industry, all those extra pages are there because they are beloved of the professionals and the watchdogs who feast on these arcane, complex monsters. They certainly do not serve the "gods of plain disclosure" or those of "transparency". I suggest that there is a lesson in my friend's story, one that should inform us of the dangers of overly complex policies and processes no matter how well-intentioned they may be.

Adam Smith argued, in *The Wealth of Nations* and elsewhere, that individuals in a free market pursue their own self-interest and in so doing they tend to promote the good of the community as a whole. He called the force behind this behaviour the "invisible hand" and saw it as an underlying principle. I trust that his shade will not be uneasy if the invisible hand is contrasted with "too many cooks spoil the broth", a comparison drawn because the proliferation of regulations seems to be rather more of the latter and less of the former.

I have argued that corporate governance is an essential element in the equation that produces an increase in shareholder value under an orderly and prudent balance of risk and reward. The law and regulations leave the strategic decisions to pursue those ends in the hands of informed and reasonable people acting in the best interests of all stakeholders, with the company as the priority. I have also argued that the differences between good management and good governance, and for that matter, common sense, are to be found in the ends sought, not in the tools, techniques and processes. Compliance with regulations is a subset of those actions, necessary, but not sufficient to guard the best interests of the company. They are not the invisible hand, and I hope as well they are not the extra cook in the kitchen.

Chairs and Tables was written for those entrusted with the oversight of small organizations. Such directorships are, in many ways, more difficult than those that overlook larger landscapes. They resolve issues of equal complexity, but the solutions must fit the constrained and limited resources that are a natural part of being smaller. As well, the directors of the small-scale company or not-for-profit face an issue that rarely surfaces for those overseeing a large company, and that is the intense demands to balance oversight with the facets of coach, mentor and facilitator, all combined with occasional tours as a stand-by executive. Think back to the chart on page 158, the shifting division of a director's time and focus between oversight and direct support to management. That is unusual and unwarranted for the directors of the large- and the well-endowed company. It has been noted elsewhere in this book, echoing the voice of Statistics Canada, that smaller undertakings, public, private and non-share, always "punch above their weight" when it comes to contributions to the country and its economy. Theirs is a tough job, and I wish them well.

Appendix One:

Thought Leaders and Experts

Ruth Armstrong	Cliff Hatch
David Atkins	Bill Hewitt
Stan Beck	Tom Hockin
Jalynn Bennett	Linda Hohol
Elinor Caplan	David Johnston
Glenna Carr	David Laidley
Ruth Corbin	Spencer Lanthier
Tom Corcoran	David Leighton
Stephen J. Dent	Marcelo Mackinlay
William Dimma	John MacNaughton
Terry Donnelly	David McFadden
Jim Farley	Helen Meyer
Bob Ferchat	Peter Mills
Colleen Fleming	Henry Pankratz
George Fierheller	Donna Parr
Sandra Foster	Elizabeth Parr-Johnston
Germaine Gibara	Carol Perry
Jim Gillies	Courtney Pratt
Anne Golden	Connie Roveto
Jim Goodfellow	Ron Smith
Cindy Gordon	Carol Stephenson
Chuck Hantho	Beverley Topping
Carol Hansell	David Williams

Titles, degrees, awards and other distinguishing features have been omitted deliberately. Similarly, first names have been replaced with diminutives and nicknames. The names of the Wise appear in this list as they are known to the communities that admire them.

Appendix Two:

Position Descriptions for the Board

Position Description for a Director

Preamble

The board of directors is responsible under law for the management of the company's business. It has the statutory authority and obligation to protect and enhance the assets of the company in the interest of all shareholders. Although directors may be elected by the shareholders to bring special expertise or a point of view to board deliberations, they are not chosen to represent a particular constituency. The best interests of the company must be paramount at all times.

The involvement and commitment of directors is shown by regular board and committee attendance, preparation for those meetings, and active participation in setting goals and requiring performance in the interest of shareholders.

Responsibilities of Directors

The board operates by delegating certain of its responsibilities to management and reserving certain powers to itself. Its principal duties fall into six categories.

Strategy determination:

- The board has the responsibility to participate, as a whole and through its committees, in developing and approving the mission of the business, its objectives and goals, and the strategy by which it proposes to reach those goals.

- The board has the responsibility to ensure congruence between shareholder expectations, company plans, and management performance.

Selection of management:

- The board is responsible for managing its own affairs, including planning its composition, selecting its chairman, nominating candidates for election to the board, appointing committees, and determining director compensation.

- The board is responsible for the appointment and replacement of the chief executive officer, for monitoring CEO performance, determining CEO compensation, and providing advice and counsel in the execution of the CEO's duties.

- The board is responsible for approving the appointment and remuneration of all corporate officers, acting upon the advice of the chief executive officer.

- The board is responsible for ensuring management succession.

Monitoring and acting:

- The board is responsible for monitoring the company's progress towards its goals, and revising and altering its direction in light of changing circumstances.

- The board is responsible for taking action when performance falls short of its goals or when other special circumstances (for example mergers and acquisitions or changes in control) warrant it.

Policies and procedures:

- The board is responsible for approving and monitoring compliance with all significant policies and procedures by which the company is operated.

- The board has a particular responsibility for ensuring that the company operates at all times within applicable laws and regulations and to the highest ethical and moral standards.

Reporting to shareholders:

- The board is responsible for ensuring that the financial performance of the company is reported to shareholders on a timely and regular basis.

- The board is responsible for ensuring that the financial results are reported fairly and in accordance with generally accepted accounting standards.

- The board is responsible for timely reporting of any other developments that have a significant and material impact on the value of the shareholders' assets.

- The board is responsible for reporting annually to shareholders on its stewardship for the preceding year.

- The board is responsible for approving any payment of dividends to shareholders.

Legal requirements:

- The board is responsible for ensuring that routine legal requirements, documents and records have been properly prepared, approved and maintained.

Position Description for a Committee Chair

The fundamental responsibility of the chair of any committee of the Board of Directors is to be responsible for the management and effective performance of the committee and provide leadership to the committee in fulfilling its charter and any other matters delegated to it by the Board.

Responsibilities

The chair of any committee of the board of directors will:

- Set committee agendas, chair committee meetings and ensure that the committee is properly organized and functions effectively and ensure that minutes are prepared for each meeting.

- As appropriate, work with the chairman of the board, the president and CEO, the CFO and the corporate secretary to establish the frequency of committee meetings and the agendas for meetings.

- As appropriate and in consultation with the committee and the chairman of the board, retain, oversee and terminate independent advisors to assist the committee in its fulfillment of its responsibilities.

- Report to the board of directors with respect to the activities of the committee and any recommendations deemed desirable by the committee.

- Lead the committee in annually reviewing and assessing the adequacy of its mandate and evaluating its effectiveness in fulfilling its mandate.

Position Description for the Chair of the Board

The chair of the board is responsible for the management, development and effective functioning of the board of directors and provides leadership in every aspect of its work. The board has the ultimate authority and responsibility for the corporation, and the chairman provides direction and leadership for the board. The chairman carries the same slate of duties and responsibilities as other directors, with additional emphasis on the following principal accountabilities.

Responsibilities

1. Responsibility for the overall operations of the board and monitoring its effectiveness; building and managing the composition and structure of the board; ensuring constant and continuous renewal of the board; setting standards of performance and job descriptions for board and committee members; managing the board and its meetings; guiding its deliberations so that appropriate strategic and policy decisions are made; and ensuring proper oversight is exercised.

2. Plans and organizes the work of the board, including:

    - setting the board's agendas and ensuring that the corporation's strategic direction, including the corporation's vision, mission and values are defined and communicated to the board for its approval and that all matters of strategic importance are dealt with regularly at the board level;
    - considering and suggesting candidates for board membership and participating in the selection of candidates to be submitted to the board for approval;
    - recommending committee composition to the board;
    - recommending board compensation after consultation with the ADC, GNC and the MRC; and
    - identifying programs for director orientation and continuing education.

3. Participating with the MRC in establishing the performance goals and assessment of the CEO in meeting agreed targets.

4. Advising management on developing corporate strategy and annual plans.

5. Ensuring that the corporation's policy with respect to regulatory compliance and its policy on ethical and moral standards is communicated to all stakeholders.

6. When asked to do so by the board, representing the company to its major stakeholders, including shareholders, policyholders, the financial community, government authorities and the public.

Appendix Three:

Board Charter — The Acme Example Inc.

Charter of the Board of Directors

General

The primary responsibility of the board of directors of the Acme Example Inc. (the Company) is to provide governance and stewardship to the Company in accordance with Canadian laws and regulations. It is the duty of the directors to exercise their business judgment in the best interests of the Company.

The Company's business is conducted by employees, managers and corporate officers led by the president and chief executive officer (CEO) with oversight from the board. The board selects the CEO and works with the CEO to select and appoint other corporate officers (the Officers) who are charged with managing the day-to-day operations of the Company. The board has the responsibility of overseeing, counselling and directing the Officers to ensure that the long-term interests of the Company and its shareholders are served. The directors and the Officers recognize that the long-term interests of the Company and its shareholders are advanced when they take into account the concerns of employees, customers, suppliers and community stakeholders.

The Board

The board's general oversight responsibilities include, but are not limited to:

- evaluating the performance of the Officers and review the Company's succession plan for the CEO and the other Officers;
- reviewing the long-range business plans of the Company and to monitor performance relative to the achievement of those plans;
- considering long-range strategic issues and risks to the Company; and

- approving policies of corporate conduct that promote and maintain the integrity of the Company.

Board Size

The size of the board will provide diverse views and opinions among directors while facilitating discussions in which each director can participate in a substantive manner. The board size will be within the limits prescribed by the Acme articles and by-laws, which currently provide that the board may have no fewer than seven and no more than 10 directors.

General Responsibilities

The board is responsible for the stewardship of the Company. In fulfilling its mandate, the board oversees major corporate plans including strategic plans, plans for management development and succession, and plans for business development. The board monitors the integrity of internal controls, management information systems, systems and procedures to identify the principal risks assumed by the business, and reviews interim and annual financial and operations results. General responsibilities include:

- Approve a mandate for the board and the chair of the board.

- Appoint a chair of the board.

- Appoint the Officers of the Company, including the CEO.

- Regularly evaluate the effectiveness and performance of the appointed Officers in their management of the operations of the Company and associated plans to cope with risks to which the company is exposed.

- Review the management succession plan and the human resources plan.

- Oversee employee compensation plans to ensure that they are consistent with sustainable achievement of business objectives, prudent management of operations and prompt ongoing assessments on the risks to which the company is exposed.

- Establish standards of business conduct and ethical behaviour of directors, Officers and employees, and ensure there is an ongoing process for ensuring compliance with these standards.

- Establish board committees and approve their mandates.

- Approve all major changes to the structure of the organization.

- Establish procedures for the approval of all significant acquisitions and major contracts and approve all significant acquisitions and major contracts outside the ordinary course of business.

- Monitor risks to the Company and ensure that management takes actions to mitigate those threats, which may include, but are not limited to, those pertaining to:

  - operations;
  - credit quality;
  - liquidity;
  - interest rate changes;
  - capital market dynamics and ongoing availability of capital;
  - adequacy of capital to operate the business; and
  - reputation risk.

- Approve all policies, including those pertaining to corporate disclosure and communications, risk management, liquidity, funding management and capital management.

- Oversee communications with shareholders, including interim and annual financial statements, filings with various securities authorities and shareholder meeting materials.

- Establish overall business objectives and consider whether they continue to be appropriate in the context of business opportunities being pursued.

- Approve management strategies and plans designed to pursue business objectives and ensure they continue to remain prudent in the context of the objectives of the business, the economic environment, available resources and reasonable achievability of results.

- Evaluate financial and operations results against budgets and forecasts in the context of business objectives, strategies and operations plans being pursued.

- Receive reports from board committees at least semi-annually.

- Declare dividends, approve stock buy-backs and new issuances of shares, including those associated with employee equity incentive programs.

- Monitor compliance documents filed with applicable regulators, including, but not limited to, the Office of the Federal Superintendent of Financial Institutions, Financial Commission of Ontario, Ontario Securities Commission and similar filings with other applicable authorities.

- Ensure there is an appropriate framework of controls in place and monitor ongoing reports on the adequacy and continuous improvement in such controls.

- Review systems plans and disaster recovery plans.

- Approve appointment of the external auditor as recommended by the ADC.

<u>Code of Conduct</u>

The board will adopt and publish a Code of Conduct to foster a climate of honesty, truthfulness and integrity, closely co-ordinated with a very similar code for the Company, but with specific details on the responsibilities of directors. It is the responsibility of the GNC and is an Appendix to this charter.

The Chair of the Board

The roles and responsibilities of the chair and of the CEO will be separate. The chair will communicate to senior management the concerns of the board, shareholders and other stakeholders; act as a resource and sounding board for the CEO and Officers; ensure that management communicates its strategy, plans and performance to the board; and facilitate the board's interaction with key management as appropriate. The chair plays a critical role on the board, leading the board in its responsibilities for the business and affairs of the Company and its oversight of management. In performing this role, the chair must work with Officers and senior management, manage the board, and promote effective relations with shareholders, other stakeholders and the public.

For further clarity, position descriptions for the chair and for the CEO will be written by the Governance and Nominating Committee (GNC) and the Management, Resources and Compensation Committee (MRC), respectively.

The Directors

The basic responsibility of the directors is to exercise their reasonable business judgment on behalf of the Company. In discharging this obligation, Directors rely on, among others, the Officers, auditors, legal counsel and other advisors.

The majority of the board will consist of directors who the board has determined to be independent. In general, an independent director must not have a material relationship with Acme or its subsidiaries, directly or indirectly.

Election of Directors

All directors will stand for election at the AGM of shareholders. The GNC will nominate a slate of director candidates for election at each annual meeting of shareholders. The board will elect directors to fill vacancies created as a result of any resignations or increases in the size of the board between annual meetings. The GNC will review and update the selection and tenure guidelines for directors from time to time and make recommendations to the board as appropriate.

Director's Commitment

Directors are expected to ensure that other commitments, including other directorships, do not interfere with their duties and responsibilities as a member of the Company's board. The CEO and other Officers must seek the approval of the GNC before accepting outside board memberships with for-profit entities. It is expected that every director will make an effort to attend each board meeting and the meeting of any committee on which the director sits. Attendance in person is preferred, but attendance by teleconference is permitted. Each director should be familiar with the agenda for each meeting, have carefully reviewed all materials distributed in advance of the meeting, and be prepared to participate meaningfully in the meeting.

Experience and Term Limits

The Acme board believes experience is a valuable asset in the oversight of the business. Accordingly, it is appropriate that a majority of the directors have experience in sectors or fields closely related to the Company's sphere of interest. Elections to the board are not subject to term limits, although the board reserves the right to ensure that fresh thinking and perspectives are always available at the board table and that the collective experience reflects the evolution of the Company and its strategy.

Director Compensation and Stock Ownership

It is the general policy of the board that director compensation should be a mix of cash and equity-based compensation with a significant portion of such compensation in the form of the Company's stock or stock-equivalent units. The form and amount of director compensation will be determined by the GNC. The GNC periodically reviews and compares the Company's board compensation to director compensation at peer companies that are also benchmarks for the Company's executive compensation program.

It is the general policy of the board that every director be a shareholder, either before nomination or within a time after joining the Board, as determined by the GNC at the time the director is recruited.

Chairs and Tables

Orientation and Continuing Education

New directors will receive a comprehensive orientation from appropriate executives and staff regarding the business affairs of the Company. In addition, particular aspects of operations are to be presented by Acme executives and staff, as part of the agenda of regular board meetings. Directors are expected to remain abreast of issues and events in the sectors where the Company has an operating interest.

Board Operations

Number of Regular Meetings

The board normally holds eight regular meetings, four of which are detailed quarterly reviews with mandatory attendance. Regular attendance is either by phone or in person, and additional meetings may be scheduled as required. The meeting schedule is published in advance of the fiscal year.

Agenda and Briefing Materials

An agenda for each board meeting and briefing materials will be distributed to each director approximately five working days prior to each meeting. Briefing materials are concise, yet sufficiently detailed to permit directors to make informed judgments. The chair will normally set the agenda for board meetings. Any director may request the inclusion of specific items.

Confidentiality

The proceedings and deliberations of the board and its committees are confidential. Each director will maintain the confidentiality of information received in connection with responsibilities as a director.

In Camera Sessions

The independent directors, as deemed appropriate, may reserve time to conduct in camera sessions following every board meeting in the absence of members of management to monitor and assess board processes and issues and to communicate to management as appropriate the results of private discussions among non-employee directors.

Access to Employees

Non-employee directors will have full access to senior management and other employees on request to discuss the business affairs of the company. The board expects there will be regular opportunities for the directors to meet with the chief executive officer and other members of management in board and committee meetings and in other formal and informal settings.

Services of Outside Consultants

In order to carry out its mandates effectively, the board directly and through its committees is empowered to engage the services of outside consultants and other advisors as appropriate, subject to board approval.

Board Assessment

The board and its committees will evaluate their own performance and effectiveness annually with the objective of continuous improvements. Generally, board performance will be measured against the following key metrics, including:

- the effectiveness with which the board functions, including satisfaction of board members regarding the functioning of the board;
- the extent to which the Acme carries out its responsibilities to shareholders, employees, customers, governments and the public; and
- the quality of communications between the board and management, including satisfaction of members of management and board members regarding this communication.

Board assessment is the responsibility of the GNC.

Board Committees

The board will appoint those committees it determines are necessary or appropriate to conduct its business. Currently, the standing committees are:

1. Audit & Disclosure Committee (ADC)
2. Management, Resources & Compensation Committee (MRC)
3. Governance & Nominations Committee (GNC)

Committees have at least three independent directors. The charter of each of these committees is set out in the Appendices. Each board committee will report to the full board on its activities, normally in the form of the minutes of its proceedings, which shall be distributed to the entire board.

Appendix Four:

The Board Calendar

The assumptions behind this calendar are a publicly-traded company with a fiscal year ending on December 31. Primary responsibility for each item is shown in parentheses, which have these meanings:

- ADC — Audit and Disclosure Committee
- MRC — Management, Resources and Compensation Committee
- GNC — Governance and Nominating Committee

1. First Quarter

a. January — the start of a new fiscal year and the wrap-up of the old

    i.   Close the books on the previous year (ADC)

        1.   Draft financial statements (ADC)

    ii.   Finalize planning for the year-end audit (ADC)

    iii.   Finalize the CEE Level performance reviews (MRC)

        1.   Determine bonuses and options (MRC)

    iv.   Board performance for the previous year (GNC)

    v.   Commence Board slate review (GNC)

b. February — an easy month

    i.   Complete Board slate for Proxy (GNC)

    ii.   Draft Consolidated Statements, core documents (ADC)

c. March — Close the previous year

    i.   Approve the Financial Statements (Board)

           1.   MD&A, AIF

    ii.   File for the previous year

2. Second Quarter

a. April — Close Q1

    i.   Approve Q1 Financial Statements (ADC)

           1.   MD&A, Message to Shareholders

    ii.   File Q1

    iii.   Prepare for AGM

           1.   Script for AGM (Chair of Board)

               a.   Motions and resolutions

b. May — the month of the Annual General Meeting

    i.   AGM in third week of May

           1.   Appoint Auditors

    ii.   New Board meets

           1.   Appoint Chair of the Board (Board)
           2.   Appoint Officers (Board)
           3.   Appoint Committees and Chairs (Board)

c. June — closing the first half

    i.   Half Year Review (Board and Management)

    ii.   Approve draft Q2 statements (ADC)

3. Third Quarter

a. July — File Q2

    i.   Approve Q2 Financial Statements (ADC)

           1.   MD&A, Message to Shareholders

ii.   File Q2

iii.   First Half Review – Board and Management

b. August — Management develops the background materials and the preliminary thinking for the strategy and planning process

c. September —

    i.   Approve draft Q3 statements (ADC)

    ii.   Corporate strategy review — Board and management

        1.   SWOT analysis

4. Fourth Quarter

a. October — complete the annual planning cycle

    i.   Approve Q3 Financial Statements (ADC)

    ii.   Review draft business plan for next year (Board)

        1.   Financial risk analysis (ADC)

        2.   Staffing implications (MRC)

b. November — set the course for the coming year

    i.   Approve draft business plan for the coming year (Board)

    ii.   Draft CEE Level goals for next year (MRC)

c. December — wrap up the year

    i.   Approve business plan and budget (Board)

    ii.   CEE Level Performance Management

        1.   Approve CEE Level goals for coming year (Board)

        2.   Commence review of past year (MRC)

Appendix Five:

Standing Committee Charters

The Audit and Disclosure Committee (ADC)

Overall Purpose and Objectives

There shall be a committee of the board of directors (the Board) of Acme Concepts Corp. (the Corporation), to be known as the Audit and Disclosure Committee (ADC) whose membership, authority and responsibilities shall be as set out in this Charter. The ADC will provide independent review and oversight of the Corporation's financial reporting process, the system of internal control and management of financial risks, and the audit process, including the selection, oversight and compensation of the Corporation's external auditors. The ADC will also assist the Board in fulfilling its responsibilities in reviewing the Corporation's process for monitoring compliance with laws and regulations and its own code of conduct. In performing its duties, the ADC will maintain effective working relationships with the Board, management, and the external auditors and monitor the independence of those auditors. The ADC will also be responsible for reviewing the Corporation's financial strategies, its financing plans and its use of the equity and debt markets.

To perform his or her role effectively, each ADC member will obtain an understanding of the responsibilities of ADC membership as well as the Corporation's business, operations and risks.

Authority

The Board authorizes the ADC, within the scope of its responsibilities, to seek any information it requires from any employee and from external parties, to retain outside legal or professional counsel and other experts and to ensure the attendance of the Corporation's officers at meetings as appropriate. The Corporation shall provide for appropriate funding, as determined by the ADC in its sole discretion, for payment of:

i.   compensation to any registered public accounting firm engaged for the purpose of preparing or issuing an audit report or performing other audit, review or attest services for the Corporation;

ii.   compensation to independent counsel and other advisors, as the ADC determines is necessary to carry out its duties; and

iii.   ordinary administrative expenses of the ADC that the ADC determines are necessary or appropriate in carrying out its duties.

Membership

The ADC shall have at least three members at all times, each of whom must be a member of the Board and must be independent as defined by promulgated best practices, by applicable law and applicable stock exchange listing rules (the listing rules), unless the Board determines that such independence is not required. A member of the ADC shall be considered independent if:

- he or she, other than in his or her capacity as a member of the ADC, Board or any other committee of the Board, does not accept, directly or indirectly, any consulting, advisory or other compensatory fee from the Corporation. The indirect acceptance of a consulting, advisory or other compensatory fee shall include acceptance of the fee by a spouse, minor child or stepchild, or child or stepchild sharing a home with the ADC member, or by an entity in which such member is a partner, member or principal or occupies a similar position and which provides accounting, consulting, legal, investment banking, financial or other advisory services or any similar services to the Corporation;
- he or she is not currently employed, and has not been employed in the past three years, by the Corporation or any of its affiliates;
- he or she is not an "affiliated person" of the Corporation or any of its subsidiaries as defined by applicable listing rules; and
- he or she meets all other requirements for independence imposed by law and the listing rules from time to time, and any requirements imposed by any Canadian body having jurisdiction over the Corporation.

No director qualifies as independent unless the Board affirmatively determines that the director does not have a material relationship with the Corporation that would interfere with the exercise of independent judgment.

All members of the ADC shall have a practical knowledge of finance and accounting and be able to read and understand fundamental financial statements from the time of their respective appointments to the ADC. In addition, members may be required to participate in continuing education if required by applicable law or the listing rules.

At least one member of the ADC shall meet the financial sophistication standards under the listing rules.

Each member of the ADC shall be appointed by the Board and shall serve until one of the following occurs: he or she shall be replaced by the Board, resigns from the ADC or resigns from the Board.

Meetings

The ADC shall meet as frequently as required, but no less than four times annually and at least quarterly. The Board shall name a chair of the ADC, who shall prepare and/or approve an agenda in advance of each meeting and shall preside over meetings of the ADC. In the absence of the chair, the ADC shall select a chairperson for that meeting. A majority of the members of the ADC shall constitute a quorum and the act of a majority of the members in attendance at a meeting where a quorum is present, shall be the act of the ADC. The ADC may also act by unanimous written consent of its members. The ADC shall maintain minutes or other records of meetings and activities of the ADC, and such minutes and records will form a part of the Minute Book of the Corporation.

The ADC shall, through its chair, report regularly to the Board following the meetings of the ADC, addressing such matters as the quality of the Corporation's financial statements, the Corporation's compliance with legal or regulatory requirements, the performance and independence of the outside auditors, the performance of any internal audit function and other matters related to the ADC's functions and responsibilities.

The ADC shall at least annually meet separately with each of the Corporation's senior executive group, the Corporation's chief financial officer and the Corporation's outside auditors in separate executive sessions to discuss any matters that the ADC or each of these groups believes should be discussed privately.

Roles and Responsibilities

The ADC's principal responsibility is one of oversight. The Corporation's management is responsible for preparing the Corporation's financial statements, and the Corporation's outside auditors are responsible for auditing and/or reviewing those financial statements. In carrying out these oversight responsibilities, the ADC is not providing any expert or special assurance as to the Corporation's financial statements or any professional certification as to the outside auditors' work. The ADC's specific responsibilities and powers are as set forth below.

General Duties and Responsibilities

- Periodically review, with management and the outside auditors, the applicable law and the listing rules relating to the qualifications, activities, responsibilities and duties of audit committees and compliance therewith, and also take, or recommend that the Board take, appropriate action to comply with such law and rules.

- Review and evaluate, at least annually, the adequacy of this Charter and make recommendations to the Board for changes to it.

- Establish procedures for:

  a. the receipt, retention and treatment of complaints received by the Corporation regarding accounting, internal accounting controls or auditing matters; and

  b. the confidential, anonymous submission by employees of the Corporation of concerns regarding questionable accounting or auditing matters.

- Retain, at the Corporation's expense, independent counsel, accountants or others for such purposes as the ADC, in its sole discretion, determines to be appropriate to carry out its responsibilities.

- Prepare annual reports of the ADC for inclusion in the proxy statements for the Corporation's annual meetings.

- Investigate any matter brought to its attention related to financial, accounting and audit matters and have full access to all books, records, facilities and personnel of the Corporation.

- Undertake such additional responsibilities as from time to time may be delegated to it by the Board, required by the Corporation's articles or by-laws or required by law or listing rules.

- As required, but no less frequently than annually, meet with the Disclosure Policy Committee to review changes proposed with respect to the disclosure policy and to confirm consistency of the disclosure policy with this Charter.

Auditor Independence

- Be directly responsible for the appointment, compensation, retention, termination and oversight, subject to the requirements of Canadian law, of the work of any outside auditor engaged by the Corporation for the purpose of preparing or issuing an audit report or performing other audit, review or attest services as such are defined in Section 7050 of the CICA Handbook. The outside auditors shall report directly to the Committee.

- Receive from the outside auditors, and then review and discuss, a formal written statement delineating all relationships between the outside auditors and the Corporation, consistent with the CICA Independence Standards, regarding relationships and services, which may affect the objectivity and independence of the outside auditors, and other applicable standards. The statement shall include a description of all services provided by the outside auditors and the related fees. The ADC shall actively discuss any disclosed relationships or services that may affect the objectivity and independence of the outside auditors.

- Pre-approve all engagement letters and fees for all auditing services (including providing comfort letters in connection with securities underwritings) and non-audit services performed by the outside auditors. Pre-approval authority may be delegated to an ADC member or a subcommittee, and any such member or subcommittee shall report any decisions to the full ADC at its next scheduled meeting. The ADC shall not approve an engagement of outside auditors to render non-audit services that are prohibited by law or the listing rules.

- Review with the outside auditors, at least annually, the auditors' internal quality control procedures and any material issues raised by the most recent internal quality peer review of the outside auditors.

Internal control

- Review annually the adequacy and quality of the Corporation's financial and accounting staffing, the need for and scope of internal audit reviews, and the plan, budget and the designations of responsibilities for any internal audit.

- Review the performance and material findings of internal audit reviews, if any.

- Review annually with the outside auditors any significant matters regarding the Corporation's internal controls and procedures over financial reporting (internal controls) that have come to their attention during the conduct of their annual audit, and review whether internal controls recommendations made by the auditors have been implemented by management.

- Review major risk exposures (whether financial, operating or otherwise) and the guidelines and policies that management has put in place to govern the process of monitoring, mitigating and reporting such exposures.

- Review and evaluate at least annually the Corporation's policies and procedures for maintaining and investing cash funds and for hedging (foreign currency, etc).

- Review disclosures made to the ADC by the Corporation's CEO and CFO during their certification process required under Multilateral Instrument 52-109, as applicable, about any significant deficiencies and material weaknesses in the design or operation of internal controls which are reasonably likely to adversely affect the

Corporation's ability to record, process, summarize and report financial information, and any fraud involving management or other employees who have a significant role in the Corporation's internal controls.

- Evaluate whether management is setting the appropriate tone at the top by communicating the importance of internal controls and ensuring that all supervisory and accounting employees understand their roles and responsibilities with respect to internal controls.

<u>Annual and Interim Financial Statements</u>

- Review, evaluate and discuss with the outside auditors and management the Corporation's audited annual financial statements and other information that is filed with Canadian securities regulatory authorities and included in the Corporation's Annual Information Return, as applicable, including the disclosures under "Management's Discussion and Analysis of Financial Condition and Results of Operations", and the results of the outside auditors' audit of the Corporation's annual financial statements, including the accompanying footnotes and the outside auditor's opinion, and determine whether to recommend to the Board that the financial statements be included in the Corporation's Annual Information Return.

- Review, evaluate and discuss the nature and extent of any significant changes in Canadian accounting principles, or the application of those accounting principles.

- Require the outside auditors to review the Corporation's interim financial statements, and review and discuss with the outside auditors and management the Corporation's interim financial statements and other information to be included in the Corporation's quarterly reports, including the disclosures under "Management's Discussion and Analysis of Financial Condition and Results of Operations", prior to filing such reports with the Ontario Securities Commission.

- Review and discuss with the Corporation's management and outside auditors significant accounting and reporting principles, practices and procedures applied in preparing the financial statements and any major changes to the Corporation's accounting or reporting principles, practices or procedures, including those required or proposed by professional or regulatory pronouncements and actions, as brought to its attention by management and/or the outside auditors.

- Review and discuss all critical accounting policies identified to the ADC by management and the outside auditors.

- Review significant accounting and reporting issues, including recent regulatory announcements and rule changes and Canadian GAAP matters and understand their effect on the financial statements.

- Discuss alternative treatments of financial information under GAAP, the ramifications of each treatment and the method preferred by the Corporation's outside auditors.

- Review the results of any material difficulties, differences or disputes with management, encountered by the outside auditors during the course of the audit or reviews and be responsible for overseeing the resolution of any difficulties, differences and disputes.

- Review the matters required to be discussed under Section 5751 of the Assurance Standards Board releases (Communications with Audit Committees), relating to the conduct of the audit.

- Review the scope, plan and procedures to be used in the annual audit and receive confirmation from the outside auditors that no limitations have been placed on the scope or nature of their audit scope, plan or procedures.

Related-party Transactions

- Review any transaction involving the Corporation and a related party (as such may be described from time to time by applicable legislation) at least once a year or upon any significant change in the transaction or relationship.

Earnings Press Releases

- Review and discuss with management and the outside auditors, prior to release, all earnings press releases of the Corporation, as well as financial information and earnings guidance, if any, provided by the Corporation to analysts or rating agencies.

Compliance with Law and Regulations

- Ensure that management has the proper systems and review processes in place so that the Corporation's financial statements, financial reports and other financial information satisfy all legal, regulatory and professional standards requirements.

- Review with the Corporation's counsel, management and independent auditors any legal or regulatory matter, including reports or correspondence that could have a material impact on the Corporation's financial statements or compliance policies.

- Report regularly to the Board with respect to any issues that arise with respect to the quality or integrity of the Corporation's financial statements, the performance and independence of the Corporation's independent auditors and internal audit function issues

<u>Administering the Whistleblower Policy</u>

- Review at least annually the Corporation's Whistleblower Policy.

- Deal with complaints made by employees and others in accordance with the Whistleblower Policy.

The Management, Resources and Compensation Committee (MRC)

Overall Purpose and Objectives

The Board of the Corporation has established a Management, Resources and Compensation Committee (the MRC) to act on its behalf regarding the president and CEO and those reporting directly to that person (the Executive Officers), with respect to: (a) appointing and compensating Executive Officers for the Corporation and its direct and indirect subsidiaries; (b) approving succession plans for Executive Officers for the Corporation and its direct and indirect subsidiaries; (c) ensuring that professional development plans are in place for all executive officers, accompanied by the appropriate professional development plans for incumbents and successors; (d) ensuring that management has developed and implemented a performance management system for the Corporation and its subsidiaries; (e) overseeing the administration of compensation and benefits plans; and (f) approving and reporting to the Board respecting the Corporation's overall human resources policies and philosophies.

Members

The Board will, in each year, appoint a minimum of three directors as members of the MRC, all three of whom will be independent directors.

The CEO of the Corporation and, to the extent the chair of the Board is not otherwise a member of the MRC, the chair, and all other directors who are not members of the MRC may attend all meetings of the MRC in an ex-officio capacity and will not vote. At the discretion of the CEO, the senior manager or executive responsible for administering human resource policies for the Company may attend the MRC meetings. The CEO will not attend in camera sessions.

Duties

As a generality, the MRC has the duty of oversight of all aspects of the Company's stance and actions with respect to its employees, and develops recommendations in this regard for the Board's approval. The MRC will have the following duties:

Executive Officers

- Review and recommend to the Board the appointment of the CEO and the direct executive reports of the CEO, regardless of their base salary.

- Recommend to the Board the CEO's compensation, including salary, incentives, benefits and other perquisites.

- Review and approve the hiring of individuals with an annual direct and indirect compensation of $150,000 or higher.

- Review, approve and report to the Board annually on management's succession plans for Executive Officers including specific development plans and career planning for potential successors.

- Review and recommend to the Board for approval the general compensation philosophy and guidelines for Executive Officers. This includes incentive plan design and other remuneration.

- Approve and report to the Board on adjustments to compensation for each Executive Officer including salary, incentives, benefits and other perquisites.

- Approve and report to the Board on any material changes to the perquisite plan for Executive Officers.

- Report on executive compensation as required in public disclosure documents.

- Approve and report to the Board on the general compensation philosophy for all employees, including base and variable pay ranges by job class, stock incentive programs and benefits.

- Develop and maintain the currency of a position description for the CEO which delineates his or her responsibilities, authorities, accountabilities and the corporate goals and objectives that the CEO is responsible for meeting and the manner in which these are linked to annual corporate goals and objectives.

- When required, the MRC recommends to the Board a candidate for appointment to the office of CEO.

CEO Performance Review

The MRC is responsible for developing a performance management and review process for the president and CEO, and for implementing this process on behalf of the Board. The process must be integrated and consistent with the performance management process for all other employees of the Corporation. Reviews are carried out at the end of the second and fourth quarters. Input is to be obtained from at least all other directors. The MRC recommends to the Board any compensation adjustments as a result of the performance reviews.

Succession Planning

The MRC ensures that a succession plan is developed specifically for the position of President and CEO. The CEO succession plan will be adjusted annually to reflect the Corporation's medium- and long-term strategic plans, and presented to the Board for approval. The CEO succession plan will, at all times, contemplate a substantial slate of candidates, internal and external, with current assessments of the readiness for the CEO role.

Corporate Human Resources

Establish compensation and recruitment policies and practices for the Corporation including establishing levels of salary, incentives, benefits and other perquisites provided to executives of the Corporation and any subsidiaries.

Employee Stock Option Plan

The employee stock option plan (SOP) has been approved and established by the Board, and the MRC will have general responsibility for the administration, amendment (other than amendments which are material or which require regulatory or shareholder approval), and making of grants under the plans, and, without limiting the foregoing, will have the following responsibilities:

- report to the Board on all matters relating to the SOP;
- interpret and administer the SOP as provided in the SOP;
- grant options to eligible persons;
- determine the exercise price, vesting terms, limitations, restrictions and conditions upon option grants;
- establish, amend and rescind any rules and regulations relating to the SOP;
- make determinations deemed necessary or desirable for the administration of the SOP; and
- correct any deficiency, inconsistency or omission in the SOP.

<u>Executive Training and Development</u>

The MRC will be accountable for ensuring that the Executive Officers of the Corporation and its subsidiaries participate in such training and development programs as the Board deems necessary to ensure high standards of governance and performance for the organization, and to ensure that a secure succession plan is in place.

<u>Executive Performance Evaluation and Assessment</u>

The MRC will oversee the evaluation and assessment of the Executive Officers in accordance with the objectives in the annual operating and ongoing plans of the business and the Board, which includes the performance standards set for officers.

Chair

The Board will, in each year, appoint the chair of the MRC from among the members of the MRC. In the chair's absence, or if the position is vacant, the MRC may select another member as chair. The chair will have the right to exercise all powers of the MRC between meetings, but will involve all other members as appropriate prior to the exercise of any powers and will, in any event, advise all other members of any decisions made or powers exercised.

Meetings

The MRC will meet at the request of its chair, but, in any event, it will meet at least quarterly to consider matters referred to it by the Board. Notices calling meetings will be sent to all MRC members, to the CEO of the Corporation, to the chair of the Board and to all other directors.

Quorum

A majority of members of the MRC, present in person, by teleconferencing or by videoconferencing, will constitute a quorum.

Removal and Vacancy

A member may resign from the MRC and may also be removed and replaced at any time by the Board, and will automatically cease to be a member as soon as the member ceases to be a director. The Board will fill vacancies on the MRC by appointment from among the directors of the Board, in accordance with Section 2 of this Charter. Subject to quorum requirements, if a vacancy exists on the MRC, the remaining members will exercise all its powers.

Experts and Advisors

Any member may, subject to the prior approval of the Board, engage an outside advisor at the expense of the Corporation to provide advice with respect to issues within the mandate of the MRC. This will include consultants engaged to advise on compensation issues, and the consultants will report directly to the MRC.

Secretary and Minutes

The corporate secretary or his delegate will act as secretary of the MRC. The minutes of the MRC will be in writing and entered into the books of the Corporation. The minutes of the MRC will be circulated to all members of the Board, redacted as may be determined necessary by the chair to remove any sensitive personnel information not otherwise material to the Board.

The Governance and Nominating Committee (GNC)

Overall Purpose and Objectives

The Board has established a Governance and Nominating Committee (the "GNC) for the purpose of providing the Board with recommendations relating to corporate governance in general, including, without limitation: (a) all matters relating to the stewardship role of the Board in respect of the management of the Corporation; (b) Board size and composition, including the director candidate selection and nomination process and the orientation of new directors; and (c) such procedures as may be necessary to allow the Board to function independently of management. The GNC will also oversee compliance with policies associated with an efficient system of corporate governance.

Members

The Board will, following the AGM of shareholders, appoint a minimum of three directors as members of the GNC. All members of the GNC will be "independent" directors in accordance with Section 1.2(1) of National Instrument 58-101 – Disclosure of Corporate Governance Practices. Members shall hold office until the next shareholders' AGM or until they are removed by the Board, or cease to be a director of the Corporation.

Authority

a.   The GNC has the authority to delegate to individual members or subcommittees of the GNC.

b.   The GNC has the authority to engage and compensate any outside advisor that it determines to be necessary or advisable to permit it to carry out its duties.

Duties

The GNC will have the following duties:

a. The GNC will review and make recommendations to the Board respecting:

- Corporate governance in general, and regarding the Board's stewardship role in the management of the Corporation, including the role and responsibilities of directors and appropriate policies and procedures for directors to carry out their duties with due diligence and in compliance with all legal and regulatory requirements.

- The size and composition of the Board, including with reference to applicable rules, regulations or guidelines promulgated by regulatory authorities related to corporate governance: (i) whether any committee responsibilities overlap; (ii) general responsibilities and functions of the Board and the directors, including position descriptions for the chair of the Board and the chair of each Board committee; (iii) the organization and responsibilities of Board committees; and (iv) the procedures for effective Board meetings to ensure that the Board functions independently of management and without conflicts of interest.

- The long-term plan for the composition of the Board that takes into consideration the competencies and skills the Board considers necessary for the Board as a whole to possess, the current strengths, skills and experience of each existing director, the competencies, skills, time commitment and resources each new nominee will bring to the boardroom and the strategic direction of the Corporation, including: (i) a written outline describing the desired qualifications, demographics, skills and experience for potential directors; (ii) the appropriate rotation of directors on Board committees; (iii) an interview process for potential candidates for Board membership; and (iv) a list of future candidates for Board membership.

- When required, a candidate for appointment to the office of chair of the Board.

- Annually, individuals qualified to become new directors and Board nominees for election as directors at the next annual meeting of shareholders.

- As required, candidates to fill any Board and committee vacancies.

- Annually, together with the chairs of other Board committees, the scope, duties and responsibilities of those committees and where advisable, any amendments thereto, as well as the establishment or disbanding of Board committees and changes to their composition, including the chairs thereof.

- Periodically, directors' and officers' third-party liability insurance coverage.

- The framework for delegating authority from the Board to management.

b. The GNC will review, approve and report to the Board on:

- The orientation process for new directors and plans for the ongoing continuing education of existing directors.

- The establishment of appropriate processes for the regular evaluation of the effectiveness and contribution of the Board and its committees.

- Annually, in conjunction with the chair of the Board, the performance of the Board as a whole, and committees of the Board.

- Annually, the performance evaluation of the chair of the Board and the chair of each Board committee.

- Together with the chair of the Board (where appropriate), concerns of individual directors about matters that are not readily or easily discussed at full Board meetings, to ensure the Board can operate independently of management.

- The corporate governance disclosure sections in the Corporation's management information circular and annual report, and any other corporate governance disclosure as required by securities regulatory requirements.

c. The GNC will oversee compliance with the Corporation's Employee Code of Conduct by officers of the Corporation, authorize any waiver granted in connection with such code, and confirm with management the appropriate disclosure of any such waiver.

d. The GNC will oversee compliance with the Corporation's Timely Disclosure, Confidentiality and Insider Trading Policy by officers and directors of the Corporation, authorize any waiver granted in connection with this policy, and confirm with management the appropriate disclosure of any such waiver.

e.   The GNC will oversee compliance with the Corporation's Board Code of Conduct by directors, monitor compliance by directors, authorize any waiver granted in connection with such code, and oversee the appropriate disclosure of any such waiver.

f.   The GNC will oversee compliance with any rules, regulations or guidelines promulgated by regulatory authorities relating to corporate governance.

g.   The GNC will receive and consider all such requests for the retention of outside advisors and experts from an individual director, the Board, and all of its committees (except for the ADC, which will notify the GNC of its actions in this regard).

h.   The GNC will annually review and assess its own performance, effectiveness and contribution, including its compliance with this Charter and will report the results thereof to the Board.

i.   The GNC will annually review and assess the adequacy of this Charter, taking into account all legislative and regulatory requirements applicable to the GNC, as well as any best practice guidelines recommended by regulators or the Toronto Stock Exchange and will recommend any changes to the Board.

Chair

The Board will, following the AGM of shareholders, appoint the chair of the GNC from among the members of the GNC. In the chair's absence, or if the position is vacant, the GNC may select another member as chair. The chair of the GNC shall be responsible for:

a.   developing and setting the agenda for GNC meetings; and
b.   determining the time, place and frequency of GNC meetings.

Meetings

The GNC will meet at the request of its chair, but, in any event, it will meet at least quarterly to consider matters referred to it by the Board.

The GNC may invite such directors, officers and employees of the Corporation and advisors as it sees fit from time to time to attend meetings of the GNC, and assist in the discussion and consideration of matters relating to the GNC.

Notices calling meetings will be sent to all GNC members and, for informational purposes, to the CEO of the Corporation, to the chair of the Board and to all other directors.

During each regularly scheduled meeting of the GNC, the GNC shall meet in camera with only GNC members present.

Quorum

A majority of members of the GNC, present in person, by teleconferencing or by videoconferencing, will constitute a quorum.

Removal and Vacancy

A member may resign from the GNC and may also be removed and replaced at any time by the Board, and will automatically cease to be a member as soon as the member ceases to be a director. The Board will fill vacancies in the GNC by appointment from among the directors of the Board in accordance with Section 2 of this Charter. Subject to quorum requirements, if a vacancy exists on the GNC, the remaining members will exercise all its powers.

Secretary and Minutes

The corporate secretary of the Corporation or such other person as may be appointed by the chair of the GNC, will act as secretary of the GNC. The minutes of the GNC will be in writing and duly entered into the books of the Corporation and will be circulated to all directors.

Appendix Six:

Regulators and Regulations

While there are multiple regulatory bodies around the world, and even more that are sources of influence, Canadian directors need watch "only" those that follow:

1. Canadian Securities Administrators (CSA): www.csa-acvm.ca

2. Canadian Public Accountability Board (CPAB): www.cpab-ccrc.ca

3. Canadian Institute of Chartered Accountants (CICA)

   • Canadian Accounting Standards Board

       - Emerging Issues Committee

4. International Accounting Standards Board (IASB): www.iasb.org

   • International Financial Reporting Standards (IFRS)

5. Public Company Accounting Oversight Board (PCAOB)

Appendix Seven:

Sources and References

Legislative and Regulatory

Concern about, and interest in, corporate governance is hardly new, with significant studies, commissions and other research providing the data, information and suggestions that have had a profound effect on laws and regulation over the years. The following selections are in chronological order.

The Attorney General's Committee on Securities Legislation in Ontario, Office of the Attorney General of Ontario, 1967, also known as the "Lawrence Report".

Duties and Responsibilities of Boards of Directors in Canada, the Conference Board of Canada, 1974.

Report of the Inquiry into the Collapse of the CCB and Northlands Bank, led by Willard Estey on behalf of the Ministry of Supply and Services, 1986, also known as the "Estey Report".

Financial Aspects of Corporate Governance, Adrian Cadbury, for the Financial Reporting Council of the London Stock Exchange, 1992, also known as the "Cadbury Report".

Where Were the Directors?: Guidelines for Improved Corporate Governance in Canada, Report of the Toronto Stock Exchange Committee on Corporate Governance in Canada, December 1994, also called the "Dey Report".

Report on Corporate Governance, 1999 — Five Years to the Dey, Toronto Stock Exchange and Institute for Corporate Directors, June 1999.

NACD Blue Ribbon Commissions — various reports by the National Association of Corporate Directors, 2001–2005.

Chairs and Tables

Beyond Compliance: Building a Governance Culture, the Joint Committee on Corporate Governance, CICA, also known as the "Saucier Report", 2001.

Report of the NYSE Corporate Accountability and Listing Standards Committee, New York Stock Exchange, June 2002.

Principles of Good Corporate Governance and Best Practice Recommendations, Australian Stock Exchange Corporate Governance Council, March 2003.

OECD Principles of Corporate Governance, Organisation for Economic Co-operation and Development Steering Group on Corporate Governance, 2004.

Corporate Governance in New Zealand: Principles and Guidelines, New Zealand Securities Commission, Wellington, February 2004.

Bibliography

Boardroom Renaissance: Power, Morality and Performance in the Modern Corporation, James Gillies, McGraw-Hill Ryerson and the National Centre for Management Research and Development, 1992.

Costing Human Resources: The Financial Impact of Behavior in Organizations, Wayne F. Cascio. PWS-Kent Publishing, 1991.

Corporate Boards: New Strategies for Adding Value at the Top, Jay A. Conger, Edward E. Lawler III and David L. Finegold, Jossey-Bass Inc. 2001.

Director's Duties in Canada: Managing Risk, 2nd Edition, Margo Priest and Hartley R. Nathan, CCH Canada Limited, 2002.

EVA: The Real Key to Creating Wealth, Al Ehrbar, John Wiley & Sons, 1998.

Excellence in the Boardroom: Best Practices in Corporate Directorship, William A. Dimma, John Wiley & Sons Canada Ltd., 2002.

Improving Corporate Boards: The Boardroom Insider Guidebook, Ralph D. Ward, John Wiley & Sons, Inc., 2000

Inside the Boardroom: How Boards Really Work and the Coming Revolution in Corporate Governance, Richard Leblanc and James Gillies, John Wiley & Sons Canada Ltd., 2005.

Making Boards Work: What Directors Must Do To Make Canadian Boards More Effective, David S. R. Leighton and Donald H. Thain, McGraw-Hill Ryerson Limited, 1997.

Tougher Boards for Tougher Times: Corporate Governance in the Post-Enron Era, William A. Dimma, John Wiley and Sons Canada Ltd., 2006.

Sources and References

Welcome to the Board: Your Guide to Effective Participation, Fisher Howe, Jossey-Bass, 1995.

What Directors Need To Know: Corporate Governance, Carol Hansell, Carswell, 2003.

Glossary of Terms

ABCA: Alberta Business Corporations Act

AcSB: Accounting Standards Board

ADC: audit and disclosure committee

AMF: L'Autorité des marches financiers

AGM: annual general meeting

AIF: annual information form

ainsi soit-il: French for so be it

bête noir: literally, French for " black beast" and refers to someone or something unwanted or even hated, a pet peeve or strong annoyance.

bon vivant: a person indulging in good living (in French, literally, a "good liver")

CA: Chartered Accountant

CBCA: Canada Business Corporations Act

CD&A: compensation, discussion & analysis

CEE Suite: this term is used through this book to mean the CEO and his or her direct reports, ie, the CFO, the CTO, the CMO and those with an executive vice president title.

CEI: Competitive Enterprise Institute

CICA: Canadian Institute of Chartered Accountants

CIPF: Canadian Investor Protection Fund

CNQ: Canadian Trading and Quotation Systems, Inc.

corporate dashboard: a summary of the key performance indicators (sometimes shortened to KPI) displayed in a compact and easily-read format

CPC: capital pool company

CRTC: Canadian Radio-television and Telecommunications Commission

CSA: Canadian Securities Administrators

D&O insurance: director's and officer's insurance

DCP: disclosure controls and procedures

de rigueur: required by custom or etiquette (in French, literally, "of strictness")

DIP: director information package

DOC (Duty of Care): the expectation that directors will act in the manner of a reasonably prudent person in comparable circumstances, exercising their judgement and doing the best they possibly can

DRIT: directors return on invested time

DOT: Duty of Trust

EBITDA: Earnings Before Interest, Depreciation or Taxes

EDGAR: Electronic Data Gathering, Analysis and Retrieval System

EIC: Emerging Issues Committee, a major, ongoing committee of the CICA

ERM: Enterprise Risk Management system

ESOP: employee stock option plan

fiduciary: a person who holds a position of trust with respect to someone else or something that secures trust

GAAP: generally accepted accounting principles

GNC: Governance and Nominations Committee

Glossary of Terms

IASB: International Accounting Standards Board

ICD: Institute for Corporate Directors

ICD.D.: Institute for Corporate Directors Designation

ICFR: Internal Control over Financial Reporting

ICG: Institute of Corporate Governance

IDA: Investment Dealers Association of Canada

IFSR: International Financial Reporting Standards

IP: intellectual properly referring to various legal entitlements which attach to investions, writing, brand names, recorded media etc.

IPO: initial public offering

ISO 9000: family of standards for quality management systems maintained by ISO, the International Organization for Standardization and is administered by accreditation and certification bodies

KPI: key performance indicators

laissez faire: a French phrase meaning to let things pass, it is an economic policy or doctrine that opposes government interference in, or regulation of, business or commerce beyond what is necessary for a free-enterprise system to regulate itself.

MD&A: management discussion and analysis

ME: Montreal Exchange

MFDA: Mutual Fund Dealers Association

modus operandi: the way a thing operates; in Latin, "way of operating"

MRC: management resources and compensation

NASDAQ: National Association of Securities Dealers Automated Quotations

NDA: non-disclosure agreement

NFP: not-for-profit

NYSE: New York Stock Exchange

OBCA: Ontario Business Corporations Act

Occam's razor: a principle attributed to the 14th-century English logician and Franciscan friar William of Ockham. The principle states that the explanation of any phenomenon should make as few assumptions as possible, eliminating those that make no difference in the observable predictions of the explanatory hypothesis or theory. The principle is often expressed in Latin as the *lex parsimoniae* ("law of parsimony" or "law of succinctness"): *"entia non sunt multiplicanda praeter necessitatem"*, or "entities should not be multiplied beyond necessity".

This is often paraphrased as "All other things being equal, the simplest solution is the best." In other words, when multiple competing theories are equal in other respects, the principle recommends selecting the theory that introduces the fewest assumptions and postulates the fewest entities. It is in this sense that Occam's razor is usually understood.

OSC: Ontario Securities Commission

PCAOB: Public Company Accounting Oversight Board

PIF: personal information form

***primus inter pares*:** Latin, translates to "first among equals"

***raison d'être*:** a purpose or reason that accounts for or justifies, or originally caused, a thing's existence (in French, literally, "reason for being")

RCAF: Royal Canadian Air Force

RS: Market Regulation Services Inc.

RSU: restricted stock units

RTO: reverse takeover

SBU: Strategic Business Unit

SEC: Securities and Exchange Commission

SEDAR: System for Electronic Document Analysis and Retrieval

SEDI: System for Electronic Disclosure by Insiders

SMB: small- and medium-sized business

SOX: Sarbanes-Oxley Act

SRO: self regulatory organization

Glossary of Terms

SSL: Secure Socket Layer

SWOT: Strengths, Weaknesses, Opportunities, Threats

TIL: "Things I Like" list

TRIPS: Trade-Related Aspects of Intellectual Property Rights

TSX: Toronto Stock Exchange

TSX-V: TSX Venture Exchange

un aûtre chapeau: literally, in French, "another hat"

VAR: value added reseller

WTO: World Trade Organization

XBRL: eXtensible Business Reporting Language